Getting Organized in Vietnam

The **Institute of Southeast Asian Studies (ISEAS)** was established as an autonomous organization in 1968. It is a regional research centre for scholars and other specialists concerned with modern Southeast Asia, particularly the many-faceted problems of stability and security, economic development, and political and social change. The Institute's research programmes are the Regional Economic Studies (RES, including ASEAN and APEC), Regional Strategic and Political Studies (RSPS), and Regional Social and Cultural Studies (RSCS).

ISEAS Publications, an established academic press, has issued more than 1,000 books and journals. It is the largest scholarly publisher of research about Southeast Asia from within the region. ISEAS Publications works with many other academic and trade publishers and distributors to disseminate important research and analyses from and about Southeast Asia to the rest of the world.

The **Vietnam Update** is a series of annual conferences that focus on recent economic, political and social conditions in Vietnam and provide in-depth analysis on a theme of particular relevance to Vietnam's socio-economic development. In recent years, the Vietnam Update has been organized in conjunction with ISEAS.

The **Research School of Pacific and Asian Studies (RSPAS)** is Australia's pre-eminent centre for research and postgraduate training on the Asia-Pacific region. Priority areas of the School are Southeast Asia, Northeast Asia and the Southwest Pacific. There are nine major disciplines represented in the School: Anthropology, Archaeology, Economics, History, Human Geography, International Relations, Linguistics, Political Science and Strategic & Defence Studies. One of the four original research schools that formed The Australian National University when it was established in 1947, RSPAS has maintained a strong record of research excellence.

Vietnam Update Series

Getting Organized in Vietnam

Moving in and around the Socialist State

edited by **Benedict J. Tria Kerkvliet**
Russell H.K. Heng
David W.H. Koh

ISEAS
INSTITUTE OF SOUTHEAST ASIAN STUDIES
SINGAPORE

First published in Singapore in 2003 by
Institute of Southeast Asian Studies
30 Heng Mui Keng Terrace
Pasir Panjang
Singapore 119614

Internet e-mail: publish@iseas.edu.sg
World Wide Web: http://bookshop.iseas.edu.sg

ISEAS Library Cataloguing-in-Publication Data

Getting organized in Vietnam : moving in and around the socialist state/ edited by Benedict J. Tria Kerkvliet, Russell H.K. Heng and David W.H. Koh.
1. Associations, institutions, etc.—Vietnam.
2. Non-governmental organizations—Vietnam.
3. Labor unions—Vietnam.
4. Social service—Vietnam.
5. Vietnam—Economic conditions
6. Vietnam—Politics and government—1975-
I. Kerkvliet, Benedict J.
II. Heng, Russell H.K. (Russell Hiang-Khng)
III. Koh, David W.H. (David Wee Hock)
JQ824 G39 2003

ISBN 981-230-165-8 (soft cover)
ISBN 981-230-235-2 (hard cover)

Typeset by International Typesetters Pte Ltd
Printed in Singapore by Seng Lee Press Pte Ltd

Contents

Preface

Beginning in 1990, the Australian National University (ANU) has been holding its series of Vietnam Update conferences almost every year. The chapters in this volume began as papers presented at the Vietnam Update 2001 held at the Institute of Southeast Asian Studies (ISEAS) in Singapore on 19–20 November. The theme of that particular Update was "Governance in Vietnam: The Role of Organizations".

By the time of the Vietnam Update 2003, there would have been 10 conferences, each focused on a particular theme. Over the years, the Update has looked at agriculture, education, law, civil society, mass media, urban culture, local government, and social differentiation, to name just a few of the themes. Conference proceedings have resulted in eight publications (books and monographs). The specialized nature of ANU's Vietnam Update is its hallmark, attesting to a capacity to draw on a critical mass of experts, both Vietnamese and non-Vietnamese, to explore specific topics. It also underlines the university's long record in researching Vietnam.

The 2001 Update was the first time the conference left the shores of Australia. Holding the conference in Singapore tapped into the island's strategic location in the region and drew a greater attendance from people working in Vietnam and other Southeast Asian countries. Since then, ISEAS has continued to co-host the conference in Canberra in 2002 and 2003. This book underlines how fruitful this ANU-ISEAS collaboration has been. More titles will be available when the volumes from the 2002 and 2003 Updates are published.

Finally, we would like to thank all those who funded the Vietnam Update 2001: the Australian Agency for International Development (AusAID), ISEAS and the ANU's Research School of Pacific and Asian

Studies. We are also grateful to staff members of both ANU and ISEAS who rendered invaluable organizational, editorial, and secretarial support.

Organizing Committee, Vietnam Update 2001
Professors Benedict J. Tria Kerkvliet and David G. Marr,
Research School of Pacific and Asian Studies, ANU
Drs Russell H.K. Heng and David Koh,
Institute of Southeast Asian Studies

Abbreviations

AIC	Association of Industry and Commerce, later UAIC, Hoi Cong Ky Nghe Gia
AIDS	acquired immune deficiency syndrome
AusAID	Australian Agency for International Development
AVF	Association of Vietnamese Folklorists, Hoi Van Nghe Dan Gian Viet Nam
CCRD	Centre for Rural Communities Research and Development, Trung Tam Nghieu Cuu va Phat Trien Cong Dong Nong Thon
CDB	Commune Development Boards
CGOP	Committee for Government Organization and Personnel (since mid-2001, the Ministry for Home Affairs)
CHESH	Centre for Human Ecology Studies of Highlands, Trung tam nghien cuu sinh thai nhan van vung
CIEE	Council on International Educational Exchange
CIEM	Central Institute of Economic Management, Vien Nghien Cuu Quan Ly Kinh Te Trung Uong
CIRD	Centre for Indigenous Knowledge Research and Development, Trung tam nghien cuu kien thuc ban dia va phat
CMEA	Council for Mutual Economic Assistance
CRES	Centre for Resource Management and Environmental Studies
DOLISA	Department of Labour, War Invalids and Social Affairs
Eco-eco	Institute of Ecological Economy
EIU	Economist Intelligence Unit
FAO	Food and Agriculture Organization
FDI	foreign direct investment

GDP	gross domestic product
GRINGOS	government-run-and-inspired NGOs
HEDO	Highland Educational Development Organization
HIV	human immunodeficiency virus
HUAIC	Hanoi Union of Associations of Industry and Commerce, Hiep Hoi Cong Thuong Thanh Pho Ha Noi
HVO	Health Volunteers Overseas
ICCO	Interchurch Organization for Cooperation and Development
IPF	indicative planning figure
IPM	Integrated Pest Management (an FAO programme)
LDG	local development group
LPDI	Law on Promotion of Domestic Investment
MARD	Ministry of Agriculture and Rural Development
MOLISA	Ministry of Labour, War Invalids and Social Affairs
MOSTE	Ministry of Science, Technology and Environment
NASC	National Assembly Standing Committee
NCCD	National Coordination Committee of Disability
NEDCEN	Non-state Economic Development Centre
NEZ	New Economic Zone
NGO	non-governmental organization, *co quan phi chinh phu*
ODA	overseas development assistance
ODTA	Office of Disability Technical Assistance
PACCOM	People's Aid Coordinating Committee
PAM	Programme Alimentaire Mondiale
PDP	Progress of Disabled People (of Hoi An), Tien Bo Nguoi Khuyet Tat Hoi An
PO	peoples' organization
PWDs	people with disabilities
RDSC	Rural Development Services Centre
RIDEF	Rural Infrastructure Development Fund
RIDU	Rural Infrastructure Development Unit
SAP-VN	Social Assistance Program for Vietnam
SOEs	state-owned enterprise
SPC	State Planning Committee
TEW	Towards Ethnic Women, Trung tam huong toi phu nu dan toc thieu so

UAIC	Union of Associations of Industry and Commerce, formerly AIC, Hiep Hoi Cong Thuong Thanh Pho Ho Chi Minh
UNCDF	United Nations Capital Development Fund
UNDP	United Nations Development Program
UNESCAP	United Nations Economic and Social Commission for Asia and the Pacific
USAID	United States Agency for International Development
VACVINA	Vietnam Gardening Association, Hoi Lam Vuon Viet Nam
VCCI	Vietnam Chamber of Commerce and Industry, Phong Thuong Mai va Cong Nghiep Viet Nam
VCP	Vietnam Communist Party, Dang Cong San Viet Nam
VFF	Vietnam Fatherland Front, Mat Tran To Quoc Viet Nam
VGCL	Vietnam General Confederation of Labour, Tong Lien Doan Lao Dong Viet Nam
VINASA	Vietnam Software Association, Hiep Hoi Doanh Nghiep Phan Mem Viet Nam
VNAH	Vietnam Assistance for the Handicapped
VND	Vietnam Dong
VUFO	Vietnam Union of Friendship Organizations, Hoi lien minh cac Hoi huu nghi Viet Nam
VUSTA	Vietnam Union of Science and Technology Associations, Lien Hiep Cac Hoi Khoa Hoc Ky Thuat Viet Nam
VULAA	Vietnam Union of Literature and Arts Associations, Lien Hiep Cac Hoi Van Hoc Nghe Thuat Viet Nam

Introduction: Grappling with Organizations and the State in Contemporary Vietnam

Benedict J. Tria Kerkvliet

In the early 1990s, observers began to comment on the increasing diversity of groups and associations in Vietnam. Phan Dai Doan, a distinguished professor of history in Hanoi, marvelled in 1994 at the "abundant and complex forms of organizations" that had emerged in rural villages following the end of collectivized farming. Unlike during the agricultural collective period, he found that villagers were joining together for mutual assistance, animal husbandry, charity work, religious activities, and adult education, among other purposes.[1] Meanwhile, Carole Beaulieu spotted what looked like NGOs (non-government organizations). People in Hanoi and elsewhere, she said, were creating "what they believed were independent organizations" and they felt free "to decide their own agenda and to raise money to act".[2] During the rest of the decade, evidence accumulated that the numbers and range of associations and groups were expanding.

To look at this phenomenon, scholars of Vietnam at the Australian National University and Singapore's Institute of Southeast Asian Studies made organizations the theme of the Vietnam Update conference held in November 2001. The chapters that follow began as presentations to that gathering.[3] The conference was one of two looking at aspects of governance in Vietnam.[4] Governance has several meanings and many features. Two aspects stood out for us: the ability of government authorities and institutions to make and implement policies and regulations that serve citizens and the country at large; and the accountability of authorities and institutions to the citizens and the public generally. We reasoned that one way to examine governance is to analyze organizations that claim to speak on behalf of certain sectors of the public, represent their interests, provide linkages between citizens and government, and enable people to hold authorities accountable. Our call for papers invited analyses of organizations in Vietnam that do these things or at least claim to. They could be government-created, government-linked, non-government, or other types of organizations, associations and groups. Presenters were asked to examine one or more of the following issues: relations between such organizations and the state, relations among the organizations themselves, orientations of the organizations, and effectiveness and significance of the organizations' activities.

The purpose of this chapter is to locate the rest of the book in the literature to date about organizations in Vietnam since the late 1980s. I shall focus on their growth, relations between them and officialdom, and the effectiveness of their activities. I shall also reflect on what the chapters here and related literature tell us about civil society in contemporary Vietnam.

From the late 1950s in the north and 1975 in the south until the mid-1980s, Vietnam's political-economic system had little room or opportunity for people to form voluntary organizations and associations. With few exceptions, only those established by the country's Communist Party and other agencies of the state were permitted. Even Catholic churches and parishioners had to be in a religious organization that the Communist Party government created for that purpose. It also established the Buddhist Church of Vietnam (Giao Hoi Phat Giao Viet Nam), which all Buddhists were supposed to join in order to practice their religion. One exception to this organizational rule is the Unified Buddhist Church of Vietnam (Giao Hoi Phat Giao Viet Nam Thong Nhat). Many monks and lay members of this organization, which had begun in 1951, refused to join the state-instigated Buddhist church and have managed to maintain their older one despite the government's periodic persecutions, which includes imprisoning and in other ways confining numerous leaders.[5]

During the 1980s, the decollectivization of agriculture, deregulation of prices for goods and services, and other aspects of what officials called "renovation" (*doi moi*) significantly changed Vietnam's political economy and society. Besides much more latitude to establish their own businesses, farm independently, and operate in a "free market," Vietnamese also increasingly found more opportunity to move about, form groups, and be involved in activities of their own choosing. This larger space for individual and group activity is reflected in legislation and regulations, which have moved considerably away from sharp restrictions on such self-generated activities of the late 1950s.[6] Among the early new regulations, analysts say, were some general directives and circulars from the Council of Ministers and other government bodies in 1989 and 1990. Subsequently, especially in 1992 and 1996–99, the Communist Party and its government provided more specific regulations about how associations and other organizations should be established and what their responsibilities and liberties are.[7]

It would be incorrect to conclude, however, that new organizations came only after the state liberalized rules and regulations. That may be the case for some groups, such as issue-oriented ones engaged in research and consulting, suggests Joerg Wischermann and Nguyen Quang Vinh's chapter in this book, but not others, such as those involved in social work and public welfare. People often formed associations that were not legally provided for. Consequently, some observers have noted, officials end up adjusting rules and regulations in order to catch up with changes already happening on the ground.[8] Government officials themselves complained in 1990 that people were establishing "clubs" (*cau lac bo*) that acted as though they were approved "associations" (*hoi*) yet they had no documentation or permission. Meanwhile some approved associations were creating other groups without any consent from authorities.[9] Eight years later, in 1998, says Thaveeporn Vasavakul's chapter in this book, Communist Party officials were still complaining about the "chaotic situation" of associations being created without authorization and engaging in activities beyond their charter.

So far as I know, no one has compiled an extensive list of registered, let alone unregistered, organizations active in Vietnam. The largest efforts to estimate the extent of organizations and what they do are two recent surveys. One, conducted by Adam Fforde and Nguyen Dinh Huan, looked for farmers' organizations in three sample provinces. The two analysts were particularly interested in identifying cooperation among rural people for making a living and doing other economic activities. About half of the farmers they interviewed in Long An, a southern province, were in various kinds "cooperative groups" (*to hop tac*) that were entirely voluntary. Comparable percentages were 20 in Ninh Binh, a northern province, and 5 in Quang Tri, a province in the central region.[10] These groups, which are also called teams and associated groups, were typically composed of several farming households working together in such activities as preparing and distributing seed, irrigating, planting, harvesting, livestock and poultry raising, and lending and borrowing tools and money. Many were recognized, even encouraged, by local authorities; others were not. Most of these groups apparently began in the 1990s. The study also found that nearly all farming households in Quang Tri and Ninh Binh provinces, but virtually none in Long An province, were in "new-style cooperatives" (*hop tac xa kieu moi*).[11] Most informants, however, were not active in these organizations nor in them voluntarily. These cooperatives were largely the creations of local officials, who were following instructions that national authorities issued in 1996–97.

The second survey, conducted by Wischermann and Nguyen Quang Vinh and their colleagues, was confined to organizations in the nation's two major urban centres, Ho Chi Minh City and Hanoi. The study, which is elaborated in a chapter of this book, found more than 700 organizations in the two cities. That is not, the authors stress, an exhaustive count. Their sample of the organizations suggests that most began after 1986. The number increased sharply and swiftly in Ho Chi Minh City during 1987–89. In Hanoi, the rise was graduated and peaked in the mid-1990s. The study does not attempt to estimate the percentage of city residents involved in these organizations.

In one of the first known published attempts to categorize organizations active in Vietnam by the mid-1990s, Mark Sidel came up with nine clusters: party-led mass organizations; research and training projects supported by senior state officials; more independent policy research and teaching groups; quasi-state or quasi-private educational institutions, peasant associations and collectives (including state-founded ones, voluntary ones, and ethnic and clan groups); "social activism and social service networks"; professional and business associations, religious groups; and "political activism groups" challenging the state and

Communist Party. The last, Sidel stressed, are either quickly suppressed by authorities or co-opted by them and turned into something else.[12] The general term he uses for all of these types is "policy and development-oriented groups".

Subsequent analysts have tried to develop a more streamlined typology and find a more felicitous term to encompass all types of organizations. In this book, Wischermann and Nguyen Quang Vinh propose "civic organization" as the general term; Vasavakul offers "popular organization". Both terms refer to much the same range of groups. The typologies Wischermann/Vinh and Vasavakul offer, however, are different, except that both identify mass organizations attached to the Communist Party as one type. Wischermann and Vinh have two other types clustered according to constituencies: professional associations and business associations. Their fourth type, issue-oriented organizations, includes research centres, development and social work groups, and religious associations. Vasavakul's typology draws primarily on official terminology. Besides mass organizations, it includes popular associations, non-state research institutes and centres, and political-social-professional organizations. The last of those, Vasavakul says, are usually groupings of popular associations. They are "political" in the sense that the state considers each the representative of its member associations, a recognition that also entitles the organization to some state funding. A fifth category in her typology is "non-governmental organization" (NGO).

Sidel purposefully does not use "non-government organization", saying in 1995 that it was not apt for groups he was then aware of. Beaulieu, writing at about the same time, was not sure whether the term was appropriate or not. The main reason for hesitating to use it was lack of clarity as to whether any organizations were really "non-government". Subsequent analysts, however, have talked about non-government organizations, largely because individuals and groups in Vietnam have themselves been using the term to describe their own or other people's groups. For instance, Michael Gray outlined in 1999 "the range of Vietnamese organizations which use the term 'NGO' in describing themselves...."[13] In her chapter in this book, Vasavakul adopts the term "NGO" to portray some groups that are also in other clusters within her typology because that is how "Vietnamese practitioners...describe themselves for various purposes". One gets the impression from Gray, Vasavakul, and other analysts that by the late 1990s, the term NGO had became rather coveted even by groups that are obviously connected to the government, the Communist Party, and other state institutions. Leaders of some may see a NGO as a way to camouflage activities that are supposed to be "non-government" but actually were not. For other activists, claiming, even insisting, to being members of a NGO may be part of their effort to increase their distance from state institutions and thwart authorities' efforts to control or direct them.

This brings me to the question of the relationship between organizations, especially registered or officially recognized ones, and the state. Three dimensions to consider are how an organization began, its affiliation, and its funding. Mass organizations are clearly linked to the state in all three respects. An example is the Vietnam General Confederation of Labour (VGCL) discussed in Eva Hansson's chapter. It is a creation of, attached to, and funded by, the Fatherland Front and the Communist Party.

Some other organizations in Vietnam are only weakly connected to the state. They are established outside of the party, the government, or other state agencies. Their funding too is from outside official circles, except when they have contracts and consultancies to do projects for particular state agencies. One of the first such organizations is Xa Me, "an entirely private initiative" that started in the early 1990s in Hanoi to help street children.[14] Another early example is Toward Ethnic Women (TEW), the advocacy group for minority people examined in Gray's chapter in this book. More recent examples are groups of disabled people discussed in Ivo Vasiljev's chapter. The main and usually rather tenuous connection these organizations have to the state is an affiliation with an official agency. That is how they become legal. It may be akin to governments in "liberal democracies" requiring organizations of all kinds to register with an authorized agency. TEW is affiliated with the Ethnology Institute, which is located in the state's National Center for Social Sciences and Humanities of Vietnam. That institute, Gray says, has "played little if any role in" TEW. Disabled people's associations often acquire legal status by becoming a branch of another recognized organization. The one featured in Vasiljev's chapter, the Progress of Disabled People of Hoi An, is an example of an organization not connected to any government or other part of the state. Its legal status, or at least de facto official recognition, comes from it being connected to a registered business, an arrangement that may become more common as private businesses spread. The boundary between self-help and other social and community-oriented associations and businesses, Vasiljev says, "has become rather fuzzy".

Most formal organizations are somewhere between the state-sponsored mass organizations and the ones tenuously linked to the state. Consequently, determining how independent or not they are of the state—whether they are "government" or "non-government"—is difficult. A large proportion of groups calling themselves NGOs in the mid-1990s began as organizations within state institutions.[15] Most of those are probably still linked, formally speaking, to the state. Membership of the rural "local development groups" discussed in Scott Fritzen's chapter includes some local officials as well as representatives of ordinary villagers; funding for the groups comes from development projects financed largely by foreign NGOs, United Nations agencies, and the governments of Vietnam and other countries. Numerous organizations surveyed in Wischermann and Vinh's chapter have multiple sources of funding, including regular allocations from state agencies. The Vietnam Union of Science and Technology Associations (VUSTA) and other "political-social-professional organizations" in Vasavakul's typology receive government subsidies. But they also derive income from their own activities, donations, and membership fees. Most associations within VUSTA, meanwhile, do not get financial support from the state, not even from the umbrella organization itself. Some VUSTA associations, however, do get state funding. Also creating ambiguity is the affiliations of organizations within these semi-state sponsored umbrella unions. The Centre for Rural Communities Research and Development (CCRD), for instance, describes itself as an NGO. Yet it is affiliated with the Vietnam Gardening Association, which in turn is a member of VUSTA.[16] So, is the centre really non-government?

In part, the answer for it and organizations like it must be in relative terms. Compared to some of the mutual assistance groups among villagers that are not registered or officially recognized, the CCRD is certainly less "non-government". Compared to Vietnam's mass organizations, however, it is more "non-government". The CCRD began not as a creation of a state agency. It is a creation of several natural and social scientists from various institutions who are interested in rural issues. They secure their own funding for CCRD projects. The group's main connection to the state is its affiliation with an organization that is itself a state-recognized institution but not state-funded, and which, in turn, is affiliated with still another organization that is closely linked to the state. Another part of the answer is to consider what is going on inside the organization. Evidence in Vasavakul's chapter indicates that CCRD is not an extension of the Ministry of Agricultural and Rural Development or other state agencies and that it is an advocate for the rural communities its members work with, not for state policies and programmes. In short, it is doing the kind of things that organizations widely regarded as "non-government" do in the Philippines, Thailand, Japan, and other countries.

It is worth identifying a subcategory of NGOs called "people's organizations" (POs). The latter are groups and associations that people form to do things they want or need to do together for themselves. Often they are not registered with, or formally recognized by, government or other state officials. If they are, they are otherwise not connected or only loosely so to the state; in that respect they are NGOs. What distinguishes them from other NGOs is that their constituencies are their own members. Unlike other NGOs, they are not trying to support or act on behalf of other constituencies. Examples are the cooperative teams and other voluntary organizations villagers form for their farming and other economic endeavours; religious associations among fellow believers to engage in shared rituals, care for their temples, and worship together; and associations formed by and for people in particular professions. An example of a PO detailed in this book is the Progress of Disabled People of Hoi An, one of several self-help organizations among disabled people in urban areas of Vietnam.[17]

Even organizations that have more linkages to, and funding from, state institutions than NGOs and POs cannot be automatically dismissed as mouthpieces for, and agents of, Communist Party and government officials. Close examination is required of what is going on inside—the organizations' activities and the discussions, even debates, among people in them about state–society relations.[18] Scholars analyzing the People's Republic of China and the Union of Soviet Socialist Republics have found that government organizations and other state agencies frequently became places where discussion, criticisms, and actions grew against prevailing policies and even the political system itself. Within these state institutions, people were challenging the ideas and policies of the ruling elite.[19] In other words, being preoccupied with apparently close relationships between an organization and the state runs the risk of overlooking a lot of what is actually going on and the political significance of that organization.[20]

Take, for example, the Vietnam General Confederation of Labour (VGCL), one of the largest mass organizations in the country. In some respects, it seems to be entirely dominated by the Communist Party and its government. Further studies reveal debates and struggles within the organization over its relationship to the party and the state.[21] Evidence has emerged that the VGCL is shifting away from being largely an organization transmitting central policy down to workers and toward being more responsive to workers' pressures for better working conditions and other improvements. In this book, Hansson's chapter suggests that this change has not been fast or far enough for many workers themselves. Their discontent and efforts to form their own unions adds to the internal dynamics within VCGL that a cursory look at the organization would miss.

The Vietnam Chamber of Commerce and Industry (VCCI) is another organization in which relations with the state are in flux. It began in 1960 as an office within the Ministry of Foreign Trade.[22] By the late 1990s, new statutes said it was "an independent, non-governmental organization". State agencies still "supervise" the organization. Yet, reports Jonathan Stromseth in this book, nearly 60 per cent of the Chamber's members are private companies and 80 per cent of its income comes from members' dues and from the Chamber's earnings generated by selling its services. Only 20 per cent of its funds comes from the government. Moreover, members within the organization have been agitating for Chamber leaders to take stronger stances against state policies and for business interests. They press Chamber leaders, for instance, to oppose complicated licensing procedures, fight state intervention in companies, and insist that companies be entitled to do any business not specifically prohibited by law rather than being limited to only activities permitted by law.

A closely related point is that a group's orientation is significant even if it is formally linked to the state. In the VGCL, national and local leaders for decades were primarily oriented to implementing labour policies of the Communist Party and its government and conveying sentiments of workers back to the national authorities. In recent years, however, struggles have developed within the organization over this position. Pressures from ordinary workers as well as among leaders themselves at various levels are pushing to turn VGCL into an advocacy organization for workers. Similar struggles may be going on in other official mass organizations, such as the Women's Association and Peasants' Association, although research on the matter remains skimpy.[23]

Some organizations structurally connected to the state have become quite clearly oriented to constituencies in society. Originally, the main purpose of the Vietnam Chamber of Commerce and Industry was to promote economic relations between Vietnam and other countries. Now its main mission is to represent the interests of the growing Vietnamese business community during government and party policy deliberations. Another example is the Association for Vietnamese Folklorists (AVF), one of the cases in Vasavakul's chapter. Established in 1966 as a state sponsored professional organization, AVF is a member of the Vietnam Union of Literature and Arts Associations, which is a state-funded organization of professional groups. Over the years the AVF developed strong connections with particular rural areas. As villages in some of these places began in the late 1980s to revive religious traditions that authorities had previously discouraged and repressed, the AVF became more involved in helping the revival. The AVF evolved from being a channel between the state and villagers to being an advocate for people who wanted to engage in religious practices that officials were still opposing.

A message from some studies in this book and elsewhere is that organizations not relying on the state for funding have more latitude to engage in activities and take stances different from the state's. The AVF, for instance, does not depend on the Vietnam Union of Literature and Arts Association or any other state agency for funding. Issue-oriented organizations in Hanoi with little or no state funds have "more room to manoeuvre," Wischermann and Vinh suggest, than do other associations in the same city that need government financing. TEW's funding is largely from a Dutch NGO. This, says Gray, allows TEW "financial freedom" in which "to move and test new ideas...." A related message, as the VCCI and CCRD examples illustrate, is that organizations with significant non-state funding have other constituencies to be conscious of. That also enhances their ability to stand further away from the state. Not that zero state funding is required for some autonomy. Indeed, non-government organizations in Vietnam, as in other countries, frequently have contracts with their governments to do particular projects. The point is that diversified funding gives organizations more leeway. Foreign NGOs, which have stimulated Vietnamese organizations in many ways, are a common source of alternative funding. Other funders include international organizations, such as the United Nations and the World Bank, and other states, such as the development agencies of Australia, Canada, and Sweden.[24] Since the late 1990s, even the United States International Development Agency (USAID) has funded, indirectly if not directly, activities of organizations of disabled people and other groups.

Turning now to the effectiveness of organizations in contemporary Vietnam, I see five patterns. One concerns POs based in particular communities. Although few studies have been done of them, available evidence suggests that many accomplish at least some of what their members want. Groups and associations among farming households, Fforde and Nguyen Dinh Huan find, are "clearly of importance" to members, providing valuable mutual assistance and services for their livelihoods.[25] Numerous local organizations among villagers engaged in related trades and marketing similar products have assisted members to increase their income and enlarge their circle of suppliers and customers.[26] Members of the organization "Progress of Disabled People in Hoi An" support each other and help themselves to study and find jobs.[27] In villages and towns across the country, associations of local Buddhists, Catholics, and people of other religious beliefs have built and refurbished sites of worship, revived rituals, and organized festivals.[28] Even people's organizations with more overt political objectives have had some success. Numerous demonstrations by villagers protesting against corrupt and abusive local authorities have contributed to putting corruption on the national agenda of governmental reforms and keeping it there. Among the protests were a series of large demonstrations in Thai Binh province that started in 1996 and turned violent in 1997.[29] Among other outcomes, the national government punished nearly 2,000 local officials and launched a "grassroots democratization" programme, which is still ongoing.

People's organizations have also encountered problems, obstacles, and failures. Many of them no doubt have internal squabbles over responsibilities, leadership, money, and other matters. Some split or disintegrate because of internal conflicts and divisions. These subjects have yet to be studied. Some research has been done on struggles religious organizations have had with authorities who object to their practices and in some cases to their very existence.[30] Many organizations among villagers opposed to corruption, abusive officials, and land confiscations by state agencies have failed to get their way. The unrest in Thai Binh was itself an outcome of villagers' inability to obtain remedies to their grievances through hundreds of petitions and small demonstrations against particular officials. Research thus far is too scanty to support any generalizations about what accounts for the successes and failures of such public protests.

A second pattern regarding effectiveness is organizations offering unconventional ideas and models. These alternatives, of course, are not inevitably influential or even necessarily good. Some that take off, however, have had positive results. The Centre for Rural Communities Research and Development, for instance, devised alternative energy technologies that three thousand families in seventeen provinces have adopted and the national government has now endorsed.[31] Non-government organizations involved with ethnic minority groups typically view development differently from the government's agenda. Rather than supporting resettlement and other top-down programmes, they stress human ecology, projects that are largely generated within minority communities, and putting communities in touch with others like them inside and outside Vietnam.[32] Some of these organizations have successfully put their ideas into practice in several communities. Although many government officials may be cold to these ideas and approaches, others have worked with the organizations. The Progress of Disabled People of Hoi An, to take another example, emphasizes members helping themselves, which is different from the charity approach of government and Communist Party organizations.[33] An organization can itself be an alternative that inspires others to act. Foreign NGOs helped to arouse Vietnamese individuals to form similar groups. And those domestic organizations have provided examples for still others to be formed.

The Local Development Groups (LDGs) examined in Fritzen's chapter of this book are a third pattern. The groups' purpose is to be an interface between local governments and rural populations in places where government and foreign donor development projects are being done, make the projects more responsive to people's needs, and assure that expenditures are transparent and funds are properly used. Members include representatives from local government offices and from the residents of the areas where the projects are being carried out. Research findings suggest that these groups on their own are not particularly effective in fulfilling their purpose. Their success depends considerably on the circumstances surrounding the development projects. One condition common to several successful groups is that they had strong backing from key provincial authorities.

This relates to leadership, a fourth pattern regarding effectiveness. In the case of the LDGs, the important locus of leadership was the government body in charge of the projects. Having what Fritzen calls a "reform champion" there enhances the chance that a LDG can do what it is supposed to accomplish. More generally, one can say that the attitude and stance of government leaders condition whether public organizations with varying degrees of distance from state institutions can function effectively. By allowing, even encouraging, such organizations to develop, government and party leaders enhance the possibility that they are useful to their members or others they are trying to serve. While this remark may be obvious, it is worth stating lest we forget that not too many years ago the Communist Party and its government took nearly the opposite stance, which squashed, prevented, or drove underground many organizational activities that exist openly today. Leadership within groups also conditions their effectiveness. Research on this is meagre but suggestive. TEW and the Progress of Disabled People of Hoi An, two organizations detailed in Gray and Vasiljev's chapters, owe their success in no small measure to their energetic and committed leaders. Very likely, the quality of leadership affects other organizations as well. Weak leadership can severely hamper a group; strong leadership can greatly help it.

Strong leaders, however, can end up contributing to the downfall of an organization if they or their supporters stand in the way of producing or recruiting new leaders who can take over and keep the group going from one generation to another. In other words, strong leaders need to be wise enough to facilitate a leadership turnover and the institutionalization of their organizations. Otherwise the organizations are likely to collapse when leaders depart. In the 1920s–30s, Vietnamese writers complained that one significant reason why their compatriots could rarely establish long-lasting organizations was that the passing of a founding leader was followed by squabbles among contending successors, splits among factions, and disintegration.[34] To date, research on contemporary Vietnam has not probed into this matter.

Another criticism in the early 20th century was that organizations rarely extended beyond a small network of relatives, village mates, or friends.[35] Being rather inward looking, these groups could not readily work with others, even those with whom they had shared interests. Whether true or not then, research suggests that at least some organizations today have a different pattern, the last in my list. They are relatively large organizations that reach out to other groups and individuals in the process of trying to advance their objectives. One example is the Vietnam Chamber of Commerce and Industry. It has numerous branches across the country that interact with each other and with the national office in Hanoi. Although its branch offices sometimes compete with other associations of business people in Ho Chi Minh City and elsewhere, the Chamber also makes concerted efforts to have liaisons with business associations whether affiliated with it or not. Having such an extensive network strengthens the Chamber's efforts to represent business interests when Communist Party and government officials invite it to participate in national policy-making deliberations.[36] Another illustration is the Association of Vietnamese Folklorists. It too has branches in various parts of the country, and they interact with other organizations and groups, ranging from research institutes to village associations. These connections, together with other AVF activities, contribute to the organization's ability to influence national party and government leaders to permit cultural practices that previously had been banned.[37] Both the Chamber and the AVF originated, as indicated earlier, within state institutions. Even though their relationship to the state has become much more distant, that origin may have facilitated their extensive networks. Other organizations that began quite independently, however, are also engaging in collaborative activities. The Progress of Disabled People of Hoi An, for instance, has connections to similar people's organizations elsewhere in the country. And these groups are working with interested NGOs, aided by some foreign and Vietnamese government agencies, to network with even more organizations interested in disabled people.[38]

I end this chapter by considering the implications of organizations for civil society in Vietnam. Carlyle Thayer, a long-time analyst of politics in Vietnam, concluded in the early 1990s that civil society in the country had reached a "nascent stage". To develop and mature, he said, the Communist Party would need to further loosen its grip on trying to control society and create a legal system to protect civil society activities.[39] A decade later civil society features of Vietnam have become more apparent, yet still rather constrained. Before elaborating, I should state briefly what civil society is.

Although civil society is a debated concept with many meanings, much of the discussion with which I am familiar does converge around four points.[40] First, civil society refers to individuals and groups speaking, writing, teaching, and organizing about various interests and issues and doing so publicly and without (significant) state instigation and manipulation.[41] Second, such activity requires considerable civility—the give and take of contending ideas and claims with restrained exuberance and a tolerance for different opinions and practices among individuals and organizations. Resorting to repressing or killing one's opponents is not a civil society activity. Nor is violence against the state or the state's violence against people engaging in civil society activities.[42] Third, to have civil society requires an accommodating state—one that not only tolerates differences and criticisms but maintains institutions and laws that make public debate possible without violent or silencing repercussions. Finally, civil society exists in degrees. It is not something that is either present or absent. The extent to which people in a country can or do engage in civil society activities varies according to numerous conditions and circumstances.

Looking at contemporary Vietnam, I see three remarkable changes indicating further development in civil society. First, the legal infrastructure to recognize and protect organizations, particularly NGOs, is greater now than a decade ago. This is not to say the infrastructure is complete, just that it is noticeably better. A second is the expansion of newspapers, books, radio, television, film, and other communications media and much more diversity in the media's content. Though not discussed in this book, this subject is obviously important to civil society. Vietnam does not have a "free press" or "unfettered media". But neither is the press and other media completely repressed. The reality is somewhere in between and often oscillating as journalists and others struggle, sometimes successfully and other times not, to diminish state restrictions.[43]

The third change is the much greater number and variety of organizations. Arguably, many of them are engaged in private and economic endeavours and hence are not part of civil society. For instance, mutual assistance associations among farming households and organizations among fellow religious devotees to renovate temples and hold particular ceremonies may be too private to count as civil society activities. Yet aspects of these activities are part of civil society. Self-formed cooperatives among peasants provide a contrast to the cooperatives promoted by state agencies. Through their example, if not their direct statements, such voluntary organizations contribute to ongoing public deliberations about how production and distribution should be organized and by whom. Small religious groups revolving around particular sites and rituals have contributed to widespread discussions in print media, conferences, and other forums about Vietnamese culture, traditions, and religious beliefs. Those religious activities and deliberations about them have also contributed to changing official views. Meanwhile, numerous other groups have emerged that are clearly part of the widening civil society. Through their actions, meetings, conferences, and printed and verbal statements, they advance arguments and propose courses of action about rural development, ethnic relations, workers' rights, relations between communities and the state, poverty, land use and distribution, corruption, and other major issues.

Apart from corruption, this list of issues that motivate and concern groups and associations of people from various sectors of Vietnamese society does not include ones that are "political" in the sense of directly criticizing high level Communist Party leaders, government officials, military officers, and the like; questioning the single-party political system; objecting to how elections are organized and run; challenging the monopoly that state agencies have on newspapers, television, radio, and other media; and appearing to state authorities to be opposed to the present political regime. That such matters are not yet part of the public discourse indicates that civil society activities are still significantly constrained. Many Vietnamese people want them discussed; some have strong views and positions about them. Police and other agencies of the state, however, inhibit people from organizing among themselves and projecting their views in public forums, publications, or other media. If any try, authorities subject them to intimidation, coercion, if not imprisonment.

An example is the Club of Former Resistance Fighters (Cau Lac Bo Nhung Nguoi Khang Chien Cu) in Ho Chi Minh City.[44] In 1988 the Club, which had started five years earlier with a different name, openly pressed for a more democratic political system, held conferences that criticized the Communist Party's governance record, and published newsletters despite government officials forbidding them. By April 1990, authorities were arresting its key leaders and teaming up with conservative members of the club to stop its political activities. Club members who continued to be highly critical of the political system had to withdraw to private conversations among themselves. Authorities are also hostile to individuals, whether or not involved with a group, who dare publicly to criticize or question official positions on controversial political matters. Using the Internet, individual dissenters have an easier time now skirting around official media outlets to get their views circulated, particularly abroad.[45] Even so, their behaviour still exposes themselves and their families to repression.

Another indication of a constrained civil society is that organizations for the most part remain small in the number of members and limited to people living in the same vicinity. This could be due to the relatively newness of many groups. There might be societal constraints such as people preferring to associate with others they know personally. The more telling reason, however, may be that authorities are highly suspicious of organizations whose memberships are expanding and embrace people residing in many different parts of the country. Authorities countenance large organizations that are still closely linked to the state. The official mass organizations for workers, peasants, women, and youth are prominent examples. Authorities also apparently approve large organizations that pose no significant threat and indeed helps the state to make and implement policies. Examples may be the Vietnam Chamber of Commerce and Industry and the Association of Vietnamese Folklorists. A large organization of disabled people or some other sector of the population may be able to multiply and merge so long as it stays clear of politically sensitive issues. If thousands of peasants from several parts of the country, however, wanted to form an association among themselves, totally separate from the official Peasants' Association, to voice their concerns and criticisms about government policies, they are unlikely to succeed in the present environment. An indication is that no organization apparently remains among disgruntled people across hundreds of villages in Thai Binh province following unrest there in 1996–97.

Exceptional in this regard are religious organizations that are independent of the state's own religious organizations. The largest, involving millions of Vietnamese, is the United Buddhist Church of Vietnam, mentioned early in this chapter. Other organizations, though smaller, are composed of members of Catholic, Cao Dai, and other faiths. At one level, these organizations seek only to enable members to live and worship according to their religious beliefs. At another level, they defy and challenge the right of the state to interfere in their religious lives and determine what groups they must join. Their own organizations and the state currently live together in a kind of stalemate, which periodically is rocked by provocations from members on one side or the other. The situation is a kind of weather balloon for civil society. If intimidation and repression significantly ease and the independent organizations are able not just to exist but to regenerate as elderly leaders and members pass away, authorities may be signalling that they are willing to countenance a further expansion of civil society activities.

Notes

1 Phan Dai Doan, "May Suy Nghi", p. 48; also see pp. 45–9.

2 Beaulieu, "Is it an NGO?", p. 3.

3 Besides the authors of the chapters here, other presenters to the conference were Duong Trung Quoc, Adam Fforde, Russell Heng, and Nguyen Tran Bat.

4 The second one, held in November 2002, focused on local governments and authority. The organizers of both were Russell Heng, Ben Kerkvliet, David Koh, and David Marr. We gratefully acknowledge the financial and in-kind support for the conferences from the Australian Agency for International Development (AusAID), the Institute for Southeast Asian Studies in Singapore, and the Australian National University's Research School of Pacific and Asian Studies.

5 See, for instance, Thich Quang Do, *Nhan Dinh*.

6 For two recent and enlightening analyses of the Communist Party leadership's crackdown on political dissent and autonomous activities in northern Vietnam during the mid-1950s, see Kim N.B. Ninh, *A World Transformed*, chaps. 4–5; and Heng, "Of the State", ch. 3. Also see Sidel, "The Emergence", p. 300, 304, which lists some of the restrictive regulations issued in 1957.

7 Sidel, "The Emergence", pp. 301, 304; Pedersen, "Civil Society", 2000, p. 4; and Stromseth's and Vasavakul's chapters in this volume.

8 Phan Dai Doan, "May Suy Nghi", pp. 48–9; Sidel, "The Emergence", p. 300.

9 Chu Tich Hoi Dong Bo Truong, "Chi Thi So 202-CT, ve Viec Chap Hanh cac Quy Dinh cua Nha Nuoc trong Viec Lap Hoi" [President, Council of Ministers, "Instruction 202-CT regarding executing state regulations for establishing associations], 5 June 1990, in *Phap Luat ve Quyen Hoi Hop*, 1992, pp. 41–2.

10 Fforde and Nguyen, "Vietnamese Rural Society," pp. 23–32.

11 Fforde and Nguyen, "Vietnamese Rural Society," pp. 32–4.

12 Sidel, "The Emergence", pp. 294–6. In the same year as Sidel's chapter, Carlyle Thayer published a similar typology in which he acknowledged communications with Sidel on the matter. Thayer, "Mono-Organizational Socialism", p. 54.

13 Gray, "Creating Civil Society?", p. 694.

14 Nguyen Ngoc Truong, "Grassroots Organizations", p. 10.

15 Gray, "Creating Civil Society?", p. 699. Also see Beaulieu, "Is it an NGO?"

16 Vasavakul's chapter, this book.

17 See the chapter by Vasiljev. He calls the disabled people's groups NGOs because they are not connected to the state. While accepting that, I see a significant difference between those groups and an organization like TEW (discussed in Gray's chapter), which also has virtually no connection to the state. TEW is composed of people trying to support and advance the interests of ethnic minority people. It is not, however, an organization formed by minority people for their own needs. TEW is a NGO; the Progress of Disabled People is a particular type of NGO, a "people's organization". Such a distinction is common among activists and analysts of NGOs. For elaboration, see Silliman and Noble, eds, *Organizing for Democracy*, 1998.

18 I have elaborated on this in "An Approach". Making similar suggestions for how to look at organizations in China is Saich, "Negotiating the State", 2000, pp. 140–41.

19 Ding, *The Decline*, 1994, pp. 26–7; Lewin, *The Gorbachev Phenomenon*, 1988, pp. 81–97.

20 The same warning applies to organizations that appear to be very far removed from any state involvement. Closer inspection may reveal that state agencies have co-opted them. I do not have any Vietnamese examples in mind. I am recalling, though, numerous seemingly non-government organizations in the United States during the 1950s–1960s that turned out to be heavily funded by, and closely linked to, state institutions, among them the Central Intelligence Agency.

21 Greenfield, "The Development of Capitalism", 1994; Stromseth, "Reform and Response", chaps. 5 and 6, 1998; Chan and Nørland, "Vietnamese and Chinese Labour Regimes"; and Hansson's chapter in this book. Also maybe relevant

is Nielson, *Vietnamese Trade Unions*, cited in Suhong Chae, "Spinning Work", 2003, p. 345.

22 Stromseth, "Reform and Response", pp. 86–7.

23 For brief accounts of the Women's Union, see Truong Thanh Dam, "Uncertain Horizon", 1997, pp. 105–10, and Endres, "Images of Womanhood", 1999, pp. 158–65. An even briefer discussion of the Peasants' Association is in Kerkvliet, "Rural Society", 1995, pp. 87–8. For reports hinting at tensions within the Peasants' Association about its orientation, see articles in *Nong Thon Ngay Nay* [The Countryside Today], 21 October 1998, p. 8, 28 October 1998, pp. 4 ff., 27 January 1999, p. 1ff., 12 February 2001, pp. 4, 11, and 9 March 2001, pp. 3, 4.

24 See especially chapters in this book by Fritzen and Vasiljev.

25 Fforde and Nguyen, "Vietnamese Rural Society", pp. 34–5.

26 Nguyen Van Chinh, "Work without Name", 2000; Boselie, *Economic Reform*, 2003, p. 170, also here and there in other parts of chaps. 5 and 6; and DiGregorio, "Urban Harvest", 1994, chaps. 3 and 4.

27 Vasiljev's chapter, this book.

28 Malarney, "Return to the Past?", 2003, pp. 235–47, provides a lucid synthesis of these religious activities and in the process refers to much of this recent literature. A forthcoming publication to watch for is Taylor, *Goddess on the Rise*.

29 Thayer, "Report on Thai Binh"; Kerkvliet, "An Approach", 2001, pp. 265–68.

30 For a summary, see Malarney, "Return to the Past?", pp. 248–52.

31 Vasavakul's chapter, this book.

32 Beaulieu, "Is it an NGO?", pp. 6–8; Gray, "Creating Civil Society?", p. 701; Gray's chapter, this book.

33 Vasiljev's chapter, this book.

34 Woodside, "The Development of Social Organizations", 1971, p. 41.

35 Woodside, "The Development of Social Organizations", pp. 40–41.

36 Stromseth, "Reform and Response", chaps. 3 and 4; Stromseth's chapter, this book.

37 Vasavakul's chapter, this book.

38 Vasiljev's chapter, this book.

39 Thayer, "Political Reform", p. 112, 129. In the early and mid-1990s, some Vietnamese scholars were also talking about the emergence of civil society (*xa hoi dan su*) in their country. See Phan Dai Doan, "Thiet Che Chinh Tri", 1996b, pp. 48–9; and Phan Dai Doan, "Mot So Van De Ly Luan", 1996a, pp. 215–23.

40 My usage draws on the Blaney and Pasha, "Civil Society", 1993; Chamberlain, "Civil Society", 1998; Diamond, *Developing Democracy*, 1999, pp. 218–33; Keane, "Despotism and Democracy", 1988; Krygier, "The Sources of Civil Society", 1996; Kumar, "Civil Society", 1993.

[41] The public feature generally distinguishes civil society activities from social behaviour that is largely or entirely private—e.g., family life, economic endeavours, and other inward looking or personal activities. Of course private activities can contribute to civil society activities.

[42] This is not to say that such violence is never justified. It just says that violence—particularly sustained violence such as systematic repression by the state, rebellion against it, and people in one sector of society killing people in a different sector—is antithetical to civil society.

[43] Recent studies of the Vietnam's communications media include Russell Heng's illuminating analysis, "Of the State", (1999) and the informative collection edited by David Marr, *The Mass Media* (1998). For historical background to the media's situation today, see Marr, "A Passion for Modernity", 2003.

[44] Heng, "Of the State", ch. 7.

[45] Although increasing, access to the World Wide Web, where many hard-hitting critiques of the country's leaders and political system are posted, remains prohibitively expensive for a large proportion of people in Vietnam.

References

Beaulieu, Carole. "Is it an NGO? Is it a Civil Society? Is it Pluralism Wriggling Along?" Letter to the Institute of Current World Affairs, CB-26, 6 October 1994, 12pp.

Blaney, David L. and Mustapha Kamal Pasha. "Civil Society and Democracy in the Third World: Ambiguities and Historical Possibilities", *Studies in Comparative International Development* 28 (Spring 1993): 3–24.

Boselie, Dave. *Economic Reform, Agricultural Diversification and Commercialisation in Northern Vietnam, 1945–1995*. Maastricht: Shaker Publishing, 2003.

Chamberlain, Heath B. "Civil Society with Chinese Characteristics?", *The China Journal* 39 (January 1998): 69–81.

Chan, Anita and Irene Nørland. "Vietnamese and Chinese Labour Regimes: On the Road to Divergence". In *Transforming Asian Socialism: China and Vietnam Compared*, edited by Anita Chan, Benedict J. Tria Kerkvliet, and Jonathan Unger, pp. 204–28. Boulder: Rowman and Littlefield, 1999.

Diamond, Larry. *Developing Democracy: Toward Consolidation*. Baltimore: Johns Hopkins University Press, 1999.

DiGregorio, Michael R. *Urban Harvest: Recycling as a Peasant Industry in Northern Vietnam*. Occasional Paper No. 17, Environmental Series, Honolulu: East West Center, 1994.

Ding, X.L. *The Decline of Communism in China: Legitimacy Crisis, 1977–1989*. Cambridge: Cambridge University Press, 1994.

Endres, Kirsten W. "Images of Womanhood in Rural Vietnam and the Role of the Vietnamese Women's Union: A Microscopic Perspective". In *Vietnamese Villages in Transition*, edited by Bernhard Dahm and Vincent J. Houben, pp. 155–74. Passau: Department of Southeast Asian Studies, Passau University, 1999.

Fforde, Adam and Nguyen Dinh Huan. "Vietnamese Rural Society and its Institutions: Results of a Study of Cooperative Groups and Cooperatives in Three Provinces, Final Report". 19 June 2001.

Gray, Michael L. "Creating Civil Society? The Emergence of NGOs in Vietnam", *Development and Change* 30 (1999): 693–713.

Greenfield, Gerard. "The Development of Capitalism in Vietnam". In *Between Globalism and Nationalism: Socialist Register*, edited by Ralph Miliband and Leo Panitch, pp. 203–34. London: Merlin Press, 1994.

Heng, Russell Hiang-Khng. "Of the State, For the State, Yet Against the State: The Struggle Paradigm in Vietnam's Media Politics". Ph.D. dissertation, The Australian National University, 1999.

Keane, John. "Despotism and Democracy". In *Civil Society and the State*, edited by idem, pp. 55–62. London: Verso, 1988.

Kerkvliet, Benedict J. Tria. "An Approach for Analysing State-Society Relations in Vietnam", *Sojourn* 16 (October 2001): 238–78.

———. "Rural Society and State Relations". In *Vietnam's Rural Transformation*, edited by idem and Doug J. Porter, pp. 65–96. Boulder and Singapore: Westview Press and ISEAS, 1995.

Krygier, Martin. "The Sources of Civil Society", The Second Richard Krygier Memorial Lecture, Melbourne, Radio National, 29 August 1996.

Kumar, Krishan. "Civil Society: An Inquiry into the Usefulness of an Historical Term", *British Journal of Sociology* 44 (September 1993): 375–401.

Lewin, Moshe. *The Gorbachev Phenomenon*. Berkeley: University of California Press, 1988.

Malarney, Shaun Kingsley. "Return to the Past? The Dynamics of Contemporary Religious and Ritual Transformation". In *Postwar Vietnam: Dynamics of a Transforming Society*, edited by Hy V. Luong, pp. 225–56. Boulder and Singapore: Rowman and Littlefield and ISEAS, 2003.

Marr, David G. "A Passion for Modernity: Intellectuals and the Media". In *Postwar Vietnam: Dynamics of a Transforming Society*, edited by Hy V. Luong, pp. 257–95. Boulder and Singapore: Rowman and Littlefield and ISEAS, 2003.

———, ed. *The Mass Media in Vietnam*. Canberra: Dept. of Political and Social Change, The Australian National University, 1998.

Nguyen Ngoc Truong. "Grassroots Organizations in Rural and Urban Vietnam during Market Reform: An Overview of their Emergence and Relationship to the State". Paper presented at the Vietnam Update Conference, The Australian National University, Canberra, 10–11 November 1994.

Nguyen Van Chinh. "Work Without Name: Changing Patterns of Children's Work in a Northern Vietnamese Village". Ph.D. dissertation, Universiteit van Amsterdam, 2000.

Nielson, Ulla. *Vietnamese Trade Unions at a Cross Road: The Implications of Structural Change for the Relationship between the State and Trade Unions in Vietnam*. Copenhagen: The Copenhagen Business School, 1996.

Ninh, Kim N.B. *A World Transformed: The Politics of Culture in Revolutionary Vietnam, 1945–1965*. Ann Arbor: University of Michigan Press, 2002.

Phan Dai Doan. "May Suy Nghi ve Xu Ly cac Thiet Che Chinh Tri Xa Hoi Nong Thon Hien Nay" [Thoughts on dealing with today's rural social and political institutions]. In *Kinh Nghiem To Chuc Quan Ly Nong Thon Viet Nam trong Lich Su* [Historical experience of organizing and managing Vietnam's countryside], edited by Phan Dai Doan and Nguyen Quang Ngoc, pp. 42–72. Hanoi: NXB Chinh Tri Quoc Gia, 1994.

———. "Mot So Van De Ly Luan va Thuc Tien ve The Che Quan Ly Nong Thon Hien Nay" [Some theoretical and practical matters regarding managing the countryside today]. In *Quan Ly Xa Hoi Nong Thon Nuoc Ta Hien Nay: Mot So Van De va Giai Phap*, edited by Phan Dai Doan, pp. 215–56. Hanoi: NXB Chinh Tri Quoc Gia, 1996a.

———. "Thiet Che Chinh Tri—Xa Hoi Nong Thon Nuoc Ta: Thuc Trang va Quan Diem Giai Quyet" [Our nation's rural social and political institutions: realities and views on solving problems]. In *Quan Ly Xa Hoi Nong Thon Nuoc Ta Hien Nay: Mot So Van De va Giai Phap*, edited by Phan Dai Doan, pp. 11–67. Hanoi: NXB Chinh Tri Quoc Gia, 1996b.

Phap Luat ve Quyen Hoi Hop, Lap Hoi va Tu Do Tin Nguong cua Cong Dan [Laws regarding citizens' rights to assembly, to establish associations, and to religious beliefs]. Hanoi: NXB Phap Ly, 1992.

Pedersen, Katrine Riisgaard. "Civil Society and NGO Development in Vietnam". Unpublished paper, 2000, 9 pp.

Saich, Tony. "Negotiating the State: The Development of Social Organizations in China", *The China Quarterly* 161 (March 2000): 124–41.

Sidel, Mark. "The Emergence of a Nonprofit Sector and Philanthropy in the Socialist Republic of Vietnam". In *Emerging Civil Society in the Asia Pacific Community*, edited by Tadashi Yamamoto, pp. 293–304. Tokyo: Japan Center for International Exchange and Singapore: ISEAS, 1995.

Silliman, G. Sidney and Lela Garner Noble, eds. *Organizing for Democracy: NGOs, Civil Society, and the Philippine State*. Quezon City: Ateneo de Manila University Press, 1998.

Stromseth, Jonathan. "Reform and Response in Vietnam: State-Society Relations and the Changing Political Economy". Ph.D. dissertation, Columbia University, 1998.

Suhong Chae. "Spinning Work and Weaving Life: The Politics of Production in a Capitalistic Multinational Textile Factory in Vietnam". Ph.D. dissertation, The City University of New York, 2003.

Taylor, Philip. *Goddess on the Rise: Pilgrimage and Popular Religion in Vietnamese Society*. Honolulu: University of Hawai'i Press, forthcoming.

Thayer, Carlyle A. "Mono-Organizational Socialism and the State". In *Vietnam's Rural Transformation*, edited by Benedict J. Tria Kerkvliet and Doug J. Porter, pp. 39–64. Boulder and Singapore: Westview Press and ISEAS, 1995.

———. "Political Reform in Vietnam: Doi Moi and the Emergence of Civil Society". In *Development of Civil Society in Communist Systems*, edited by Robert F. Miller, pp. 110–29. North Sydney: Allen and Unwin, 1992.

———. "Report on Thai Binh", parts 1–3, posted to the Southeast Asia Discussion List, <SEASIA-L@List.MSU.EDU>, 26 August 1998.

Thich Quan Do. *Nhan Dinh ve Nhung Sai Lam Tai Hai cua Dang Cong San Viet Nam doi voi Dan Toc va Phat Giao* [Grave mistakes of the Vietnam Communist Party against the nation and Buddhism]. Paris: Phong Thong Tin Phat Giao Quoc Te; Que Me, 1995.

Truong Thanh-Dam. "Uncertain Horizon: The Women's Question in Vietnam Revisited". In *Vietnam: Reform and Transformation*, edited by Björn Beckman, Eva Hansson, and Lisa Romàn, pp. 73–116. Stockholm: Center for Pacific Asia Studies, Stockholm University, 1997.

Woodside, Alexander. "The Development of Social Organizations in Vietnamese Cities in the Late Colonial Period". *Pacific Affairs* 44 (1971): 39–64.

1

From Fence-Breaking to Networking: Interests, Popular Organizations and Policy Influences in Post-Socialist Vietnam[1]

Thaveeporn Vasavakul

Political and economic reforms beginning in the 1980s have, as correctly observed by Carlyle Thayer, led to "a loosening of the party's mono-organizational grip on society and to the explosion of private activities, which the state has found difficult to control" (Thayer 1992, p.110). In post-socialist Vietnam, this loosening provided opportunities for citizens to form groupings in pursuit of certain common interests.[2] By the end of the 1990s, the Vietnamese themselves began to use the term "non-governmental organization" (*co quan phi chinh phu*) to refer to popular organizations that were loosely connected to the party-state structure, financially self-sufficient and involved in development work once considered as falling under the jurisdiction of the party-state.

This paper focuses on how popular organizations, both state and non-state sponsored, influenced the policy-making process in the era of *doi moi*. It examines the relationship between interests, organizational networking, and policy influence. It argues that although popular organizations—state and non-state sponsored—continued to be closely associated with the party-state structure, they assumed an increasingly important role as advocates and pioneers for policy options on behalf of certain interests. Operating under the structure of the one-party state, the successful organizations were the ones that could muster political resources by both vertical networking with certain sections of the party-state hierarchy, and horizontal networking with other popular organizations. The vertical alliance provided the necessary policy support from elements within the party-state, while the horizontal alliance helped to legitimize the policy position these organizations are adopting. I argue that this model of policy influence departs from that developed under state socialism in which interest aggregation was top-down, the mobilization channels for policy influence were vertically and sectorally-based, and policy positions were expressed mostly through the method of "fence-breaking" (*pha rao*), i.e., violations of rules and regulations set up by the party-state. This influence in policy-making marks a transformation of the mono-organizational structure, from so-called "exclusionary" towards some degree of "inclusionary" corporatism.[3]

In this paper, I use the collective "popular organizations" to refer to a range of different popular groupings developed both under state socialism and during the post-socialist period. They include the five following groupings:

(a) "Mass Organizations" (*doan the*). Mass organizations are functional groups attached to the Vietnamese Communist Party such as the Youth's and Women's Unions.

(b) "Popular Association" (*hoi quan chung*). These are voluntary groupings organized around any number of distinguishing features, e.g., age, school year, hobby, occupational interests and religious beliefs. Popular associations are not new. As early as 1957, Ho Chi Minh had issued a decree to allow the setting up of associations and the decades that followed witnessed the rise of various associations along occupational lines. Under *doi moi*, new popular associations have proliferated. The degree of their connection with the party-state structure varies but most are self-supporting. Their distancing from party-state sponsorship and financing sets them apart from mass organizations. Among different types of popular associations, professional associations (*hoi nghe nghiep*) organized by intellectuals and businesses increasingly play an important role. The Association for Vietnamese Historians (Hoi Su Hoc), set up in the 1960s, and the Vietnam Gardening Association (Hoi Lam Vuon Viet Nam), set up in the 1980s, are two examples.

(c) "Non-State Research Institutes and Centres" (*vien/trung tam nghien cuu*). These are small-scale groupings organized by intellectuals and technocrats from various fields. They are run by intellectuals and technocrats who may or may not be affiliated with state-sponsored institutes and centres. Some centres and institutes are affiliated with development-oriented popular associations.

(d) "Political-Social-Professional Organizations" (*to chuc chinh tri, xa hoi va nghe nghiep*). These are large groupings usually comprising popular associations and are considered by the party-state as representative of the collective interests of their member associations. An official classification as a "political-social-professional organization" will entitle a particular grouping to receive official funding and directly participate in general policy debates. There is no evidence suggesting that this type of organization existed before the *doi moi* period. Under state socialism, the term "organization" or *to chuc* was only used to refer to *to chuc dang* meaning "party organization". The party-state's recognition of the "to chuc chinh tri, xa hoi va nghe nghiep" during the *doi moi* period marks a turning point in the political relationship between the party-state and popular organizations.[4] Vietnamese practitioners comment that professional associations with or without state sponsorship will want to negotiate for "political-social-professional organization" status because this brings them automatic state financial contributions and political influence in policy-making circles. However, in the 1990s, the number of this type of organization was very small.

(e) "Non-Governmental Organizations" (NGOs)—These are a *doi moi* product which emerged in Vietnam around the end of the 1990s. The Vietnamese use this term to refer to (b), (c), and (d) that are: loosely connected to the party-state structure, financially self-sufficient, provide services once considered to fall under the jurisdiction of the party-state, and charge fees for their professional services.[5] Unlike (a), (b), (c), and (d), the title NGO does not have official status but is a term used by Vietamese practitioners to describe themselves for various purposes.[6] Hence there can be an overlap when a professional association, a research institute, or a political-social-professional organization calls itself an NGO.

The existence of the different types of popular organizations outlined above draws attention to the potential development of vertical and horizontal networking which is the key focus of this paper. The arguments on interests, organizational networking, and policy influence put forth in this paper are drawn from a preliminary examination of the activities of the Association of Vietnamese Folklorists (AVF aka Hoi Van Nghe Dan Gian Viet Nam) and of the Centre for Rural Communities Research and Development (CCRD aka Trung Tam Nghien Cuu va Phat Trien Cong Dong Nong Thon). The two are similar in their success in advocating policies not initially supported by the party-state. The AVF's activities contributed substantially to the revival of the cult of the holy mothers, an indigenous popular cult that had been proscribed by the party-state. The CCRD experimented with alternative models in agricultural development and attempted to put forth policy alternatives. The two organizations, however, differ from one another in their official affiliation. The AVF is clearly connected with the party-state structure. It is a state-sponsored professional organization that is placed under the Vietnam Union of Literature and Arts Associations (VULAA aka Lien Hiep Cac Hoi Van Hoc Nghe Thuat Viet Nam), itself a state-sponsored umbrella organization as well as a political-social-professional organization for literature and the arts. The CCRD is registered as a research centre under the Vietnam Gardening Association (VACVINA aka Hoi Lam Vuon Viet Nam), a body registered as a popular association. VACVINA in turn comes under the Vietnam Union of Science and Technology Associations (VUSTA aka Lien Hiep Cac Hoi Khoa Hoc Ky Thuat Viet Nam), recognized as both a front organization for scientific and technical professional associations and a political-social-professional organization.[7] However CCRD, VACVINA, and VUSTA call themselves NGOs in their brochures. This paper looks at AVF's and CCRD's capacity to influence policy, given the varying degrees of state control related to these bodies and the extent to which networking within or outside the system is important.

This chapter consists of five parts. The first looks at interests and policy influence under state socialism, emphasizing the top-down nature of interest aggregation and policy-making, the absence of an active role for popular associations, the sectorally-based nature of policy interests, and the pervasive use of fence-breaking as the means to communicate policy preferences. The second part of the paper focuses on the development of non-state sponsored popular associations and the redefinition of the relationship between the state and these entities during the *doi moi* period, emphasizing the close connection between the party-state structure and all kinds of popular organizations. The third and fourth parts look at the organizational networks of the AVF and the CCRD as well as their activities. I conclude the chapter by discussing how this preliminary investigation may serve to generate hypotheses for further studies on the changing nature of the Vietnamese political system in the post-socialist era.

Policy Influence under State Socialism

Vietnam watchers have resorted to a wide range of terms to characterize the state socialist system that developed in the Democratic Republic of Vietnam (DRV, 1945–76) and the Socialist Republic of Vietnam (SRV, 1976 to the present): mono-organizational socialism, the DRV model, the Stalinist model, mobilizational authoritarianism, state corporatism, and bureaucratic authoritarianism.[8] Running through this diversity of labels is a common set of political structural features: the predominant role of the Communist Party, democratic centralism in decision-making, the interwoven nature of the party and the state, party control of social organizations, and a certain degree of coercion.

The party-state structure began to develop in the early 1950s, with the revival of the Communist Party under the name of the Vietnam Workers' Party (VWP) at its Second Congress in 1951. The years that followed witnessed the gradual development of what Dang Phong and Beresford call the "partification" of the state.[9] The Communist Party controlled the state apparatus through a set of mechanisms. The party issued directives to guide every major affair of state and supervised the state apparatus through the system of central committee commissions. It was also directly involved in the appointment, promotion, and dismissal of state officials.

Party control extended to popular organizations in the 1950s. In 1955, the Vietnam Fatherland Front (VFF aka Mat Tran To Quoc Viet Nam) was founded to function as an umbrella organization under which mass organizations such as the Women's Union, the Association of Farming Collectives, the Confederation of Labour, and the Ho Chi Minh Youth Union, were placed.[10] VFF itself was placed under the leadership of the Central Party Commission for Mass Mobilization.[11] It was, in theory, designed to serve two functions. One was to implement party and state policies in their areas of responsibility; another was to act as a transmission conduit channelling information from member organizations to the party for policy formulation purposes. The VFF has branches from central to district levels. Below that (e.g., at the enterprise, commune, school, and neighbourhood levels), only the VFF member associations such as the labour, youth and women's unions are present.

The VFF model has been replicated to gather other popular organizations with related interests into various fronts. This "front" or "*lien hiep*" strategy provides an institutional framework through which party supervision and influence can be activated. VULAA was founded in 1943 by the Indochinese Communist Party to mobilize support from intellectual circles.[12] In the 1950s and 1960s, member associations representing the different artistic professions came into being.[13] In that same period, associations covering the sciences and technology also emerged. Examples include Vietnam General Association of Medicine and Pharmacy, Vietnam Physics Society, Vietnam Association of Historians and the Vietnam Foundry and Metallurgical Association, to name just a few. In the 1970s, the Vietnam Economics Association (1974) was formed. In 1983, these scientific and technological associations were placed under another front organization, VUSTA.

Interests and Policy Influence

Among existing writings on Vietnam that explore the key features of the state socialist system, few discuss policy-making and policy influence prior to *doi moi*. Dang Phong and Beresford are rare exceptions. They outline four levels of economic decision-making: broad programmatic decisions; strategic decisions affecting the medium to long-term direction of particular sectors; shorter-term decisions affecting the macro-management of the economy or of particular sectors within it; and day-to-day decisions of economic actors (individuals or organizations) in response to policy signals received. In the context of the 1960s and 1970s, the programmatic decisions would include issues related to features of state socialism such as central planning, public and collective ownership of the means of production, and distribution according to labour productivity. The strategic decisions would include, for example, issues related to agricultural collectivization and the structure and rate of industrial investment. Short-term decisions would include particular projects or the selection of pilot models. Day-to-day decisions would include action taken by local actors to implement instructions from above. The authors argue that in reality it was difficult for an individual leader, a sector, or a social group to influence decisions on programmes and strategies. Changes at these first two levels were likely to involve large numbers of actors and interests. During the 1960s and 1970s, the third and the fourth levels of decision-making saw more inclusionary debates. Those participating in the former were mostly from the party-state structure and ranged from ministry and province-level officials to those even lower-ranking, such as the local actors in various economic sectors.[14]

Available empirical studies on pre-*doi moi* Vietnam confirm somewhat the observations put forth by Dang Phong and Beresford. The *Nhan Van Giai Pham* affair that unfolded between 1955 and 1958 can be considered as a move by Vietnamese intellectuals in educational, arts, and literary circles to challenge both the programmatic and the strategic decision-making directions of the VWP. However, this attempt failed. There was a split within the intellectual, literary and artistic sector itself, in addition to the fact that the party-state was unified in countering the attack launched by the *Nhan Van Giai Pham* group.[15] In the decades that followed, the role of intellectuals and professionals was limited. Professional associations under the umbrella of VULAA mostly followed the programmatic and strategic guidelines put forth by the party-state.[16]

Available empirical evidence also corroborates how ministries, provinces or lower-level localities could influence policy. Vinh Phuc Party Secretary Kim Ngoc's initiative in experimenting with the subcontracting system in the province in 1966 and Long An province's initiative in applying the market price system in the 1980s were cases in point. In both cases, provincial officials were backed by at least one party leader at the Politburo level, General Secretary Le Duan in the case of the Vinh Phuc experiment and Le Duc Tho in the case of Long An.[17] Adam Fforde's study of the role of state-owned enterprises and its commercialized interests in the 1980s suggest that SOE managers, themselves senior and middle-level cadres, might have put pressure on the party leaders to adopt *doi moi* as an official policy at the 1986 Sixth National Congress. Carlyle Thayer's analysis of the sectoral composition of the Central Committee members from 1951 to 1986 also suggests that at the Sixth National Congress (1986), middle-level cadres probably played an important role in pushing the reform policy forward.[18]

Existing writings also confirm Dang Phong and Beresford's observation of the role of local actors in influencing day-to-day policy implementation (White 1985, Hy Van Luong 1994, and Kerkvliet 1995). Overall, local actors' reactions to state policy had the effect, one way or another, of changing the short-term and some medium-range strategies of the party-state. However, they did not bring about changes in the "programmatic" direction. Programmatic changes require additional domestic or international pressure. In 1979, for example, resistance from southern peasants in itself would not have been sufficient to force the party-state to move towards socialist reform. Other factors at work included a series of external shocks caused by the renewal of war with China and Democratic Kampuchea; massive reductions in external assistance from the United States, China, and the Soviet Union; and the impending application of much higher international trade prices through the Council for Mutual Economic Assistance (CMEA). All these factors led to recurring economic crises.

In sum, under the state socialist system, popular organizations played a limited role in influencing policy. Available writings suggest that most functioned as transmission conduits to convey party-state policy to social groups, and to mobilize social groups to fulfill party-state policy goals. Policy influence came from within the party-state structure, for instance, from officials in ministries, provinces and lower-level localities. In this pattern, interest aggregation and articulation were top-down. Local actors also asserted policy influence by relying mostly on fence-breaking strategies to convey their policy preferences. In neither case was there any organizational networking that linked sections of the party-state to popular interests, nor was there any horizontal linkage between local actors in various locations.

Growth of Popular Organizations

The 1990s witnessed the expansion of popular organizations that had no state sponsorship. The key ones were professional, charity, friendship, and sport associations as well as non-state research centres and institutes. The political and economic reforms of *doi moi* combined to promote their growth in various ways. For example, the transition from central planning to a market economy paralyzed the provision of services that were traditionally the responsibility of the state. Popular associations in many localities filled this vacuum. There was a need to create channels for public response and comment on reform policies. A return to "Ho Chi Minh thought" on the united front strategy meant ideological support for those who want to form associations to participate in national construction.[19] International openness allowed international NGOs to operate in Vietnam in the 1980s and expand their activities in the 1990s; they served as a model for Vietnamese professional associations, research institutes, and development centres. The international NGOs also provided much-needed financial assistance to fuel the growth of Vietnamese charity and development-oriented popular organizations such as the Vietnam Red Cross Association and the Vietnam Gardening Association.

Relationship with the Party-State

The liberalization of conditions for setting up popular organizations began with Directive 01/CT from the Council of Ministers dated January 5, 1989. A series of party decrees followed, such as Resolution no. 08 issued by the Central Committee in March 1990.[20] However as the numbers grew, the situation became more complex and the party leadership felt the need for more stringent regulations. Politburo documents issued in 1998 clarified the relationship between the party-state and popular associations.[21] The Politburo called on party and state agencies to evaluate the development of popular associations since Resolution no. 08 and raised the need for new laws to address the changing situation of interests getting organized in the post-central planning era. More specifically, the party-state leadership was concerned with an increasingly chaotic situation where popular associations were set up without following proper procedures and were, technically speaking, "illegal". Many associations reportedly changed their activities without reporting to the upper echelons. Yet, many associations, once set up, were not active. Some only focused on getting state funding to develop infrastructure facilities. Some focused on administrative routine without doing any real work for members. Directive no. 42 referred specifically to the inadequacy of party leadership in these entities and wanted the *dang doan* (party board) in each organization to enforce party guidelines more forcefully.[22] The tighter regulatory regime requires a new association to seek official permission from a government agency—either the Committee for Government Organization and Personnel or the Prime Minister's Office—and have its statutes endorsed by relevant state agencies. Membership is forbidden for foreigners. In principle, the party-state expects popular associations to be of a voluntary nature, self-governing, and self-financing. However, where funding is concerned, the state will provide money if a particular association provides services that contribute to government plans.

Despite the official call for them to be voluntary and self-governing, these new associations are influenced by the organizational characteristics of the one-party socialist state. Many try to replicate the top-down hierarchical structure that descends from central through provincial, district, and commune levels. Many are staffed by retired state officials. Another feature inherited from the state socialist period is the party-state's use of the "front" system as an umbrella organization to oversee popular associations with similar or related interests and activities. Thus a new grouping will eventually be co-opted into existing umbrella entities such as the likes of VULAA or VUSTA.

However, the new associations also have features that mark a departure from the old ways. The popular associations that developed in the late 1980s and the 1990s are different in their representation, missions, and forms of participation. A growing number of them represent the interests of newly emerging sectoral or social groups, were pro-globalization and pro-capitalism in outlook, supported cultural pluralism, and increasingly assumed responsibilities not assigned to them earlier. Their new roles ranged from education or training to consultancy and development. Some popular associations were able to get involved in the process of setting and implementing policy. These features stand in contrast with the reasons for setting up some pre-*doi moi* associations. For example, the Association of Vietnamese Lawyers served mainly to represent the erstwhile DRV at international forums on legal issues and was placed under the Ministry of Foreign Affairs. The Traditional Medicine Association of Vietnam was founded by Ho Chi Minh himself, who reportedly appreciated the contribution that traditional medicine had made in the 1940s and 1950s.[23] The Vietnam Economics Association was founded as a result of the need for Vietnam to send a non-governmental delegation to attend an international economics conference.

Apart from the popular associations, all of the post-socialist popular organizations have to learn to manage a more complex environment to secure a level of success. The key factors in this process include the personal credibility of their leaders, alliances with the party and state leadership, horizontal connections and support from other organizations, and alliances with their societal constituencies.

The Association for Vietnamese Folklorists: Networks and Activities

The Association for Vietnamese Folklorists is a popular association which comes under VULAA, which is in turn under the leadership of the Party Commission for Ideology and Culture (Ban Tu Tuong Van Hoa) and the Party Commission for Organization (Bo To Chuc). Despite being located within the hierarchical party system, the AVF is quite independent of VULAA when it comes to management, finance, and personnel. This independence applies also to other professional organizations under the VULAA umbrella. The AVF has its own provincial branches, thus forming vertical hierarchical networks of its own. It is at liberty to engage horizontally with other state and non-state sponsored popular associations in the arts and literature circles. The horizontal network also covers departments within universities, research institutes and culturally-oriented popular associations as well as local cultural clubs. Because the AVF's mission concentrates on popular culture, it has also developed long-term connections with individual villages or groups of villages with a vested interest in reviving particular aspects of folk culture.

VULAA: Structure and Members

The VULAA statute, revised at its sixth national congress in 2000, states that the union is a "political, social and professional organization". It is also the Fatherland Front of literature and arts associations in Vietnam.[24] In 2001, the VULAA structure consisted of the central union structure, 10 central-level member associations, and 61 provincial and municipal unions. [25]

The VULAA central union coordinates the activities of its member associations and provincial and municipal unions. The central union's main decision-making body is its quinquennial congress. Between congresses, the union's national commission, consisting of the heads of the ten member associations and the sixty-one provincial and municipal branches of the union, meets annually. Between these annual sessions, the president, three vice presidents and the presidium (consisting of general secretaries from the ten member associations and the three municipal branch unions from Hanoi, Hue and Ho Chi Minh City) run day-to-day affairs with the assistance of a standing committee. The central union's financial resources come from the government, income generated from its activities, and contributions from individuals or domestic organizations.[26]

The ten central member associations are the Associations of Vietnamese Writers, Fine Arts, Vietnamese Musicians, Vietnamese Artists, Film Makers, Photographers, Dancers, Architects, Folklorists, and Minority Arts and Literature. Total membership was around 10,000 in 2000.[27] These member associations are independent of the central union, run their own organization, recruit their own personnel, and set membership qualifications. All publish their own newspapers and periodicals and some run their own publishing houses and clubs although the resources to do this vary.

In addition to the main task of assisting their members in professional matters, these associations advise the state on policies related to arts and culture and contribute to state cultural projects when requested. The Association of Vietnamese Musicians, for example, proposed that music be taught in kindergartens and primary schools, while the Association of Vietnamese Architects assisted the government with urban planning and legal issues related to construction. The Association of Vietnamese Writers assisted the Ministry of Education with the reform of textbooks on literature, and the Association for Minority Arts and Literature on textbooks for ethnic minority primary schools.

Both the central union and its member associations assist provincial and municipal unions on relevant professional issues. Provincial and municipal unions in turn provide assistance for their members, arranging training, creating a favourable working environment and publishing members' work. The organizational structure of the sixty-one provincial and municipal unions varies, however: some are stronger than others. The Ho Chi Minh City union, for example, has eight member associations under its supervision. Most of the provincial branch unions, however, do not have separate member associations owing to their smaller membership. The local unions' relationship with the central union varies. At the VULAA congress in 2000, members raised the need for more local representation in the leadership body and for greater coordination between central and provincial bodies.

VULAA and its Relationship with the Party-State

In theory, the party oversees the organization of VULAA's congresses with special attention given to who should be elected as office bearers. Agencies or figures of authority responsible for organizing VULAA's sixth national congress in 2000 included a Vice Prime Minister, members of the Politburo and the Central Committee, Party Commission for Ideology and Culture, Party Commission for Personnel, Committee for Government Organization and Personnel, VULAA's party board, and the leaders of member associations. All provincial branches of VULAA are placed under the leadership of respective provincial party committees. The central union and its member associations are also under the management of several government bodies such as the Committee for Government Organization and Personnel (called the Ministry of Home Affairs since mid-2001, see n.35), the Ministry of Planning and Investment, and the Ministry of Culture and Information. VULAA's statutes have to be endorsed by the Minister of the CGOP. The central union and its members receive funding directly from the Ministry of Finance. They work with the Ministry of Culture and Information on activities related to arts and culture.

In practice, the relationship between the party-state, VULAA, and its member associations is problematic. As late as 2000, a Politburo Standing Board document asked for the central union to work with both the party and the state to clarify the role and position of the party board in the union and member associations.[28] At the provincial level, party leadership seems unbalanced. At VULAA's sixth national congress in 2000, delegates complained that the party did not provide sufficient leadership. Examples cited include the lack of clear instruction for local unions on personnel and funding matters, the absence of coordination between the central and local unions, and the inconsistency of organizational procedure at all levels of the union.[29] The extent of the problems led one delegate to ask whether provincial unions were under the party or the state, or neither.[30]

But today's problems with administrative coordination do not have the same political gravity as the ideological discontent within VULAA and its member associations in the early years of *doi moi*. In the late 1980s, both the leadership and members of the Association for Vietnamese Writers criticized the party's cultural policy as outdated and not in keeping with the need for reforms. These critics painted a dark picture of the old doctrinaire socialist policy that had not produced any real art. They demanded complete freedom of expression and the complete withdrawal of the party-state from artistic and literary spheres.

This spirit of protest which characterized the initial years of *doi moi* provides the background to understanding how the relationship between the party-state and public organizations is not always a placid affair despite seemingly well-entrenched methods of supervision. Artists and their associations can and do influence policy-making. My case study of AVF, its cultural contribution in general and its contribution to the revival of the cult of the holy mothers in particular, will reveal the way in which a party-affiliated popular organization has participated in the cultural policy formation process.

AVF as Promoters of Cultural Pluralism

Set up in November 1966, AVF is a professional association of researchers and practitioners collecting, researching, developing, propagating and teaching the traditional cultural, literary and artistic values of the Vietnamese people. By the end of the 1990s, the association claimed to have completed over 15,000 written projects, each more than 100 pages long and sometimes amounting to around 40,000 pages. In addition, association members have collected over 10,000 folk songs and about 500 hours of tapes recording popular customs.[31]

Since the introduction of *doi moi*, a major party policy has been the promoting of national cultural heritage. Like other member associations under VULAA, AVF planned many activities in accord with this party line. Some examples from the 1990s include its organization of a national meeting on lullaby singing and central highlands musical meetings in Dac Lac, clubs for *cheo* performances, and exhibitions on handicraft villages. It collaborated with other VULAA member associations and provincial branch unions to organize conferences focusing on "the maintenance and development of the national cultural heritage". Emphasis was given to different parts of Vietnam. AVF propagated its concept of cultural pluralism by organizing short-term cultural training courses for its counterparts in the provinces and municipalities. These training courses focused on the cultural policy of the party and the state; the history of ethnic groups in Vietnam; the popular arts and culture of the Viet and of minorities; and specialized subjects such as folk poems, folk songs, epics and legends.[32]

This party policy provides leeway for organizations to explore a broader agenda but the case of the Cult of the Holy Mothers (Dao Mau) demonstrates the limits of what the state can accept. It also shows how the AVF mobilized support from the party leadership and formed alliances with various popular associations, state-sponsored research agencies, and local state agencies in the process of rehabilitating the cult and getting it recognized. The cult's revival underwent three stages: prohibition and fence-breaking (before 1987), experimentation (1987–1993); and public recognition (1993–2000).

Background on the Cult of the Holy Mothers

The Cult of the Holy Mothers is an indigenous belief institutionalized around the 16th century. It originally referred to the worshipping of three female deities representing the three realms of heaven (*thien phu*), earth (*dia phu*) and the high seas (*thuy phu*). To this, a fourth was added to represent the forest. The cult does not have an organized clergy. Instead of priests and missionaries, it only has *ong dong* and *ba dong* (male and female mediums) who are believed to be predestined to serve the cult. They lead the life of the laity, propagating the cult within the limited circle of their followers.

The cult itself is manifested in the ceremony called *hau bong*, which translates broadly as "receiving incarnations of the deities". When this ceremony is in session, the medium goes into a trance, awaiting spiritual possession by the deities. The ceremony includes a number of *gia* (incarnations). Each *gia* requires a specific costume and make-up, sometimes very expensive. During the ceremony, the liturgical singer plays music and sings invocations, accompanied by traditional musical instruments. In the course of an average *hau bong* session, ten to fifteen deities are incarnated in the medium. When the medium feels possessed by a deity, he or she makes appropriate signs. The assistants then dress the medium in the costume corresponding to that deity. Each deity's descent is followed by the offering of incense sticks. Then the medium incarnating a deity begins to dance to the accompaniment of liturgical music and songs played by a *cung van* (liturgical singer). At the end of the dance, participants then approach the seated medium to have fortunes told or make offerings in return for wishes granted. The deity hands out sacred gifts in the form of incense sticks. A ceremony of *hau dong* can last from two to seven hours.[33]

From Fence-Breaking to Recognition

During the socialist period, the party-state prohibited the Cult of the Holy Mothers on the grounds that it was a form of superstition. This was in keeping with an official policy to proscribe popular cultural practices considered to be superstitious or wasteful. Despite prohibition, fence-breaking was pervasive. Local followers tell of the times when they organized *hau bong* ceremonies in secret and, if necessary, bribed the local police to look the other way. The mediums recalled the times they were "invited" to the police station to discuss the matter. Some were detained, although the detention period was normally very short.

In 1987, one year after *doi moi* was officially endorsed, pressure to relax the prohibition came from local followers and attendants of the holy mother temples in various parts of the Red River delta, the centre being in Phu Giay, Nam Dinh province. Local followers, organized around informal associations called "pure heart" (*Hoi Chan Tam/Thanh Tam*), sought support from AVF.

The AVF leadership, in an attempt to liberalize the traditional cultural sphere, relied on a networking strategy. It first sought support from a party leader cum government official in the Ministry of Culture. The main argument put forth to justify the revival of the cult was that both the sacred dance movements performed by the medium, and the music itself, were forms of popular culture that needed to be studied and preserved. These arguments were also effective in mobilizing support from popular culture intellectuals working in performance arts and music associations. The idea of preserving the traditional musical element of *hau bong* also attracted support from Vietnamese composers and singers. One famous musician, Pho Duc Phuong, reportedly went so far as to use the *hau bong* style to compose pop songs. The AVF leadership, through the provincial association of folklorists in Nam Dinh, also sought support from the provincial party and state authorities that later agreed with the revival of the ceremony. Finally, the AVF worked with local cult followers in Nam Dinh to provide specific historical information about the cult. It turned out that there were two local temples claiming to be the real site of worship. A compromise was eventually made when all parties concerned agreed that on festival days, the ceremonial procession would visit both sites.

The period from 1987 to 1993 was a period of experimentation when the *hau bong* ceremony was allowed on a limited scale. The Phu Giay temple in Nam Dinh was the first to revive and perform the ceremony. Holy Mothers temples in other provinces followed. These ceremonies were considered as occasions for folklorists, musicians, and theatrical performers to "study" the dance and music. Since there had not yet been an official directive that openly permitted the ceremony to take place, some provincial authorities were uncooperative. There were cases when barricades were set up to prevent the "research" delegations and cult followers from reaching the temples, forcing them to wade through rice fields instead.

The experimentation period ended around 1993 and the period from 1993 to 2000 was considered a time of public recognition. However, at a major festival in 2001, participants found red banners being hung across the streets with a statement advising people not to follow blindly all elements considered to be superstitious practices. Also in 2001, the Cult of the Holy Mothers became a topic of an international conference. This time, a foreign delegation attended the festival in Phu Giay, taking pictures and discussing *hau bong* in conjunction with other shamanistic practices found in many minority areas in Vietnam.

The revival of the Cult of the Holy Mothers came about as a result of complex organizational networking. From the vertical connection point of view, it involved at one time or another ministerial, provincial and local-level party-state officials. It also involved the AVF and its provincial branches. From the horizontal point of view, it involved contacts between party-state circles and popular organizations; among popular organizations themselves; and between popular organizations and local followers. This complex organizational networking was buttressed by a complex set of vested interests at work. More fieldwork is needed to detail why the various parties contributed to the revival of the Cult of the Holy Mothers. At this point, however, one should not assume that all parties concerned shared the same interests. From the perspective of the local followers, it was the spiritual interest that counted. From the grassroots level party-state perspective, it could be a combination of prestige gained from liberalizing cultural practices and from the economic gains resulting from the revival; local festivals in Vietnam had long been one key source of local revenue, let alone one with such regional importance as the Cult of the Holy Mothers. From the perspective of the AVF and other professional organisations, the key concern could be academic. From the perspective of the high ranking party-state members, it could be about prestige earned within leadership circles for supporting a popular and "culturally and academically grounded" policy initiative.

Viewed within a larger framework of governance in Vietnam, the revival of the Cult of the Holy Mothers indicates a new form of policy influence. The AVF served first as an advocate for a sector of the local population, while also acting as an intermediary between the party-state structure and its constituencies. It served as a coordinator to work with potential supporters from both the party-state and intellectual sectors. Despite its position as a party-affiliated organization, the goals and actions of the AVF approximated the modus operandi of an NGO, pointing to the fact that in Vietnam the line between state-sponsored organizations and NGOs is an ill-defined one. In the shifting dynamics of *doi moi*, the identity of an organization depends on a great deal more than its formal affiliation.

Centre for Rural Communities Research and Development: Operating within Hierarchies

The CCRD is a research centre which, according to its brochure, is staffed by "a group of scientists in technology, natural science and the social science working as volunteers for the sake of the community". Its founders and members come from a wide range of disciplines and fields including construction, human geography, sociology, economics, ethnology, oceanography, agriculture and environmental sciences. Its brochure lists six advisors, two of whom are former high-ranking government officials from the Ministry of Agriculture and Rural Development, two from research institutes, one from the Ministry of Planning and Investment and one from the Vietnam Gardening Association (VACVINA).[34] The CCRD brochure calls itself "a non-governmental and non-profit organization". It does not give details about its organizational affiliations. However, it is structurally attached to VACVINA, itself registered as a popular association placed under the management of VUSTA. Situated in the VACVINA-VUSTA hierarchy, the CCRD's organizational networking, although narrower and less complicated, looks similar to that of the AVF.

VUSTA and Members

VUSTA calls itself an NGO in its brochure but like VULAA, it is recognized by the party-state as a "political-social-professional organization". Also like VULAA, VUSTA is an umbrella organization gathering together various associations. For VUSTA, member associations are groupings of scientists and intellectuals. VUSTA has four main components: the central organization, member associations, provincial unions, and centres and research institutes registered under VUSTA. The total membership is 650,000 or about half of the total number of Vietnamese intellectuals (defined as those graduating from universities).

Similar to the other umbrella organizations such as the VFF and VULAA, VUSTA is governed by statutes set down at its quinquennial congress. To run the operation, the congress elects a central council consisting of representatives from all member associations and administrative staff. The central council elects a presidium. VUSTA's budget comes from government subsidies, returns from various scientific and technological activities and enterprises, donations from individuals and institutions, and membership contributions.

The member associations of VUSTA are the professional or specialized associations (*hoi chuyen nganh*) in natural sciences, social sciences, applied sciences and technology. The number of professional associations registered with VUSTA increased from 15 in 1983 to 22 in 1988, 34 in 1992, and 49 in 2001. Member associations have their own statutes that must not contradict that of the central union. They report to the central union twice yearly. They have responsibility for their own finance, with the exception of the associations of Vietnamese Lawyers, Traditional Medicine, and Medicine and Pharmacy, which received subsidies from the government before *doi moi* and have since retained the arrangement. All other member associations receive no financial support from the state but are entitled to work for government projects for a fee. Some member associations have complex organizations, running their own research centres, private schools and universities, and newspapers. The Association of Economics under former Vice Minister Tran Phuong, for example, administers a private university, the Hanoi University of Business Management, and runs an economics newspaper. The Association of Physics runs a private university, the Dong Do, and the Union of Technology and Science Associations of Hanoi yet another, the Phuong Dong.

New professional or specialized associations are expected to seek membership in VUSTA. To set up such an association, Vietnamese scientists in a particular professional branch will consult with the central union to see whether a new association is needed. To receive preliminary approval from VUSTA, the applicant will have to show that there are at least 1,000 people interested in joining and that the new association will be able to survive financially. Once these two conditions are met, the new association will be allowed to operate for 6 to 12 months. The central union will then ask the Government Committee for Organization and Personnel (GCOP) for approval.[35] The new association has to submit its draft statute, operational procedures and a list of temporary administrative staff. The GCOP will seek advice from various ministries before making its decision.[36]

VUSTA's third component is its 28 province or municipality level unions with varying numbers of member associations ranging from 8 to 40. In Ho Chi Minh City, the union has 34 members; in Hanoi around 30.

The final component—research centres or institutes—carry out research, training, consultancy and also practical work. Setting up a centre or an institute is easier than setting up an association. The process involves submitting a proposal directly to the central union. Once the latter agrees to sponsor the centre or institute, the latter will work with the Ministry of Science, Technology, and Environment and/or the Ministry of Education and Training to get official approval. In 2000,

VUSTA had 52 such centres and institutes concentrating mainly on business management, urban and rural development, environmental issues and training, and poverty-alleviation. Some participated in government-funded projects. Most of these research centres and institutes call themselves NGOs.

VUSTA's Relationship with the Party-State

VUSTA's founder was Prof. Lt Col Tran Dai Nghia, known as a designer of modern weapons during the wars of resistance. In the 1980s, he was President of the Vietnam Commission for Science and Technology, a position comparable to that of a minister. In 1983, he suggested that the government set up a union structure to unite 15 existing associations of science and technology. The proposal was accepted. During its first ten years of existence, however, VUSTA's role was minimal because, according to VUSTA staff members, there was no "political framework" in which it could operate. This difficult time lasted from its inception to the dawn of *doi moi*.[37]

If published party documents are to be believed, the party leadership enhanced the role of VUSTA. It is possible to speculate that the party-state's move could be an attempt to resolve tension between the party-state and the scientific and technological community over the latter's demand for political openness.[38] The Secretariat's Directive no. 35/CT-TW of April 11, 1988, called for the strengthening of VUSTA's organization and activities. The directive provided a general guideline that would become the framework for VUSTA's development. It considered VUSTA a popular association with a separate administration and its own voice. Initially, the government provided some funding but the union and its association members would later become financially independent. The directive called for the Commission for Science and Technology of Vietnam, the Commission for Social Sciences and Humanities and the Vietnam Institute of Science to coordinate with VUSTA, not merely to link the union with the state but also to help the union develop into an advisory agency. It also requested the Confederation of Labour Unions, the Youth Union and other mass organizations to coordinate their work with VUSTA. The party leadership wanted VUSTA to help stabilize and develop the economy and society, following the three reform economic policies of promoting foodstuffs, consumer goods and export goods, as outlined by the Sixth National

Party Congress in 1986. The directive emphasized the role of VUSTA in supervising member associations.

However, the party-state kept VUSTA within its structure by placing the union under the leadership of the Secretariat with the assistance of the Central Party Commission for Science and Education (Ban Khoa Giao Trung Uong).[39] In 1992, the secretariat issued a directive to institutionalize the party and state leadership within VUSTA. The Party Commission for Personnel and the Commission for Science and Education were to work with the union to set up a party board within the union. It also called for the Party Commission within the state (Ban Can Su Dang)[40] to consolidate state management of the union.[41] In August 1993, the Secretariat issued another document discussing party-VUSTA relations. It accorded the union the status of a political and social organization and again recognized that each member association was a self-governed organization that entered the union on a voluntary basis. Despite the self-governing status, the party still oversaw the selection of candidates to hold office in the union. The party board of the union would work with the Party Commissions for Personnel and for Science and Education, as well as coordinating with party members working in member associations.[42] As a political-social-professional organization, the union structure received funding from the state. Its political status was also elevated somewhat as political-social-professional organizations were included in policy-making circles. VUSTA staff members, however, commented that the party-state was not legally obliged to follow the union's recommendations.

Mission beyond Affiliation

Despite its close affiliation with the party-state structure, VUSTA's mission at times allows it to engage in far-reaching advocacy autonomous of the state. The central union's first mission is to coordinate and network with various groups of scientists and organize interdisciplinary conferences and meetings. It also tries to promote the application of technology in state management and policy implementation in general. This function is carried out through member associations and research centres or institutes registered under the central union. Finally, the central union coordinates member associations to comment on government proposals or provide advice when needed as collective voices can be more influential. In the 1990s, it gave advice on numerous crucial national-level projects including the north-south power line, the Son La hydroelectric power project, the construction of the Ho Chi Minh Highway through the nature reserve forests of Cuc Phuong, and the construction of seaports. However, no mechanism exists to compel party-state officials to adopt VUSTA's recommendations.[43]

VUSTA's member associations themselves also help to provide public education and training. For example, the Traditional Medicine Association of Vietnam has classes for those interested in using its techniques. The Vietnam Association for Information Processing teaches information technology via television and helps with its teaching in schools. These professional scientific associations also assume an advisory role and comment on government proposals. They provide advice on small projects implemented by state-owned enterprises and schools. For example, the Vietnam Association for Construction commented on the technical aspect of the My Thuan bridge (Hau River) and designed the Yaly hydroelectric power station. The Vietnam Electrical Power Association organized conferences to propose options for national energy policy and provided advice on the 500 kv north-south electricity system and the hydroelectric power stations at Yaly and Son La.

The Case of VACVINA and the VAC Model

VACVINA is a professional association set up in 1986 to promote sustainable agriculture through the development of the VAC ecosystem model.[44] VAC is an acronym of three Vietnamese words: *vuon* meaning garden or orchard; *ao* meaning fish pond; and *chuong* meaning animal shed. The VAC model focuses on interactions between these three farming systems with a view to recycling and using the residue from one system as material for another.

VACVINA is an example of the first generation of Vietnamese popular associations with a clear affiliation to the party-state structure but also claiming the status of an NGO. Retired ministerial-level officials from the ministries of Agriculture, Forestry, and Marine Resources founded it. Its first president was a former National Assembly member. Beyond the central VACVINA, there are branches in 61 provinces and municipalities. In addition to the nationwide network of gardener members, VACVINA also runs five centres and three companies that support the promotion of the VAC ecosystem. VACVINA does not receive funding from the state. Most of its funding comes from its domestic clients who sign contracts with VACVINA to do development work and from VACVINA's advisory projects for local communities seeking to develop VAC farming. VACVINA voices its opinions through newspapers and conferences with the Ministry of Agriculture and Rural Development or the cabinet.

VACVINA is a member association of VUSTA but the hierarchical relationship is a loose one. VACVINA has separately established relationships with the state structure, especially with the ministries of Agriculture, Marine Resources, Forestry, Education, Finance, Planning and Investment, and Science, Technology, and Environment. VACVINA also has established relations with the party structure and like all popular organizations is obliged to follow party guidelines. Working with the party structure has its advantages since the party can put pressure on rank and file to help facilitate the operation of the association.[45] VACVINA has also worked with party-sponsored mass organizations, especially the Peasant's Union, the Women's Union and the Fatherland Front, and other popular associations such as the Association of Fertilizer Producers and the Association for Vietnamese Planters. However, VACVINA's local activities vary from province to province depending on the composition of the leadership.[46]

Since its inception in 1986, VACVINA's activities have developed in three phases. The first, from 1986 to 1988, introduced the VAC model to rural producers. At the time when the association was set up, most agricultural land still belonged to cooperatives and the area that could be considered *vuon* (suitable for the VAC model) was limited to five per cent of the land. The second phase came with decollectivization of agriculture in 1988. In the late 1980s and early 1990s, the VAC model became popular for rural development and expanded to the delta, mountain, coastal, and forest areas. Economically, the model helped to increase the income of rural households; socially, it became a poverty reduction mechanism; and ecologically, it claimed to promote conditions for sustainable development. By the mid-1990s, the VAC model was applied nationwide by various groups. Colleges of agriculture have a department focusing on the VAC model. During the third phase of its development, which began roughly in the mid-1990s, it became the baseline for advice and assessment of other rural models of development. VACVINA also advised the state on plans for rural development.

Centre for Rural Communities Research and Development

CCRD consists of a group of volunteer scientists who work in the areas of technology, natural and social sciences. The organizational structure of CCRD shows signs of both vertical and horizontal networking. Vertically, CCRD includes in its advisory board some key state officials from the Ministry of Agriculture and Rural Development and the Ministry of Planning and Investment. It is one of VACVINA's five centres and carries out its activities within the framework of the resolutions of VACVINA congresses. CCRD also relies on the VACVINA structure at the provincial, district, and commune levels when carrying out its projects. In practice, the hierarchical relationship is poorly defined. CCRD is responsible for its own finances; this is one of the bases for CCRD's staff members to highlight its claim to NGO status. It has direct connections with rural producers while VACVINA's provincial branches, mostly staffed by active and retired state officials and members of farmer associations, do not.[47] Horizontally, CCRD incorporates into its management committee a network of technocrats and scientists from the fields of engineering, agricultural economics, oceanography, environmental sciences, human geography, sociology, and ethnology. CCRD also worked with both local authorities and local producers to propagate its development models.

CCRD's mission focuses on three areas: poverty alleviation in rural Vietnam; improvement of local community capacity through education; and promotion of environmentally sustainable development strategies. Its poverty reduction activities are based on the assumption that poverty comes from old ways of thinking and producers' refusal to risk entering the market. CCRD thus works to persuade local producers to move from self-sufficiency to production for the market. This involves moving away from mono-crop (rice) production (*doc canh lua*). Its plans for environmental protection in rural areas are based on the ecological principles of interconnection between multiple agricultural activities.

Believing in the VAC model, CCRD technocrats worked to develop it in various forms. In the delta, the VAC model was well accepted and spread quickly after land was decollectivized in 1988. In mountain areas, CCRD encouraged the planting of vegetables and fruit trees in minority villages. CCRD also advocated the so-called VACR—VAC in the forests (VAC Rung)—a plan carried out in 1994 to serve as an alternative to the government's unsuccessful attempts at reforestation. In 1980, the government promulgated Decision 327 on reforestation, subcontracting forest land to peasants and giving them 25 kilograms of rice for every hectare of land. Peasants accepted the handout but when they had consumed the rice, they returned to exploiting the forests. CCRD's VACR model divides forest areas into three separate sections reserved for growing: forest trees; or forest and fruit trees; or forest trees, fruit trees and other foodstuffs; as well as for animal husbandry. The VACR concept was based on the assumption that the government needs to provide peasants with the means of subsistence by allowing them to grow fruit trees wherever the land was suitable. As well as having commercial value, fruit trees afforded some protection for the soil.

The Ministry of Agriculture and Rural Development allowed the model to operate. A pilot project, *nong lam ket hop*, was carried out in Tuyen Quang province. In 2000, CCRD claimed that the VAC method solved the problems that Decision 327 failed to solve. Three hundred hectares of forest had been distributed among twenty-two families who replanted the forest land. Each family's annual income came from the production of about 300 fruit trees, each of which generated 2–300,000 VND (around US$13–15) a year. These families also grew other food crops, tended eighteen to twenty French geese and had between three and five beehives, each of which produced ten litres of honey per harvest. Since honey could be harvested twice a year, the income from raising bees was substantial.

Based on the VAC concept, CCRD has also experimented on several other rural projects with potential commercial value. These include the biogas programme (*bio-gas*), the combination of rice cultivation with duck rearing (*lua-vit*), the bamboo charcoal project (*than tre*), and a project to grow fruit in swampy land (*vuon u*). The biogas programme involves turning animal manure into gas for cooking, thus helping to keep rural areas clean, reduce women's work, and save energy; by 2000, it had been adopted by more than 3,000 families in 17 provinces. The *lua vit* project focuses on increasing duck production by raising ducklings in rice fields since only fully-grown birds damage crops. The project also emphasizes the production of rice without chemical fertilizers as duck manure helps fertilize the fields. The bamboo charcoal project is environmentally driven as the growing of bamboo prevents soil erosion and bamboo charcoal is non-polluting. The fruit-growing project is part of the effort to diversify farmers' income by getting farmers to switch from rice growing to fruit growing.

So far, the biogas project has been the only one that has received official government recognition as a model for rural development. In 2002, it was discussed in a public conference and received official endorsement by the Ministry of Agriculture and Rural Development. Of the other experiments, reforestation is considered too "limited" in scope; merging rice cultivation with duck rearing was good for the environment but the cost for producing the rice was too high; and the bamboo charcoal project could not be expanded until rural producers could find a market for the product. Finally, the fruit growing project went against the grain of a deeply entrenched habit in the Red River Delta to rely on rice cultivation and the central government's emphasis on food security in the Red River Delta.

CCRD has worked slowly, moving step by step, capitalizing on its vertical and horizontal networks. Michael Gray observes that the party-state structure is effective in getting work done and that NGOs will necessarily make use of this structure. Gray's observation is confirmed as CCRD's vertical connections with VACVINA did facilitate its operations at the grassroots level. CCRD, through VACVINA and its connections with the Ministry of Agriculture and Rural Development, was also able to draw policy-makers' attention to its initial experimental results.[48] However, the success of its projects depend, first and foremost, on the expertise and effectiveness of the scientists in the organization, i.e., its horizontal network of collaborators. The projects' success also depend on the degree of benefits they offer to the locality. This is particularly crucial as CCRD's projects have to be funded by the local clients themselves. Recently, CCRD has begun to network with international NGOs to solicit support and promotion for some of its projects.

Conclusion

The preliminary investigation of the AVF and the CCRD indicates continuity in popular organizations' affiliation with the party-state structure on the one hand and changes in their activities and role in policy-making on the other. The two cases, at first glance, show that the party-state retained its leadership over popular organizations and its directives continued to affect their activities. It relied on a number of mechanisms to regulate the new socio-economic and professional groupings that have emerged. In each case, an umbrella organization called a front was set up, a party board was required in associations classified as social and political organizations, and party members within the various types of popular organizations helped maintain the party line. However, in practice, party control has become increasingly indirect. The VCP worked with associations through an umbrella organization and increasingly relied on rule by consultation and negotiation (and probably rule by law, once the Law on Associations is promulgated). It delegated the management of popular organizations—both state and non-state sponsored—to state organs. Despite the hierarchical structure of both VUSTA and VULAA, the relationship between the union structure and member associations was far from hierarchical. The recent history of the AVF and the relationship between the central unions of VUSTA, VACVINA, and CCRD show that the member associations had their own established party-state and horizontal connections and that their activities were not necessarily carried out through the union structure.

Although most popular organizations, both with and without state sponsorship, adhered to general policy guidelines issued by the party and assisted the party-state in fulfilling certain policy goals, new forms of participation were also introduced. The central unions and their member associations began to assume, in varying degrees, the role of educators, trainers, advisers, consultants and evaluators. The extent of VUSTA's participation in the 1990s is remarkable compared with its absence in the 1980s, when it was seen as "too weak". By the year 2000, it had become customary for the government leadership, especially the Prime Minister's office, to expect ministries submitting proposals to ask for written comments from VUSTA first. The advisory role of VUSTA and its member associations has been institutionalized, and it is likely that this role will be extended.

Whatever the degree of state sponsorship, popular organizations tried to test how far they could assert their influence when the mono-organizational grip was loosened. In this regard, the AVF and CCRD can both lay claim to some success. Several common factors underline that. The first was the fact that they were linked with one form of grassroots constituency or another, and were serving as intermediaries to voice popular interests to the upper hierarchy. Another was their ability to muster support through their networking attempts. They were also successful because their policy options were supported by certain sections of the party-state leadership. However, whether these newly acquired roles will be further institutionalized and legalized, and if so how much, remains a question.

The two case studies suggest some analytical directions for further investigation of the Vietnamese political system under *doi moi*. The first direction is the need to rethink the relationship between the party-state and popular organizations. Vietnam watchers are mostly skeptical when analyzing popular organizations because these organizations' close connections with the party-state structure gives the impression that they are merely government subcontractors (Eva Hansson's assessment of the Vietnam trade union movement in chapter 5 of this book is an example). However, the emphasis on the structural affiliations between the party-state and popular organizations is not analytically useful in exploring the degree and nature of polical change in transitional Vietnam. This preliminary study suggests that with the right vertical and horizontal political resources, both the AVF and the CCRD were able to operate and influence policy-making. Regardless of their "official" status and affiliations, popular organizations' ability to represent particular interests and to provide alternative policy options to those advocated by the party-state may be among the most crucial signs that show the changing nature of the political system in *doi moi* Vietnam.

The second analytical direction deals with the evolutionary nature of change in the political system. The Vietnamese political system in the 1990s still contains remnants of the old state socialist structural features and practices, the key aspects of which are the remaining predominant party-state structure and party-state networks. The two cases suggest that the current party-state structure both imposes constraints and provides opportunities for popular organizations to operate. The pertinent question then is how do popular organizations maintain their identity as "popular" while availing themselves of the resources and opportunities by networking with the party-state structure.

The third direction deals with the need to unpack the concept of the party-state and society. Vietnam watchers have observed that the one-party state was not, and is not, monolithic. Yet, so far, very few studies have attempted to disaggregate the concept of the party-state and societal groups in the process of analyzing policy-making. Benedict Kerkvliet has grouped existing approches to Vietnamese politics under three rubrics based on the degree of popular influences on decision making: the "dominating state", "mobilizational corporatism" and "society-state dialogue".[49] Interestingly, all three approaches take the party-state and society as monolithic entities. Unpacking the concepts "state" and "society" will enable Vietnam watchers to focus on "interest" and the relationship between "interest" and "organizational networking". The two cases suggest that in the era of *doi moi*, interests have become more diversified within the party-state structure and society. These different interests within and outside the party-state structure may or may not be oppositional to one another. A close look at interests will also allow Vietnam watchers to develop a more sophisticated approach to discuss bargaining and trade-offs as a basis for organizational networking during the post-socialist period.

Notes

I would like to thank Ben Kerkvliet for his comments on an ealier draft and Russell Heng for his editorial assistance. I remain responsible for the shortcomings in this chapter.

1 While Vietnam is in name still a socialist country, I used the term "post-socialist" because many of the classic features of Marxist-Leninist inspired socialism are no longer useful in understanding the present-day realities of the country. However this is entirely my interpretation and not necessarily shared by other scholars. For example, in their choice of title for this book, the editors accept that Vietnam is still a "socialist state".

2 See Nguyen Khac Mai, *Vi tri, vai tro cac hiep hoi quan chung o nuoc ta* [The Position and Role of Popular Associations in Vietnam], (Hanoi: Lao Dong, 1996).

3 Andrew MacIntyre makes a distinction between "exclusionary" and "inclusionary" corporatism when he compares the relationship between the state and business in Indonesia under the New Order, and in Thailand under semi-democracy. "Exclusionary" corporatism refers to the situation in which business representative bodies operate as instruments of the state rather than as vehicles for the advancement of business interests. "Inclusionary" corporatism refers to the institutional arrangements for broad collective business input into the policy process along liberal

or societal corporatist lines. See MacIntyre's "Power, Prosperity and Patrimonialism: Business and Government in Indonesia", in *Business and Government in Industrialising Asia*, edited by Andrew MacIntyre. (Ithaca, NY: Cornell University Press, 1994), pp. 244–67, especially pp. 252 and 263.

4 Please note that (a) and (d) are *to chuc* (organizations) and (b) is a *hoi* (association). In the Vietnamese language, there is a key distinction between these two terms. *Hoi* or "association" is commonly used to refer to "non-political" popular groupings while the term *to chuc* or "organization" implies a political status.

5 See, for example, VUSTA's brochure (Hanoi, 2000).

6 The Vietnamese practitioners interviewed give the impression that the label "NGO" is useful when they need to solicit technical assistance, project assignment, and fund-raising from non-state and foreign sources.

7 Information on the activities of the AVF, the CCRD, and their affiliations was gathered from mid-1999 to early 2002. I was a frequent visitor and a regular attendant at the performances carried out at the Holy Mother temples in Hanoi, Hung Yen, Hoa Binh, Thai Binh and Nam Dinh. I also had a chance to exchange ideas with intellectuals working on the Cult of the Holy Mothers and to attend the international workshop organized in April 2001 entitled "Mother Goddess Worship and the Phu Giay Festival" (Tin nguong tho mau va le hoi Phu Giay). I first came in contact with CCRD in my capacity as Resident Director of the Council on International Educational Exchange (CIEE) programme in Hanoi, which I served from the 1998 to the 2002 academic year. I consider CCRD's approaches to development, different from those adopted by the government, sufficient to grant it status as an NGO. Information on the CCRD is drawn from lectures provided by CCRD staff members, field trips to CCRD project sites, especially in Vinh Phuc and Hai Phong, and discussions with rural inhabitants who were beneficiaries of CCRD projects. Information on the activities of VUSTA, VACVINA, and VULAA is drawn from my interviews with the organizations' staff members in October 2001 and from their brochures.

8 See writings by Carlye Thayer, Adam Fforde, William Turley, Gareth Porter, and Benedict Kerkvliet. During the post-socialist period, Vietnamese scholars use the term *quan lieu bao cap*, or the bureaucratic subsidizing system, to refer to the state prior to *doi moi*.

9 For a good description of the development of the party-state structure, see chapters 1 and 2 of Dang Phong and Melanie Beresford, *Authority Relations and Economic Decision-Making in Vietnam*.

10 These organizations had been placed under the leadership of the Indochinese Communist Party as early as 1930. See Huynh Kim Khanh, *Vietnamese*

Communism, 1925–1945 (Ithaca, NY: Cornell University Press, 1982), p. 139. After 1975, the Association of Vietnamese Veterans was added.

11 Mat Tran To Quoc Viet Nam, *Ky Niem (1994–1998)*, pp. 29–30.

12 The VULAA was originally called the Cultural Association for National Salvation [Hoi Van Hoa Cuu Quoc]. It took its present name in 1957.

13 Examples included the associations of Vietnamese Architects, Fine Arts, Vietnamese Writers, Performance Theatre, and Vietnamese Musicians in the 1950s, and the associations of Vietnamese Photographers, Folklorists, and Film Makers in the 1960s.

14 Dang Phong and Beresford, pp. 52–84. See also their observation on how the system of "dual subordination" gave flexibility to local officials in making and implementing policy.

15 For a detailed discussion of the event, see Georges Boudarel, "Intellectual Dissidence in the 1950s: The *Nhan Van Giai Pham* Affair", pp. 154–74.

16 For a summary of the intellectual sector's contribution to the formation of official nationalism, see Thaveeporn Vasavakul, "Vietnam: The Changing Models of Legitimation", pp. 257–89.

17 On Kim Ngoc, see Dang Phong and Beresford, p. 62. The comment on Long An is drawn from my November 2002 interview with provincial authorities who had served in Long An in the 1970s and 1980s.

18 Adam Fforde, "The Political Economy of 'Reform' in Vietnam: Some Reflections", pp. 293–323; Carlyle Thayer, "The Regularisation of Politics: Continuity and Change in the Party's Central Committee, 1951–1986", pp. 177–93.

19 "Chu tich Ho Chi Minh noi ve cong tac mat tran" (President Ho Chi Minh talking about the Front's tasks), in *Mat Tran To Quoc Viet Nam, Ky Niem Dai Hoi IV (1994–1998)* [The Vietnam Fatherland Front, Records from the Fourth Congress, 1994–1999], pp. 118–30; Ho Chi Minh, "Dan Van" [Mass mobilization], in ibid., pp. 131–3.

20 *Nghi quyet so 08B/NQ-TW (Khoa VI) ngay 27-3-1990 ve doi moi cong tac quan chung cua Dang, tang cuong moi quan he giua Dang va nhan dan* [Resolution no. 08B/NQ-TW (session VI) of 27 March 1990 on the Reform of the Party's Mass Mobilization Work and the Strengthening of the Relationship between the Party and the People].

21 Two examples include *Thong Bao so 143/TB-TW ngay 5-6-1998 y kien cua thuong vu Bo Chinh Tri ve to chuc, hoat dong va quan ly cac hoi nghe nghiep* [Announcement no. 143/TB-TW of 5 June 1998 Regarding the Politburo's Opinions on the Organization, Activities, and Management of Professional Associations), in *Mot so van kien cua Dang ve cong tac dan van* [Party Documents on Mass Mobilization], pp. 699–700; and *Chi thi so 42/CT-TW ngay 6-10-1998 cua Bo Chinh Tri ve viec tang cuong su lanh dao cua Dang doi voi to chuc va hoat*

dong cua cac hoi quan chung [Directive no. 42/CT-TW of 6 October 1998 of the Politburo on the Strengthening of the Party Leadership in the Organization of Activities of Popular Associations], in *Mot so van kien cua Dang ve cong tac dan van* [Party Documents on Mass Mobilization Work], pp. 701–4.

22 *Dang doan* is a party mechanism set up within the National Assembly as well as non-state organizations including popular organizations.

23 Interview with staff members at the Association of Vietnamese Traditional Medicine, October 2001, Hanoi.

24 Decision no. 66/2000/QD-BTCCBCP of November 1, 2000.

25 *50 Nam Lien Hiep cac Hoi Van Hoc-Nghe Thuat Viet Nam, 1948–1998* [50 Years of the Union and Vietnam's Literary and Arts Associations] (Hanoi: Hoi Nha Van, 1998) and Lien Hiep Cac Hoi Van Hoc Nghe Thuat Viet Nam, *Dai Hoi VI Lien Hiep Cac Hoi Van Hoc Nghe Thuat Viet Nam (Ky Yeu)* [The Sixth Congress of the Vietnam Union of Literature and Arts Associations, Records] (Hanoi: Hoi Nha Van, 2000).

26 See "Dieu Le" (Regulations) in *Dai Hoi VI*, pp. 125–9.

27 See "Tien len mot chang duong phat trien moi cua van hoc nghe thuat nuoc ta" [Advancing One Step in the Development of Literature and the Arts], in *Dai Hoi VI*, p. 22. The distribution is as follows: 700 in the Association of Vietnamese Writers; 1,500 in the Association of Fine Arts; 700 in the Association of Vietnamese Musicians; 1,800 in the Association of Performing Arts; around 800 in the Association of Vietnamese Cinematography; 480 in the Association of Vietnamese Photographers; 450 in the Association for Vietnamese Dancers; 2,200 in the Association of Vietnamese Architects; 900 in the Association of Vietnamese Folklorists; and 430 in the Association for Minority Arts and Literature.

28 See "Y kien Thuong Vu Bo Chinh Tri ve to chuc Dai Hoi Lien Hiep Cac Hoi Van Hoc, Nghe Thuat Viet Nam lan thu VI" [Opinion of the Politburo Standing Committee on the Organization of the Congress of VULAA], in *Dai Hoi VI* (The Sixth Congress), pp. 5–6.

29 *Dai Hoi VI* (The Sixth Congress), pp. 80–83 and 86–7.

30 Ibid., pp. 80–83; 86–7; and 113–21.

31 *50 nam*, pp. 224–7.

32 Ibid., pp. 228–9.

33 Details on different aspects of *hau bong* can be found in *Vietnamese Studies*, no. 1 (1999) and *Van Hoa Dan Gian* [Popular Culture], no. 4 (2001). Information in this section is also drawn from the author's observations of *hau bong* between 1999 and 2001.

34 See the CCRD brochure.

35 The CGOP was elevated to the status of a Ministry, the Ministry of Home Affairs, in mid-2001. The existing Ministry of Home Affairs then became the Ministry of Public Security (Bo Cong An).

[36] Most of the new associations in the late 1990s were set up through VUSTA. The only exception is the case of the Association for Vietnam-Southeast Asian Studies (Hoi Viet Nam-Dong Nam A Hoc) which was founded in 1998. Its permit was signed by the Prime Minister. The key founder is Prof. Pham Duc Duong, a prominent linguist, who had also served as the Director of the Institute of Southeast Asian Studies in the 1980s. Structurally, the Association consists of the central office, member associations, and provincial branches. According to my interview with Prof. Duong, there were debates at its first congress whether the Association should become a VUSTA member association; the advantage centred around the expansion of the Association's networking abilities. Then, member associations decided not stay within VUSTA's umbrella. Interview with the author, Hanoi, November, 2001.

[37] Interview with VUSTA staff members, October 2001, Hanoi. VUSTA staff members did not explain the phrase "legal and political framework". It is likely that they were referring to political openness in general and the leadership's uncertainty as to how much leeway it should give to VUSTA.

[38] Although a lot of research has been done to examine the relationship between the party-state and social scientists, journalists, and writers in the wake of *doi moi*, little work has been done to analyze the relationship between the party-state and the Vietnamese scientific and technological community. One may recall how prominent Phan Dinh Dieu, an eminent mathematician, was in the struggle for greater intellectual freedom in the late 1980s and 1990s.

[39] *Chi thi so 35/CT-TW ngay 11-4-1998 cua Ban Bi Thu ve cung co to chuc va day manh hoat dong cua Lien Hiep cac Hoi Khoa Hoc va Ky Thuat Viet Nam* [Directive no. 35/CT-TW of April 11 1998 of the Secretariat Strengthening Activities of VUSTA] in *Mot so van kien cua dang* [Party documents], pp. 659–62.

[40] The term *ban can su dang*, or party commission within the state, is used to refer to party units within government bodies.

[41] *Thong bao so 37/TB-TW ngay 20-11-1992 Y kien cua Ban Bi Thu ve to chuc va hoat dong cua Lien Hiep cac Hoi Khoa Hoc va Ky That Viet Nam* [Announcement no. 37/TB-TW of November 20 1992 on the Opinions of the Secretariat on the Organization and Activities of VUSTA) in ibid., pp. 669–71.

[42] *Thong bao so 52/TB-TW ngay 31-8-1993 Y kien cua Ban Bi Thu ve Dai Hoi lan thu III cua Lien Hiep cac Hoi Khoa Hoc va Ky That Viet Nam* [Announcement no. 52/TB-TW of 20 November 1992 on the Opinions of the Secretariat on VUSTA's Third National Congress] in ibid., pp. 680–84.

[43] It is not compulsory for state agencies to seek advice or to send their proposals for comments and recommendations from VUSTA.

[44] Information from this section is based on VACVINA's brochure and an interview with VACVINA staff members in November 2001 in Hanoi.

[45] Interview with VACVINA staff members, November 2001, Hanoi.

46 In Quang Ngai province in central Vietnam, for example, the majority of VACVINA members are from the provincial Department of Agriculture and Rural Development. According to state cum VACVINA affiliates, the lack of funding made it impossible for VACVINA to expand its activities. (Interview with provincial officials in the Department of Agriculture and Rural Development in Quang Ngai provincial town, November 2002.)

47 The perception of CCRD as being "independent" from the VACVINA hierarchy can be detected from one key CCRD staff member's reaction to the case of embezzlement of Australian development funds by VACVINA's branch members in Ha Tinh a few years ago. In the key CCRD staff member's words, "that Australia-VACVINA scandal did exist,"...but "within the system of VACVINA, there are numerous dependent and independent units operating. CCRD belongs to the latter. The scandal did not have anything to do with CCRD." Private communication with CCRD staff members, May, 2003.

48 See Michael Gray, "Creating Civil Society? The Emergence of NGOs in Vietnam", *Development and Change* 30 (1999): 693–713.

49 See Benedict Kerkvliet, "An Approach for Analysing State-Society Relations in Vietnam", *Sojourn* 16, no. 2 (October 2001): 238–78. For preliminary attempts to "unpack" the state at the top leadership level, see Carlyle Thayer's analysis on sectoral politics and Vasavakul's elaboration of the concept, as well as Vasavakul's "Political of Public Administration reform in Vietnam". By 2003, however, the situtation had become more complicated. For a preliminary move to unpack the state at the middle and grassroots levels, see David Koh "Negotiating the Socialist State in Vietnam through Local Adminstrators: The Case of *Karaoke* shops", *Sojourn* 16, op. cit., pp. 279–305 and Russell Hiang-Khng Heng, "Media Negotiating the State: In the Name of the Law in Anticipation", *Sojourn* 16, pp. 213–78.

References

50 nam Lien Hiep Cac Hoi Van Hoc Nghe Thuat Viet Nam, 1948–1998. Hanoi: Hoi Nha Van, 1998.

Ban Dan Van Trung Uong. *Mot so van kien cua dang ve cong tac dan van (1976–2000)*. Hanoi: Chinh Tri Quoc Gia, 2000.

Bo Van Hoa-Thong Tin. *Duong loi van hoa van nghe cua Dang Cong San Viet Nam*. Hanoi: Van Hoa-Thong Tin, 1995.

Boudarel, Georges. "Intellectual Dissidence in the 1950s: The *Nhan Van Giai Pham* Affair". *Vietnam Forum* 13 (1990): 154–74.

Dang Cong San Viet Nam. *Van Kien Hoi Nghi lan thu nam Ban chap hanh Trung Uong Khoa VIII*. Hanoi: Chinh Tri Quoc, Gia, 1998.

Dang Phong and Melanie Beresford. *Authority Relations and Economic Decision-Making in Vietnam: An Historical Perspective.* Copenhagen: NIAS, 1998.

Fforde, Adam. "The Political Economy of 'Reform' in Vietnam: Some Reflections". In *The Challenge of Reform in Indochina* edited by Börje Ljunggren. Cambridge, MA: HIID, 1993.

Gray, Michael. "Creating Civil Society? The Emergence of NGOs in Vietnam". *Development and Change* 30 (1999): 693–713.

Hoi Lam Vuon Viet Nam (VACVINA). *Dieu le Hoi Lam Vuon Viet Nam (VACVINA).* Hanoi: Nong Nghiep, 1998.

Hoi Van Nghe Dan Gian Viet Nam. *Dieu Le Hoi Van Nghe Dan Gian Viet Nam, Khoa IV (2000–2005).* Hanoi, 2000.

Hy Van Luong. "The Marxist State and the Dialogic Re-structuring of Culture in Rural Vietnam". In *Indochina: Social and Cultural Change,* edited by David Elliott. Claremont, CA: The Keck Centre for International and Strategic Studies, 1994, pp. 79–117.

Kerkvliet, Benedict. "Village-State Relations in Vietnam: The Effect of Everyday Politics on Decollectivisation". *Journal of Asian Studies* 54, no. 2 (May 1995): 396–418.

Le Mau Han. Dang Cong San Viet Nam. *Cac Dai Hoi va Hoi Nghi Trung Uong.* Hanoi: Chinh Tri Quoc Gia. 1998.

Lien Hiep Cac Hoi Van Hoc Nghe Thuat Viet Nam. *Dai Hoi VI Lien Hiep Cac Hoi Van Hoc Nghe Thuat Viet Nam (Ky yeu).* Hanoi: Van Hoc, 2000.

Mat Tran To Quoc Viet Nam. *Ky Niem Dai Hoi IV (1994–1998).* Hanoi: Lao Dong, 1994.

———. *Mat Tran To Quoc Viet Nam trong su nghiep doi moi.* Hanoi: Chinh Tri Quoc Gia, 1993.

Nguyen Khac Mai. *Vi tri, vai tro cac hiep hoi quan chung o nuoc ta* [The Position and Role of Popular Associations in Vietnam]. Hanoi: Lao Dong, 1996.

Phan Xuan Son (chu bien). *Cac doan the nhan dan voi viec bao dam dan chu o co so hien nay* [People's Organizations and the Task of Protecting Grassroots Democracy Today]. Hanoi: Chinh Tri Quoc Gia, 2002.

Thayer, Carlyle. "The Regularisation of Politics: Continuity and Change in the Party's Central Committee, 1951–1986". In *Postwar Vietnam,* edited by David Marr and Christine White. Ithaca, NY: Cornell Southeast Asia Program, 1987.

———. "Political Reform in Vietnam: *Doi Moi* and the Emergence of Civil Society". In *The Developments of Civil Society in Communist Systems,* edited by Robert F. Miller. Sydney: Allen and Unwin, 1992, pp. 110–29.

Tran Minh Vy. *Mot so quy dinh phat luat ve quan ly to chuc hoat dong cua cac hoi, doan the xa hoi* [Some Legal Rules on the Management of Activities by Associations and Mass Organizations]. Hanoi: Lao Dong, 2002.

VACVINA. Brochure, n.d.

Vasavakul, Thaveeporn. "Vietnam: The Changing Model of Legitimation". In *Political Legitimacy in Southeast Asia*, edited by Muthiah Alagappa. Stanford, CA: Stanford University Press, 1995.

VUSTA. Brochure. Hanoi, 2000.

White, Christine. "Agricultural Planning, Pricing Policy and Co-operatives in Vietnam". *World Development* 13, no. 1 (1985): 97–114.

2

Business Associations and Policy-Making in Vietnam

Jonathan R. Stromseth

Since *doi moi* began in 1986, the Vietnamese political authorities have implemented reforms aimed at expanding the scope and modalities of interest representation in Vietnam. These reforms can be seen in official efforts to rejuvenate traditional mass organizations, to encourage the development of new representative groups in sectors where mass organizations do not exist, and, especially, to intensify the participation of these organizations in policy and law-making. During the 1990s, it became common for government-appointed drafting committees to distribute draft laws to mass organizations and other groups, such as the Vietnam Chamber of Commerce and Industry (Phong Thuong Mai va Cong Nghiep Viet Nam), in order to solicit comments on the content of drafts. In 1994, Adam Fforde summed up these changes succinctly by observing that "public organizations such as the Chamber of Commerce and Industry... have been given scope to voice political opinions and participate in law-making. Thus mechanisms have been created for criticizing, drafting and redrafting laws as an overt means to 'change the rules.'"[1] By the late 1990s, the government was facilitating more direct business representation in law-making by inviting leaders of the Chamber of Commerce to serve as official members of legislative drafting committees.

This chapter argues that the changing role of business associations and other groups is indicative of an emerging "corporatism" in Vietnam. Broadly speaking, corporatism may be defined as a pattern of organizing interests and influence in which the state gives favoured status to certain interest groups. This institutional pattern typically involves tripartite consultations among representatives of business, labour, and government over economic policy. The state may grant representational monopolies to interest groups within their respective economic sectors or social categories, but, in exchange, these groups must operate within parameters determined by the state and often through leaders chosen or approved by the state. Sometimes the state itself even creates the interest groups. Above all, corporatism emphasizes interest group harmony over conflict and seeks to achieve this by incorporating organizations representing important sectors of society into the decision-making structure of the state. Corporatist arrangements often have been observed in developing countries undergoing rapid economic development, where governments have sought to maintain stability by forging close relations with new social forces being spawned by modernization and industrialization.[2]

With their emphasis on social order and rapid economic growth, it is not surprising that a number of East Asian states—notably South Korea, Taiwan, and Singapore—have exhibited strong corporatist tendencies at different stages in their development histories. To suggest that Vietnam is now also exhibiting corporatist characteristics is not to argue that state–society relations are undergoing a wholesale change; rather, it is to argue that these relations are shifting incrementally away from the traditional Leninist practice in which mass organizations serve as mobilizational instruments of the authorities by transmitting official policies and laws to society.[3] More precisely, it is to argue that, in addition to this mobilizational role, mass organizations and other groups are beginning to articulate the interests of society to the government during the *formulation* of policies and laws. State–society relations in Vietnam are thus moving toward a mixed or hybrid pattern that exhibits characteristics both of its Leninist tradition and of an emerging corporatism. This pattern is emerging largely due to official efforts to cope with new social pressures generated by economic reforms, and to foster interest group harmony through expanded opportunities for interest representation.[4]

In the context of market economic reforms and the development of a domestic private sector, this chapter examines the emerging policy-making role of Vietnamese business associations in general and the Chamber of Commerce and Industry in particular. The chapter first describes the origins, structure, and development of the Chamber of Commerce and three other groups that typify the current environment. Subsequently, it describes how changes to the operating mandate of the Chamber of Commerce, coupled with broader reforms to the country's legal framework, have led to a dramatic increase in interest representation on business issues. Finally, the chapter examines the involvement of Vietnamese business associations in specific policy-making contexts. The main case study assesses the extent to which the Chamber of Commerce participated in and influenced the drafting of the Law on Promotion of Domestic Investment, implemented in 1995. Subsequent discussion focuses on the drafting of the much-heralded Enterprise Law, which came into effect in January 2000, and the landmark resolution of the Fifth Plenum of the Central Committee of the Vietnamese Communist Party. Issued in March 2002, this resolution has provided the strongest political endorsement yet for the development of the domestic private sector in Vietnam.

The chapter shows that as the political leadership in Vietnam has sought to pull officially-sponsored business associations into corporatist forms of policy-making and interest representation, some of these associations have responded by articulating strong demands on their constituents' behalf. The intensity of this response appears to suggest that bottom-up pressures are reinforcing the evolving pattern of increased representation, with the associations being pushed to assume stronger advocacy roles by their constituencies in Vietnamese society.[5]

Origins and Development of Business Associations

The past decade has witnessed a steady growth of business associations in Vietnam. Although the precise figure is unknown, the total number of business associations is estimated to be approaching 200 nationwide.[6] Most prominent is the Vietnam Chamber of Commerce and Industry, the officially sanctioned "representative" of the national business community and the largest association organized on a horizontal basis (i.e., amalgamating businesses across industries and sectors). Others include municipal associations, such as the Union of Associations of Industry and Commerce of Ho Chi Minh City (Hiep Hoi Cong Thuong Thanh Pho Ho Chi Minh) and the Hanoi Union of Associations of Industry and Commerce (Hiep Hoi Cong Thuong Thanh Pho Ha Noi), as well as vertically organized sectoral associations representing such industries as textiles and garments, software, and food processing. Vietnamese business associations must secure numerous permissions and approvals from the government to become established, and some have been established or cultivated by the government itself.

Like business associations elsewhere, Vietnamese associations are engaged in two broad areas of activity: (i) interest representation; and (ii) providing business services to their members in areas such as management training, technical consultation, and information dissemination. According to a new study on the status and performance of Vietnamese business associations, the associations are relatively weak in providing business services to members, but are performing fairly well—in some notable cases, such as the Chamber of Commerce and the municipal associations noted above—in carrying out interest representation.[7] Before exploring how Vietnamese business associations represent the interests of their members in policy-making, the chapter first summarizes the origins, structure, and development of four associations that exemplify the present environment, starting with the Chamber of Commerce.

Though it did not gain prominence until the early 1990s, the Chamber of Commerce was established by official decree on April 29, 1960. In its original statutes, issued in 1963, the Chamber was described as a self-governing economic organization and its main purpose was to promote economic relations between the country and the rest of the world, including non-socialist countries. Its current statutes, revised most recently in 1997, reflect the Chamber's close and sometimes confusing relations with the government. On the one hand, the statutes indicate that the Chamber is "an independent, non-governmental organization" operating with financial autonomy; on the other, the statues note that it carries out its activities "with the support and under the supervision of the Vietnamese State", and is required to conduct "activities which are assigned by the Vietnamese

State...."[8] (Of its approximately US$2.5 million annual budget in 2001, 20 per cent was provided by the government, 20 per cent came from membership dues, and 60 per cent was generated by service fees and related activities.) In addition, some of the Chamber's senior staff have worked in the government, and many are members of the Communist Party. The current president, Doan Duy Thanh, is himself a former member of the Party Central Committee and previously served as Minister of Trade and Deputy Prime Minister. Recommended by the party and government, he became the president of the Chamber in 1993.[9]

The Chamber provides a broad range of services to businesses including matchmaking between domestic and foreign partners; information provision through its biweekly newspaper, *Dien Dan Doanh Nghiep* (Business Forum); technical and legal consulting; and organizing seminars, training courses, and trade fairs and exhibitions. However, the Chamber's primary function is to carry out a dialogue with government and represent the interests of Vietnamese businesses, of all economic sectors, in the formulation of policies and laws. To carry out these various activities, the Chamber employs 437 staff, with 160 working in Hanoi, and maintains branch offices in Ho Chi Minh City, Da Nang, Hai Phong, and Can Tho and representative offices in Vinh, Nha Trang and Vung Tau. Membership in the Chamber is voluntary and has grown from 93 enterprises in 1963, to 700 in 1992, 1,600 in 1995, and 6,700 in 2002. Of the current enterprise total, 54 per cent are private companies and the remainder are state-owned enterprises (in contrast, only 20 per cent of members came from the private sector in the mid-1990s). The Chamber's membership also includes other Vietnamese business associations—101 at present count—many of which possess substantial memberships themselves.[10]

In addition to the Chamber's branch offices in various cities and provinces, a number of municipal business associations emerged during *doi moi* with close links to city people's committees. One is the Union of Associations of Industry and Commerce of Ho Chi Minh City, established in 1989 as the Association of Industrialists (Hoi Cong Ky Nghe Gia). The group changed its name to the Association of Industry and Commerce (AIC) in 1994, and it was later reorganized and renamed the Union of Associations of Industry and Commerce (UAIC) with its membership divided into sectoral associations under this umbrella. The impetus for forming the organization, as indicated in a foreword to its 1994 statutes, was Politburo Resolution no. 16, dated 15 July 1988. This resolution stated that "national bourgeoisie, small owners and individual producers should voluntarily join together to establish industrialists' associations, which should be organized in developed industrial centres, first in Hanoi and Ho Chi Minh City."[11] To implement the resolution, the Vietnam Fatherland Front (VFF) Committee of Ho Chi Minh City invited a group of pre-1975 industrialists to attend a meeting and encouraged them to form an association. They welcomed this opportunity and drafted statutes for the new association in coordination with the local authorities. Some of the founding members had been members of a prominent business association in the former Saigon, called the General Association of Industrialists (Tong Doan Cong Ky Nghe).[12]

A People's Committee document that accompanies the group's statutes indicates that it "operates under the direction and sponsorship of the Vietnam Fatherland Front Committee of Ho Chi Minh City and according to statutes...that are approved by the City People's Committee." Its purpose is to unite the city's business community, foster mutual assistance, and mobilize its members to invest in business production. In addition, it is expected to represent the aspirations of its members by making recommendations to draft policies and laws, and to "contribute to stability and socioeconomic development" by participating in the mass activities of the country.[13] Towards this end, the UAIC meets regularly with the city People's Committee to voice the grievances and policy concerns of local business people, and sometimes has the opportunity to advance business interests to the national government. It also cooperates with city trade unions to mediate relations between workers and enterprise owners in accordance with Vietnamese labour laws. At present, the UAIC has twelve affiliated sectoral associations—including the Leather Shoes Association, Rubber-Plastics Association, and Food Processing Association—and a membership of about 1,700 companies, 90 per cent of which are private.[14]

Although the aforementioned Politburo resolution also called for an industrialists' association to be organized in Hanoi, the Hanoi Union of Associations of Industry and Commerce (HUAIC) was not established until early 1996. Press reports at the time described the HUAIC as being "under the Hanoi People's Committee", and said it was founded "to promote the development of the private sector and to ensure that the state- and non-state sectors enjoy equal business opportunities." The group's outspoken Vice President and Secretary General, Vu Duy Thai, explained that the HUAIC was established because "complaints and proposals from separate private enterprises are not significant enough to catch the attention of the government, [and] that is why we have to join hands to raise our common voice in order to speak out our concerns and interests."[15] One of the first actions of the HUAIC was to formulate a set of proposals for private sector promotion to be submitted to the Eighth Party Congress in June 1996. The HUAIC excludes state firms from its membership, which is comprised of 875 private enterprises at present. It seeks to provide business promotion services to its members in addition to representing their interests to the government, but its capacity to provide these services is constrained by insufficient funds. Unlike the Chamber of Commerce, the HUAIC receives no government funding and must rely on membership dues of approximately US$30 per year.[16]

Despite having common origins, similar names, and analogous relations with their respective people's committees, there is no formal relationship between the HUAIC and the UAIC of Ho Chi Minh City. However, they do occasionally share information and experiences. In the process of establishing the HUAIC, for example, its founders visited the UAIC of Ho Chi Minh City to learn about the group's development since 1989.[17]

A more recent example of the formation of a business association is the Vietnam Software Association (VINASA, Hiep Hoi Doanh Nghiep Phan Mem Viet Nam), formally inaugurated in April 2002. In early 2001, a group of leading software companies decided to team up and lobby for the establishment of this association. Following steps outlined in existing regulations on the formation of associations in Vietnam, the group first needed to obtain the approval of the line ministry overseeing information technology (IT) activities in Vietnam (then the Ministry of Science, Technology and Environment or MOSTE) for the list of individuals in its preparatory committee (chaired by Truong Gia Binh, CEO and President of the FPT Corporation). After securing this approval in June 2001, the preparatory committee submitted an application to the Government Committee on Organization and Personnel (GCOP) for a licence to establish the association.[18] To support its application, it also solicited positive written recommendations from MOSTE, the Ministry of Industry, the Economic Commission of the Party Central Committee, and the Chamber of Commerce. With all of this paperwork completed, the GCOP issued a decision in August 2001 approving the establishment of the software association, and VINASA organized its inaugural congress in April 2002 in Hanoi.[19]

According to its official website, VINASA was established for the purpose of connecting software businesses in Vietnam into one bloc and "acting as a bridge between software businesses and the state, representing its members in making recommendations and raising opinions in the policy-making of the state regarding the software industry."[20] While it is too early to assess the policy effectiveness of this new sectoral association, it has already begun advancing strong demands to the government on behalf of its members. At its inaugural congress, attended by Deputy Prime Minister Pham Gia Khiem and other senior officials, VINASA pushed the government to lower Internet costs, spend more of the government budget on software development, and provide tax exemptions to companies purchasing new software for their business operations.[21] VINASA also has begun meeting with local and national authorities in an effort to improve policy and enhance government support for the Vietnamese software industry. In May 2002, for instance, VINASA's Executive Committee met with Hoang Van Nghien, Chair of the Hanoi People's Committee, to make recommendations on software development and encourage the People's Committee to allot land for creating a VINASA software centre in Hanoi. A similar meeting was held in June 2002 between VINASA and Nguyen Thien Nhan, Standing Deputy Chair of the Ho Chi Minh City People's Committee. The same month, VINASA was invited to be an official member of the National Steering Board for implementing Politburo Directive no. 58 on the acceleration of IT development in Vietnam.[22]

The establishment of VINASA illustrates the multiple steps and cumbersome procedures that confront business people wishing to form a new business association in Vietnam. It is a process that can be navigated successfully by business people with strong political connections, but sets out serious obstacles for those without such relationships. Yet, while laws and regulations make it difficult to establish business associations in Vietnam, they also can afford these associations, once established, with considerable opportunities to participate in the making of new policies and laws. These opportunities for participation are explored further in the section below, focusing on the Chamber of Commerce.

Modes of Representation and Participation in Policy-Making

The formal participation of the Chamber of Commerce in policy and law-making began in the early 1990s, and was facilitated by official efforts to draw the Chamber into corporatist patterns of interest representation. These efforts are reflected in presentations and instructions given by senior officials from the government and Party at meetings of the Chamber, as reprinted in *Dien Dan Doanh Nghiep* and other public documents. At the same time, the Chamber's policy-making role has been facilitated by broader changes to the legal framework in Vietnam during the 1990s—changes that allowed for greater participation in the country's legislative process by mass organizations, business associations, and other groups.

The Chamber of Commerce began undertaking its policy-making function after convening its Second National Congress, a watershed event held in Hanoi in April 1993, when the Chamber officially became *the* representative of the national business community. The Office of Government was instrumental in bringing about this change, with current Prime Minister Phan Van Khai playing a key role.[23] Having ascended to the Politburo in 1991, Khai was then serving as Standing Deputy Prime Minister with responsibility for economic and trade issues. He attended the congress with numerous other senior officials, including Minister of Trade Le Van Triet. In his keynote speech to the Congress, Khai spoke about the 30-year history of the Chamber and about the changes that the government expected of the Chamber in the future. He commended the organization for having promoted business relations with foreign countries. But now, he said, the Chamber "is being asked to improve its organization and further reform its mode of operation. It is hoped that the present convention will usher in a new period of development of the Chamber of Commerce and Industry in breadth and depth, in response to the expectation of the business community and the government."[24] In particular, Khai emphasized the importance of the Chamber's new responsibility as the representative of the Vietnamese business community. He called on the Chamber, as "the representative of business enterprises, to make its voice heard by way of recommending to the government amendments and additions to the current mechanism and policies."[25]

The nature of the Chamber's representative function was further defined at its Executive Committee meeting in September 1995. Attending the meeting was Vu Oanh, then a Politburo member and head of the Party's Mass Mobilization Commission. The Chamber welcomed Oanh so that he could "directly communicate the instructions of the Politburo and the Secretariat regarding the organization and activities of the Chamber of Commerce and Industry."[26] In his speech to the Committee, Oanh confirmed that the Chamber was the "highest representative of the business community and the appropriate instrument for the Party and state to gather and guide the business community from all economic sectors of the country in the cause of building the economy..."[27] He also encouraged the Chamber to take on an explicitly corporatist role in labour relations:

> Apart from functioning as the promotional and representative organization of the business community in economic and business relations, the Chamber of Commerce must strive to undertake the function of a labour-using organization (employers' organization) in labour relations. The Chamber must coordinate well with the General Confederation of Labour of Vietnam and with government agencies on the basis of guaranteeing the interests and creating cooperative relations between the business community and employees. The establishment of cooperative relations between the business community (employers) and labourers on the scale of the national economy as well as in each enterprise is a crucial factor for ensuring stable and effective development of the economy.[28]

In other words, Oanh was encouraging a more specific function for the Chamber of Commerce: in addition to promoting trade and representing the business community in a general sense, it also would have the specific role of representing employers in the development and management of cooperative labour relations. And it would do so, as his comments suggest, in order to help maintain social stability while achieving positive economic growth.

The emphasis on enhancing the Chamber's representative role continued at its Third National Congress, convened in March 1997. As at the Second Congress, the most senior official was Deputy Prime Minister Phan Van Khai. He was accompanied by Pham The Duyet, a Politburo member who recently had replaced Vu Oanh as head of the Central Committee's Mass Mobilization Commission. In his speech to the Congress, Pham The Duyet noted that he had attended the meeting of the Politburo Standing Board which had listened to the report on preparations for the event. He acknowledged the Chamber's concrete contributions to economic policy in the past, and urged the organization to increase its participation in the policy-making process in the future.[29] In his speech, Phan Van Khai recognized the Chamber as the "largest representative organization" of the Vietnamese business community; however, he also pressed the Chamber to gather more business associations into its organization. Associations could be members according to the Chamber's 1993 statutes, but very few had joined by 1997. To help foster economic growth, Khai also emphasized the importance of close cooperation between the government and the business community:

> The experience of other countries and of our country both show that economies will develop dynamically and steadily at high growth levels when close cooperative relations are established between the government and the business community. The government is ready to cooperate and listen closely to the opinions of the business community in many ways, and one of the most important ways is through the representative organization, the Chamber of Commerce and Industry of Vietnam. The [government] also hopes that enterprises will cooperate with the government in efforts to speed up the process of renovation with the general aim of making the people rich, the country strong, and the society just and civilized.[30]

In sum, presentations by senior officials at the Third Congress continued to focus on enhancing the Chamber's role as the representative of the Vietnamese business community. As suggested in the remarks of Phan Van Khai above, moreover, the country's political leadership clearly subscribed to a corporatist vision of government-business relations, viewing "close cooperative relations" as essential to the country's economic growth. In this vision, the Chamber of Commerce occupied a pre-eminent position—expected not only to participate in national policy-making as the peak organization representing all Vietnamese business, but also to attract and absorb other domestic business associations into its membership structure.

Alongside these officially sponsored changes in the political role and operating mandate of the Chamber of Commerce, reforms have taken place in the broader legal framework of Vietnam during *doi moi* which allow mass organizations, business associations, and other groups to participate more extensively in the country's legislative process.[31]

Regulations for soliciting public opinions on draft laws first appeared in August 1988,[32] and the process was codified into law when the National Assembly passed the Law on the Promulgation of Legal Documents in November 1996. Article 30 of the law stipulates that the "Vietnam Fatherland Front and its member organizations [i.e., mass organizations and other groups] shall have the right to make comments on the bills and draft ordinances." When draft legislation is "related to the functions, tasks and powers" of these organizations, drafting committees also are required to "send the drafts to the Vietnam Fatherland Front and its member organizations for comment."[33]

Procedures for gathering opinions from the public generally are set out in Articles 39–41, which together comprise Section Six of the Law. This section, titled "Soliciting Public Comments on Bills and Draft Ordinances", stipulates that the National Assembly or the Standing Committee of the National Assembly (NASC) shall decide on which draft legislation the government should solicit public comments. The NASC also determines the content, scope, mode and time of the solicitation and has overall direction of the process. For their part, citizens can offer comments through "their agencies or organizations" or can mail their comments directly to the Office of the National Assembly, the drafting committee, or to the mass media. During the solicitation process, the VFF and its member organizations, social and economic organizations, state agencies, and People's Armed Forces units are responsible for creating conditions for citizens to offer comments on draft legislation. Finally, the Office of the National Assembly is responsible for gathering all of the public comments. Then the drafting committee coordinates with the evaluating agency (i.e., one of the seven specialized committees of the National Assembly) "in studying and accepting the public comments, revising the draft document and making a report to the Standing Committee of the National Assembly."[34]

In addition to these general legislative provisions, the government has promulgated two regulations aimed at enhancing the political participation of business associations in particular. The first, Government Decision no. 310, pertains only to the Chamber of Commerce and was issued by the Prime Minister three months after the Chamber's Second National Congress in 1993. The regulation calls on the Chamber to offer policy recommendations to national and local organs of the government, and requires these organs to provide the Chamber with the documents and information needed to fulfill this task. The decision also affirms that the Chamber would be invited to take part in government meetings where relevant matters were to be discussed. Meanwhile, the President of the Chamber is "responsible for reporting to the Prime Minister every six months, on the development situation of the business community and on the activity of the Chamber, and sending a report on the existing state of business enterprises to the government organs and people's committees concerned."[35]

The second regulation, Directive no. 16 of the Prime Minister, was issued in March 1998 and calls for the role of the Chamber of Commerce and other business associations to be strengthened in terms of identifying business problems that arise, collecting the opinions of business people, and forwarding recommendations to the Prime Minister and government agencies. The regulation requires ministries and drafting bodies to consult with the Chamber and other business associations when drafting new legal documents affecting the business community.[36] (Two months later, the Office of Government also issued an official letter [*cong van*] requiring ministries and drafting bodies to consult stakeholders when drafting new legal documents to ensure that laws and regulations are drafted well and can be implemented successfully. "For legal documents related to enterprises," the instruction said, "it is required to obtain comments from enterprises through the Vietnam Chamber of Commerce and Industry, relevant business associations, or directly from enterprises.")[37]

Based on the above regulations, there are three basic processes by which the Chamber of Commerce carries out interest representation and engages in policy-making in Vietnam. It does so by (i) organizing large public meetings where business people have an opportunity to voice their grievances directly to the Prime Minister and other senior ministers; (ii) participating in governmental meetings and meeting privately with the Prime Minister; and (iii) recommending changes to draft laws and regulations.

Public Meetings between Business Community and Prime Minister

The first way in which the Chamber carries out interest representation is by organizing annual public meetings between the business community and the Prime Minister, Deputy Prime Minister, and senior ministers, in which there are frank exchanges on policy issues. Each year, starting four to six months in advance of these meetings, the Chamber carries out a national survey on problems facing the business community, and organizes several preparatory workshops to analyze these problems and develop specific policy proposals for submission to the Prime Minister. As reported in the Vietnamese press, business people from both the private and state sectors attend these gatherings, often voicing strong complaints to the Prime Minister or his deputies. Business people have voiced many well-known private sector grievances at these meetings—namely limited access to land, insufficient bank credit, high taxes, restrictions on foreign trade, and difficulties in establishing a business.

Government Meetings and Private Meetings with Prime Minister

The Chamber's President also is invited to attend government meetings when issues affecting the business community are on the agenda, such as trade policy or implementation of the Enterprise Law. In addition, he meets directly with the Prime Minister every six months to discuss the needs of the business community as well as the internal affairs of the Chamber, including the tasks that the Prime Minister expects the Chamber to fulfill and the support that the Chamber expects to receive from the government. Aside from these regularly scheduled meetings, the President can meet with the Prime Minister on an emergency basis as pressing issues arise.[38]

Recommending Changes to Draft Laws and Regulations

The most tangible way in which the Chamber represents the interests of the business community is by recommending changes to draft laws and regulations. As discussed above, ministries and other government agencies that are drafting new legal documents are required to share drafts with the Chamber so that it can examine the draft documents and propose changes. Once the Chamber receives a draft document from the government, it usually circulates the document within the business community. In some cases, the Chamber limits circulation to members of its Advisory Board and Executive Committee, who are given between two and four weeks to respond with written comments. For particularly important documents, the Chamber also solicits opinions from the business community at large. It does this in two ways. First, it distributes the documents to its branch offices throughout the country, instructing them to share the document with local members, hold discussions, and reply with a written report. Second, it organizes public meetings so that its members, and any other interested business people, can gather to discuss the draft legal document. Attendees often include government officials involved in the drafting, who are invited to introduce and explain the main contents of the draft. After convening these meetings and receiving written reports from its branch offices and from members of its Advisory Board and Executive Committee, the Chamber synthesizes what it considers to be the most salient recommendations into a single report, and then dispatches it to the government organ that is responsible for the drafting.[39]

Since the late 1990s, moreover, the government has facilitated more direct business participation in law-making by inviting Chamber officials to serve as official members of the drafting bodies themselves. As discussed later in this chapter, senior Chamber staff served on both the steering committee and drafting group of the Enterprise Law, which came into effect in January 2000. During the drafting of the amended Labour Code, passed by the National Assembly in April 2002, the Chamber of Commerce also was invited to participate in the steering and drafting bodies as the official representative of Vietnamese employers. Other members were drawn from the Vietnam General Confederation of Labour (VGCL), which represented employee interests, as well as the Ministry of Justice and the Ministry of Labour, War Invalids and Social Affairs. Following these examples, Chamber staff are now serving on an increasing number of committees that are drafting new laws or ordinances in accordance with the National Assembly's legislative programme. In the Assembly's legislative programme for 2002, for example, the Chamber participated in eight committees drafting new legislation—including the draft competition law and a draft ordinance on commercial arbitration.[40]

In sum, the Vietnamese government has implemented far-reaching reforms during *doi moi* that have led not only to dramatic changes in the operating mandate of the Chamber of Commerce, but also to new corporatist arrangements which provide the Chamber with increasing opportunities to participate in policy and law-making.[41] In practice, the Chamber may comment on numerous drafts of the same legislation over extended periods. As discussed in the next section, it offered comments and suggested changes to several drafts of the Law on Promotion of Domestic Investment (LPDI). However, the main comment period usually occurs shortly before draft legislation is submitted to the National

Assembly for a vote, and begins when full texts of the drafts are published in national newspapers. Once newspapers published the draft LPDI, for instance, the Chamber organized public meetings in Hanoi and Ho Chi Minh City, and it instructed its branch offices to hold discussions with members and reply to headquarters with a written report. Subsequently, the Chamber summarized the main comments and recommendations into a comprehensive report and presented it to the government.

The Law on Promotion of Domestic Investment

This section investigates the participation of the Chamber of Commerce in the drafting of the LPDI, enacted in June 1994 and put into effect in January 1995. The making of this law is an important case study on the topic of business associations and policy-making in Vietnam, as it was the first time that the Chamber organized membership meetings for the purpose of contributing opinions to a draft law. Before examining the Chamber's role in the making of the law, the section first describes the drafting process, identifies the key players involved, and discusses the political and economic exigencies that prompted the law's creation.

The stated goal of the LPDI was to mobilize latent capital and concentrate investment into manufacturing sectors and geographical regions that had been targeted for priority development. In other words, in addition to increasing the overall level of domestic investment, the government aimed to reduce regional economic inequalities by channelling investment into relatively underdeveloped areas, such as remote mountainous regions inhabited by national minorities, and to exploit the country's comparative advantage by directing investment into priority export sectors.[42]

Broadly speaking, the law's drafters hoped to accomplish these goals in three ways. First, they offered enhanced legal guarantees to domestic investors, including increased protection against the nationalization of investor assets, in an effort to boost the confidence of Vietnamese business people in the investment environment. Second, they established various forms of governmental assistance for domestic investment, such as credit guarantees for banks and an "investment assistance fund" designed to extend mid and long-term loans for investment projects. Third and most importantly, they created specific categories of investment projects (e.g., aquaculture, infrastructure, and production for export) that would be eligible to receive preferential tax treatment—most notably exemptions or reductions of profit and revenue tax and, in more limited instances, import tax exemptions for machinery, equipment, and material imported for use in production. The precise level of tax relief that a particular project received would vary according to the number of preferential categories that it satisfied. It would also depend on the geographic location of the investment. In this way, the drafters intended to use tax incentives as a "tool" or "lever" to encourage business people to invest in regions and sectors that were prioritized by the state.

Disagreement existed over whether state-owned enterprises (SOEs) should be included among the beneficiaries of the law and receive the same preferential treatment as private sector investment. Initially, the drafters intended that the LPDI would promote the private sector and that SOEs would be guided by a forthcoming Law on State Enterprises. But opposition to excluding SOEs emerged early in the drafting process due to concern that SOEs could lose their "leading role" in the economy if denied the privileges offered by the LPDI. In the end, SOEs were included among the beneficiaries: Article 4 of the final legislation indicates that the law covers "investment for setting up production and business establishments by all economic sectors."[43] Yet, the law still has limited applicability to SOEs. According to a 1995 Ministry of Justice report, a state enterprise may "only receive promotion for the part of investment capital that the enterprise possesses itself and not for capital supplied by the [state] budget."[44] And while a number of the law's provisions are apparently relevant to SOEs (e.g., tax incentives), others are not (e.g., protections against the nationalization of investor assets). In any case, since *all* provisions of the law are relevant to the private sector, it is a good test case of the extent to which the Chamber represents private sector interests to the government during the law-making process.

In addition to the economic arguments for promoting domestic investment, there was a strong political motivation behind the new legislation: to satisfy the demand of Vietnamese investors that the legal environment between domestic and foreign investment be equalized. The Chamber of Commerce vigorously asserted this demand during the drafting process, as did National Assembly deputies, and it emerged as a central theme in the press reports that covered the process. In essence, Vietnamese business people were unhappy that the Foreign Investment Law, promulgated in 1987 and amended in 1990 and 1992, bestowed foreign investors with investment privileges that domestic investors could not receive. They wanted a level playing field—especially in the area of tax relief—and they expected the new law to bring this about. As the Ministry of Justice report acknowledged:

> Privileges which the state reserved for foreign investors have put domestic investors in a disadvantageous position in competition. They must carry out activities in an investment environment with many difficulties (regarding capital, floor-space, technology transfers, import-export, etc.), and meanwhile they are unable to receive tax and credit privileges that foreigners receive. This is completely contrary to the principle of equality of the market economic system. Domestic investors demand to receive equal treatment to be able to invest in a more favourable and transparent legal environment.[45]

Vietnamese investors were particularly unhappy that so much time had passed between the promulgation of the Foreign Investment Law and the drafting of the LPDI. In a May 1994 interview in *Thoi Bao Kinh Te Viet Nam* (Vietnam Economic Times), a journalist asked a senior government official whether he believed the law was coming out late. In response, the official indicated that this was "the correct occasion" for issuing the law because it coincided with a new stage of industrialization and modernization as well as a large influx of foreign investment. Other recently promulgated laws had also established a solid foundation for the domestic investment law, the official said.[46] A journalist writing about the drafting process in the same newspaper offered a more cynical spin, characterizing the situation as "better late than never."[47]

Drafting of the LPDI officially began in 1993 after the National Assembly voted to include the investment law in its annual legislative programme. Overall drafting responsibility was assigned to the State Planning Committee (SPC), which was then a government agency of ministerial rank charged with formulating national socio-economic development strategies. Specific responsibility fell to the Central Institute of Economic Management (CIEM)—an internal institute of the SPC which Doan Duy Thanh had headed from 1991 until he became president of the Chamber in April 1993. To prepare for drafting the LPDI, the Institute studied the investment promotion policies of other countries (notably Indonesia, Malaysia, Singapore, Thailand, South Korea, and the Federal Republic of Germany) and organized public seminars in Hanoi and Ho Chi Minh City, where its staff gathered the opinions and proposals of legal specialists, business people, scholars, and officials from central and local-level state offices. The Institute also conducted a survey of 300 private sector enterprises operating in Hanoi and Ho Chi Minh City.[48]

The formal drafting committee was composed of SPC Chairman Do Quoc Sam as well as ministers and vice-ministers whose areas of responsibility included investment matters. An inter-agency working group, acting as a subsidiary of the drafting committee, was responsible for the actual drafting. This group included approximately ten economic and legal specialists drawn from CIEM itself, other SPC departments, the Economic and Budgetary Committee and the Legal Committee of the National Assembly, the Ministry of Justice, the Ministry of Finance, the Office of Government, the State Committee for Cooperation and Investment, and the Economic Commission of the Party Central Committee. The higher-level drafting committee convened periodically throughout the drafting process to review the latest drafts put forward by the working group. Once the committee considered a draft to be satisfactory, SPC Chairman Do Quoc Sam would present it to a session of government for review.[49]

The first such occasion occurred on 28 November 1993, when the standing body of the government reviewed the fourth draft of the law. Soon thereafter, the drafting committee circulated the fifth draft to members of the government, and numerous ministries responded with suggested changes to the document. Upon completing the seventh draft in mid-December, the drafting committee submitted the draft law to the Fourth Session of the Ninth National Assembly—not for open debate but simply to obtain written comments from individual deputies, each of whom received copies of the draft.[50]

Another body actively participating in the drafting process was the Economic and Budgetary Committee of the National Assembly. As the legislative committee assigned to examine the draft, it convened several meetings to inspect the draft at various stages of its development. In addition, it solicited the views of private entrepreneurs, directors of state enterprises, and chairmen of people's councils and people's committees from various cities and provinces, and forwarded these views to the drafting committee.[51]

With the LPDI expected to be debated and put before a vote at the next National Assembly session, scheduled to open in late May, the National Assembly Standing Committee decided to publish the eleventh draft in *Nhan Dan* (The People) in mid-April and called on the public to contribute opinions by 10 May.[52] The publication of draft laws for public consultation is limited to especially important legislation due to cost and time constraints. In addition to soliciting the views of private individuals and governmental organs around the country, the NASC requests the opinions of mass organizations and other socio-economic groups, such as the Chamber of Commerce, whose areas of operation or expertise are pertinent to the content of the draft. The Chamber appears to have taken full advantage of this invitation. Although it had reviewed and commented on earlier drafts, the public consultation process offered the Chamber its greatest opportunity to influence the drafting process. In response to an official letter from the Office of the National Assembly requesting its input, the Chamber circulated the draft law to members of its Executive Committee and Advisory Board and asked them for written comments. It also distributed the draft to membership departments of its branch offices throughout the country, instructing them to share the document with local members, hold discussions, and reply with a written report. In Hanoi, the Chamber organized a public meeting so that its members, and any other interested business people, could gather to discuss the draft law. Invitees included officials from CIEM, who kicked off the discussion by introducing and explaining the main contents of the draft. The Chamber organized a similar meeting at its branch office in Ho Chi Minh City shortly thereafter.[53]

After convening these meetings and receiving other reactions in writing, the Chamber synthesized the recommendations into a single report and dispatched it to the State Planning Committee and the Office of the National Assembly on 10 May 1994. The introductory section of the report stressed the importance of promulgating the draft as quickly as possible. It also indicated that while the "majority of opinions" viewed the eleventh draft as an improvement from previous drafts, some believed that it still contained a number of shortcomings. For example, the promotionary investment measures enumerated in the draft are characterized as "trivial", and the draft is criticized for placing too much emphasis on what "the state provides" rather than what "citizens have the right to receive". The introduction also devoted considerable print to critical opinions of a more general nature. These admonished state offices for harassing business people; asserted that the state should not interfere in the production processes of businesses if they did nothing to violate the law; called for a more favourable legal environment with tight procedures and short inspection periods; proposed transforming the system of "asking permission" to establish new businesses to a system of "registering" businesses; and demanded that all privileges provided to foreign investors also be offered to Vietnamese entrepreneurs.[54]

The main section of the report moved through the draft law chapter by chapter and article by article, offering forty proposed changes on issues ranging from the level of preferential tax treatment to the protection of investor assets from nationalization. While gathering opinions on these issues, the Chamber sought to achieve a consensus on the perspectives that it would advance in its report. Where this was not possible, it would present each of the contending viewpoints. For example, the Chamber presented two perspectives on the question of whether SOEs should be included among the beneficiaries of the law. The first perspective, reflecting the dominance of SOEs in its membership at that time, affirmed that "the beneficiaries of the law should include all state enterprises because now they are not supplied with budget capital as in the past". In contrast, the second perspective argued against the inclusion of SOEs because "this would allow the state to offer preferential treatment to itself."[55]

Viewed in its entirety, the recommendation report of the Chamber of Commerce indicates that when the Chamber is invited to participate in the law-making process, it does represent the interests of the business community to the government. Indeed, as will be shown in the pages ahead, the report reveals an organization that is ready to advance tough proposals on behalf of business interests.

The Chamber was not the only organization invited to contribute proposals to the drafting committee. By 11 May, the end of the period for public debate, the drafting committee had received seventeen reports from state offices and National Assembly delegations, seven reports published in the media,[56] and one letter from a private citizen. The Vietnam Lawyers' Association and the AIC of Ho Chi Minh City contributed reports as well. On 12 May, the drafting committee and Economic and Budgetary Committee of the National Assembly jointly sent a document summarizing these reports to the National Assembly Standing Committee.[57] According to this report, a widespread perspective expressed in the recommendation reports was that Vietnamese lacked confidence in current legal protections for investment and viewed the required administrative procedures to be excessively difficult and cumbersome.

Prompted by these outside recommendations, the drafting committee reconvened to revise the draft before submitting it to the National Assembly for debate. On 30 May, the committee issued a significantly revised draft with twenty-six articles (hereafter referred to as the "revised draft"), down from forty-three articles in the published draft.[58] Three days later, on 2 June, it issued its official Presentation Report to the Assembly. This detailed report not only described the drafting process and the general content of the draft law; it also identified the most controversial issues and explained why the committee adopted the positions contained in the draft and rejected opposing ones.[59] For its part, the Assembly's Economic and Budgetary Committee met in full session in Hanoi on 23 May and 1 June to continue examining the draft law and to prepare a lengthy Examination Report. The finished report, also dated 2 June and providing the opinions of committee members on a number of important issues, was addressed to the full Assembly.[60]

The National Assembly officially opened the fifth session of its ninth term on 26 May, although debate on the draft law on domestic investment did not begin until 6 June. Many deputies voiced strong opposition to various aspects of the draft law when debate got underway in the assembly hall that afternoon.[61] The drafting committee's working group carefully monitored these debates and collected written opinions submitted by the deputies. By 13 June, the drafting committee had completed a summary report on the changes recommended in the Assembly, which it sent to the NASC for review.[62] Combined with press accounts, the various reports noted above offer a window into the law-making process of Vietnam. In particular, they reveal the existence of sharply divided perspectives over a series of issues and show how these issues were ultimately resolved.

In the following pages, two of the more divisive issues—protection against the nationalization of investor assets and the types of investment projects that would qualify for preferential treatment—are discussed first as they are presented in the Chamber's recommendation report and then as they are cited in other reports and debated at the National Assembly. During the drafting process, other divisive issues included the levels of tax privileges offered to qualified projects and the eligibility of domestic enterprises to receive import tax exemptions on inputs to be used in production.

Nationalization

On 4 April, two weeks before the draft law was published in *Nhan Dan*, a CIEM official remarked in a newspaper interview that the LPDI would "unleash a flood of investment" because it affirmed that the capital and property of investors would not be nationalized or requisitioned.[63] Article 6 of the published draft did provide that "investment capital and property created from the lawful investments of investors shall not be nationalized", but it also added that the state may "make a compulsory purchase or compulsory requisition" of an investor's property "for reasons of national defense, security and national interest". In this event, the investor would be compensated "according to the market price prevailing at the time of the compulsory purchase or requisition and shall be afforded favourable conditions to invest in an appropriate field or area."[64]

The Chamber of Commerce criticized the language on nationalization in its recommendation report, asserting that the guarantees offered in the draft fell short of those provided in the Foreign Investment Law. In particular, the Chamber proposed that the drafters "eliminate 'compulsory purchase' and 'compulsory requisition' and simply pledge not to nationalize property (as in the Foreign Investment Law), so that investors can feel assured". The Chamber also indicated that if the language allowing for such purchases or requisitions could not be removed, then the draft should include more concrete provisions for compensating investors than general pledges to create favourable conditions. Specifically, it called for compensation to businesses for losses arising from a "compulsory purchase" as well as stipulations about the state's responsibility to provide compensation in a timely manner so that businesses could invest in other areas. "If compensation is delayed", the Chamber added, "then the state must pay the interest on money borrowed from the bank from the moment it was decided to purchase the property."[65]

Other outside contributors also raised concerns about the draft law's guarantees against nationalization, although they tended to seek further information on the subject rather than advance tough demands. In the end, the content of Article 6 remained virtually unchanged from the published draft to the final law passed by the National Assembly on 22 June. In its Presentation Report to the Assembly, the drafting committee stressed that the LPDI's protections against nationalization not only mirrored the protections offered in the 1992 Constitution,[66] but also went a step further by stipulating that "favourable conditions" would be created for investors to invest elsewhere in the rare circumstances where nationalization actually occurred.[67] For its part, the 1995 Ministry of Justice report indicated that Article 6 both institutionalized the 1992 constitutional provisions on nationalization and inherited the guarantees first offered in the 1987 Foreign Investment Law.[68] What the ministry report failed to mention was that the Foreign Investment Law does not include conditions or circumstances in which the state may carry out nationalization "for reasons of national defense, security and national interest"; it simply offers a blanket guarantee that an "enterprise with foreign-owned capital shall not be nationalized."[69]

Given that no other contributors, committees or deputies strongly objected to the LPDI's provisions on nationalization, it is not surprising that the drafting committee disregarded the Chamber's demand that the LDPI provide guarantees equal to those in the Foreign Investment Law or at least offer more specific forms of compensation. Nevertheless, the Chamber's contribution on this issue demonstrated that it was ready to advance tough demands on behalf of business interests—even on such sensitive subjects as the right of private investors to protect their property from the reach of the state.

Projects Eligible for Preferential Treatment

The Chamber also advanced proposals for expanding the number of investment areas that are entitled to receive privileges from the state, as listed in Article 8 of the published draft and Article 9 of both the revised draft issued on 30 May and the final law.[70] These proposals reveal instances where the drafting committee incorporated the Chamber's perspectives into the law and also demonstrate how recommendations by other contributors, especially deputies to the National Assembly, reinforced the Chamber's efforts. In the two project areas discussed briefly below, the first (labour-intensive projects) describes a situation where the drafting committee accepted the Chamber's proposed change into the revised draft and also retained this change in the final law. In the second project area (science and technology), the committee did not accept the Chamber's proposal into the revised draft, although the change does appear in the final law.

Labour-intensive Projects. Toward the end of its recommendation report, the Chamber enumerated a list of issues that it felt the draft had yet to address adequately. One of these concerned the lack of measures for promoting labour-intensive investment projects. "There should be an additional investment area receiving privileges," the Chamber proposed, "that includes trades and professions which, although not generating high economic efficiency, do have a significant social impact, i.e., attracting many workers, creating jobs, and mitigating the problem of unemployment."[71] Other outside contributors also proposed that projects helping to boost employment be included among the privileged investment areas.[72] The drafting committee responded to these recommendations by adding labour-intensive projects to the list of privileged investment projects in the revised draft issued on 30 May.[73] It did so by awarding privileged treatment, in Article 9(3) of the new draft, to projects "setting up production and business establishments that create many jobs". Meanwhile, press reports indicate that the labour issue arose only once during the National Assembly debates. This occurred on 7 June when Deputy Duong Viet Trung, a member of the Chamber's Executive Committee and Director of the Can Tho Agricultural Foodstuffs Export Company, affirmed that privileges were needed for investment projects which set up production establishments using many labourers; he added that these establishments also must "use domestic raw materials."[74] Although the drafting committee ignored his proposal for utilizing domestic materials, labour-intensive projects did remain among the privileged investment areas listed in the final law.

Science and Technology. In addition to labour-intensive projects, the Chamber proposed that "research and the application of new science and technology" should be added to the projects being promoted by the law.[75] The drafting committee did not accept the Chamber's proposed change into the revised draft, but the change does appear among the privileged areas found in the final law. Specifically, Article 9(1b) of the law lists "scientific and technological research" among the privileged investment categories, and Article 9(3), the same article that previously focused only on labour-intensive projects, now also promoted projects "setting up production and business establishments that use modern technology..."[76] This last-minute change almost certainly resulted from the fact that National Assembly deputies focused attention on the technology issue during the debates that occurred on June 6. Though the deputies did not address the specific question of scientific research during the debates, they did advocate that privileges be granted for projects utilizing modern technology.[77]

On 22 June 1994, the day the National Assembly passed the draft LPDI into law, a *Nhan Dan* reporter interviewed Doan Duy Thanh, President of the Chamber of Commerce, to obtain his perspectives on the new law. The interview appeared on the newspaper's front page the following day. Asked whether the law contained any points that might undercut the confidence of Vietnamese investors in the investment environment, Thanh indicated that while the National Assembly had defined the contents of the law quite clearly, problems of interpretation remained. Referring to Article 6 (where the law indicates that the state may make a compulsory purchase or requisition of an investor's property "for reasons of national defence, security and national interest"), he asked what the phrase "national defence, security and national interest" meant in a practical sense. More pointedly, he questioned what the state does that is *not* for reasons of national defence, security and national interest. "If [the law] is stated in such a general way, then investors will not feel assured", he said.[78] Still, Thanh acknowledged that the National Assembly had devoted considerable time to debating the law and that many business people and experts had contributed their opinions during the drafting process. Because the law had been drafted in this way, he said, it had established a basic foundation for building confidence among investors.[79]

In evaluating the Chamber's participation in the drafting of the LPDI, it is useful to ask two questions. First, did the organization actually represent the interests of the Vietnamese business community? Second, did it influence the end result? With regard to influence, precise measurement is complicated by the fact that the draft law was revised and rearranged extensively during the closing weeks of the drafting process. Furthermore, isolating the individual impact of the Chamber is difficult because it encountered the most success when its proposals coincided with proposals advanced by other organizations, such as the AIC of Ho Chi Minh City, and by deputies to the National Assembly. However, whether through its own influence or in concert with the influence of other interests, some of the Chamber's recommendations did find their way into the final law. Though the drafting committee ignored the Chamber's proposals on the nationalization issue, it did incorporate the Chamber's perspectives on the categories of projects which are eligible to receive preferential tax treatment (labour-intensive projects and those utilizing modern technology) as well as on tax exemptions for reinvestment.[80]

More generally, the Chamber clearly did represent the interests of the Vietnamese business community during the drafting process. Indeed, it articulated tough demands to the drafting committee over a wide range of issues. The Chamber's demands were particularly strong where it called for a "level playing field" between domestic business people and foreign investors, including the sensitive issue, applicable only to the private sector, of whether Vietnamese investors would receive increased protection against the nationalization of private assets. Its extensive participation resulted from official efforts to develop corporatist patterns of interest representation in economic policy-making—first by anointing the Chamber as the officially-sanctioned "representative" of the national business community, and then by facilitating the Chamber's participation in an actual law-making process. Once given the opportunity to participate in this process, however, the Chamber articulated the grievances of the Vietnamese business community in very strong terms.

The Enterprise Law

Implementation of the LPDI met with mixed results in the years immediately following its enactment by the National Assembly, as few businesses took advantage of the preferential tax treatment and other benefits provided in the law. Business people complained that the tax privileges were not sufficiently attractive, while the procedures for securing these privileges were difficult and complicated. The government responded by amending the LPDI in 1998, and the amended law broadened the list of investment areas eligible for preferential treatment; enhanced the level of government support provided through investment assistance funds; and improved the preferential tax treatment by offering greater tax exemptions and reductions over longer investment periods.[81] At a more fundamental level, there also was a growing recognition among policy-makers that there simply were not enough private enterprises established in Vietnam which could apply for and benefit from the investment privileges, thereby limiting the law's impact. New private enterprises had to be licensed under the Law on Private Enterprises or the Law on Companies, both of which were enacted in December 1990 and amended in July 1994, and these laws set out restrictive conditions for the establishment of private firms.[82] Less than 30,000 had been officially registered by the late 1990s. In order to enhance the impact of the LPDI and generate more domestic investment (among other reasons), a consensus was emerging on the need to create a new legal framework for the private sector that would ease entry procedures and allow more private firms to come into existence. This legal framework would soon be codified in a new Enterprise Law.[83]

The drafting of the Enterprise Law grew out of an earlier and less ambitious plan to further amend the Private Enterprise Law and Company Law. The government had instructed relevant ministries in 1995 to coordinate with Party agencies, the Office of the National Assembly, and the Chamber of Commerce to conduct studies on further amending these laws. Eventually, in January 1998, the government established a steering committee to accomplish this task. The committee was headed by the Minister of Planning and Investment, and official members included vice ministers of relevant ministries (notably the Ministry of Finance, Ministry of Trade, and Ministry of Industry) as well as representatives from the Office of Government and the Chamber of Commerce. From the Chamber, the committee position was filled by Vice President Pham Chi Lan. Others invited "to participate" were representatives from the Economic Commission of the Party Central Committee, two National Assembly committees, and the VGCL. Later that year, however, the government proposed that instead of amending the Private Enterprise Law and Company Law, the steering committee should create an entirely new law, called the Enterprise Law, building on the foundation of the original two laws.[84]

By including a senior official of the Chamber of Commerce on the steering committee, the government had opened up a more direct channel for business association participation in the country's legislative process. Previously, as illustrated in the drafting of the LPDI, the Chamber could participate by organizing public meetings among its members, soliciting their opinions on draft laws, synthesizing these opinions into a recommendation report, and forwarding the report to the drafting agency. This time, the Chamber not only had a Vice President on the formal steering committee, but the head of its legal department was a member of the drafting group that actually composed the law. Once again, CIEM served as the home base of these drafting bodies during the drafting process.[85]

With representatives serving on both the steering committee and the drafting group, the Chamber was able to participate in and influence the drafting process more directly than in the past through verbal interventions at working meetings of these bodies. Throughout the drafting process, the Chamber's representatives pushed hard to create a law that would improve the operating environment for Vietnam's private sector. Against sharp resistance from the Ministry of Finance, for instance, they pushed to eliminate minimal capital requirements for establishing a new business. They also argued for replacing the complicated system of licensing new enterprises with a streamlined registration system; called for simplified procedures of reporting by businesses to the government; said that state inspections of businesses should be limited and clearly stipulated in the law in order to prevent abuses by officials; and, more generally, insisted on codifying the principle that entrepreneurs can do any business activities not prohibited by law (as opposed to doing only what is permitted by law). In most cases, the Chamber and its allies in the government were successful in ensuring that these recommendations appeared in the final version of the Enterprise Law—often replacing restrictive or vague provisions that existed in the earlier Private Enterprise Law and Company Law.[86]

As with the Law on Promotion of Domestic Investment, the Chamber of Commerce was not the only business association participating in the drafting process. While the Chamber was the sole business association with officials serving directly on the steering committee and drafting group, other business associations participated by commenting on drafts, organizing membership meetings, and sending recommendation reports to the drafting bodies. One of these associations was the HUAIC. Early on, CIEM provided the HUAIC with drafts of the Enterprise Law as they were completed, and the HUAIC responded by making comments and suggested changes on the draft itself and then returning the edited draft to CIEM. Subsequently, the HUAIC submitted two recommendation reports, one in February 1999 and another in April 1999. In its April report, the HUAIC stressed the importance of changing the state management of business operations from the old mechanism (characterized by asking permission and waiting for approval) to basic state functions in a market economy (described as setting the legal framework, establishing tax liabilities, protecting the environment, and ensuring obligations to society).[87]

New provisions on minimal capital requirements and state inspections illustrate the stark difference between the legal framework represented by the old Company Law and Private Enterprise Law, on the one hand, and the framework represented by the new Enterprise Law, on the other. In terms of capital, the original laws required the founders of a new firm to prove that they possessed legal capital that was "sufficient for the scale, branches and areas of the business."[88] These capital requirements applied to all businesses, and ranged from about US$3,000 to US$100,000 depending on the business field. However, the Enterprise Law eliminates capital requirements for most businesses by stipulating that they are necessary only in specific fields identified in other laws and regulations (e.g., banking and financial leasing). In contrast to the original two laws, the Enterprise Law also provides transparent provisions on state inspections of private enterprises. Specifically, Article 117 states that financial inspections "shall be conducted no more than once each year for each enterprise". Furthermore, if an official "issues an inspection decision not in accordance with the law or takes advantage of the inspection to gain personal benefits, harass or obstruct the operation of an enterprise, such person shall, depending on the seriousness of the breach, be disciplined or examined for penal liability; and must compensate the enterprise for any damage caused in accordance with the law."[89]

However, the most important innovation of the Enterprise Law involves the change from a cumbersome and protracted system of licensing new enterprises to a streamlined registration system. The old system effectively required business people to secure approvals from numerous authorities prior to registration, allowing officials to collect extra fees and other concessions at various stages of the licensing process. By contrast, the Enterprise Law allows most businesses simply to submit an application for registration to a specialized registration agency set up in each province. The law also requires the registration agencies to respond to these applications within specified time periods. This legal innovation has removed a key barrier that had been hindering private sector development in Vietnam throughout the 1990s. Though licences are still required in some "conditional" sectors (such as hospitals and pharmacies) related to the public interest, the overall number is being reduced based on recommendations from an official task force working on enforcement of the Enterprise Law. By mid-2002, the government had eliminated about 160 licences that were previously associated with the registration of private companies.[90]

The Enterprise Law was passed by the National Assembly on 12 June 1999 and took effect on 1 January 2000. Implementation has brought the average time needed for business registration down from 90 days to one week and the average cost from US$690 to US$35. The response to such improvements in the business environment has been dramatic: about 36,000 private companies registered in the two years following its implementation in January 2000, compared to only 6,000 in the two years before 2000. These firms had a total registered capital equivalent to US$2 billion, or 6 per cent of Vietnam's GDP, and have created hundreds of thousands of new jobs. Estimates suggest that the Vietnamese private sector now accounts for 8 per cent of GDP and employs about one million people. Spurred by the Enterprise Law, it also has generated 43 per cent of export growth in the past two years. In addition, domestic private investment has risen by 3 per cent of GDP since the Enterprise Law came into effect. Although enforcement of the law has been not been uniform throughout the country, with reports of poor compliance in some areas (manifested in repeated and improper state inspections, for example), it is widely viewed as an economic success by both Vietnamese and foreign observers.[91]

Party Fifth Plenum

The participation of the Chamber of Commerce and other business associations in policy-making is not limited to laws drafted by the government-appointed committees, such as the Enterprise Law and the LPDI, but also includes important resolutions issued by the Central Committee of the Vietnamese Communist Party. This participation was clearly demonstrated in the drafting of the Party resolution issued by the Fifth Plenum, held from 18 February to 23 March 2002, which strongly endorsed further development of the domestic private sector.

Central Committee plenums are convened every six months on a thematic basis, and this was the first plenum to focus on private sector development. The most conspicuous outcome—stated in the official resolution of the plenum and widely reported in the domestic and international press—was the decision to allow private business owners who already are Party members to retain their membership. Previously, Party regulations had discouraged members from engaging in business activities by forbidding them from undertaking "exploitative" activities. Although business owners still are not allowed to join the Party as new members, as they now can in China, the decision was seen by the business community as an important step in recognizing the legitimate role of the private sector in contributing to the country's economic development.[92]

The Fifth Plenum Resolution also made other significant policy statements of both a general and specific nature. For instance, while confirming that the state sector would continue to play the "leading role" in the country's "socialist-oriented market economy", it declared that the private sector is an important component of the national economy, affirmed that all economic sectors should be treated equally, and recognized that the private sector is a significant contributor to job creation, income generation, and budget revenues. More specifically, the resolution stipulated that state inspections of private enterprises should be minimized; reconfirmed the right of private enterprises to mortgage land-use rights for bank loans; instructed that certificates of land-use rights be issued more expeditiously; called for simplified lending procedures as well as the provision of guarantees and consultancy services for the private sector; and stated that laws and regulations should be amended to distinguish clearly between civil and criminal violations, thereby avoiding the prevalent criminalization of commercial decisions and disputes involving enterprises and banks.[93]

In addition, the resolution stated that "the role of the Vietnam Chamber of Commerce and Industry and business associations should be promoted". This would be accomplished through support programmes for enhancing the capacity of business associations, and by allowing business associations to expand their operations to deliver public services currently provided by state agencies. To promote business associations and facilitate this expanded role, the resolution also stipulated that a regulation on the organization and operation of business associations should be promulgated soon.[94]

Prior to the Fifth Plenum, the Politburo instructed Truong Tan Sang, a Politburo member and head of the Economic Commission of the Party Central Committee, to prepare a report on the current status of private sector development in Vietnam. In response, the Economic Commission established a steering committee (headed by Sang) and a drafting committee to draft both this report, which would be submitted to the plenum for discussion, and the plenum resolution itself. When drafting the private sector report and resolution, the Commission solicited opinions from government ministries and agencies, local government authorities, and the business community. The Commission obtained opinions from the business community in four ways: (i) it appointed Chamber of Commerce officials to serve on the steering committee and the drafting committee; (ii) it distributed the draft documents to business associations and solicited their views and comments; (iii) it arranged seminars and workshops in which Party leaders and members of the drafting bodies could meet with representatives of business associations and enterprises to listen to their comments and suggestions; and (iv) it organized field trips to visit private enterprises and speak with business people themselves. The Commission worked most intensively with the Chamber of Commerce, but also consulted municipal business associations and sectoral associations representing such industries as textiles and garments, leather goods, and fisheries.[95]

For example, the HUAIC accompanied Truong Tan Sang to visit twenty-four of its member enterprises in order to provide a close view of the problems facing the private sector in Hanoi. The HUAIC also participated in two workshops, both attended by Sang and organized by the Hanoi People's Committee. At one of these meetings, convened in late October 2001, the HUAIC's Vice President and Secretary General, Vu Duy Thai, delivered a presentation on the current status of private sector businesses in Hanoi. His presentation described the dramatic increase in private enterprises established in the city since the Enterprise Law came into effect in January 2000, but also enumerated serious problems that continued to hinder private sector growth—including state enterprise monopolies over key intermediate sectors (e.g., electricity, water, petrol, telecommunications, and transportation); high input costs; poor business promotion services; and unreasonable conditions restricting the flow of credit.[96] In addition to participating in these meetings, the HUAIC submitted a formal recommendation report to the Economic

Commission regarding the private sector. Just before the conclusion of the Fifth Plenum, Vu Duy Thai also published an article in the association's newspaper, *Doanh Nghiep va Kinh Te Thu Do* (Capital Business and Economy), in which he wrote that private business people were "expecting a lot" from the plenum in terms of achieving a consensus on the importance of private sector for the country's market economy. Only by achieving such consensus, he wrote, would it be possible "to remove old ideas existing in society and unnecessary barriers which have constrained the reform program of the Party and state concerning the multi-component economy, including private sector development."[97]

While the Economic Commission consulted municipal associations such as the HUAIC and UAIC of Ho Chi Minh City in the months leading to the Fifth Plenum, the Chamber of Commerce was given a special role on the drafting bodies noted above: the Chamber's President was appointed as vice chair of the steering committee, and its Executive Vice President, Vu Tien Loc, served on both the steering committee and the drafting committee. During the drafting of the private sector report and the plenum resolution, the Chamber supplied the drafting bodies with research on the private sector, including a synthesis of reports that it had solicited from its branch offices around the country, and facilitated direct consultations with its private sector members. In addition, the Chamber's representatives advanced a broad range of policy recommendations while serving on the drafting bodies themselves—e.g., improving the country's land policies to facilitate private sector growth. They also raised three issues pertaining to business associations in particular: (i) that Vietnamese business associations should be promoted; (ii) that public services for supporting enterprises should be transferred from state agencies to business associations; and (iii) that the government should issue a regulation to improve the legal framework for business associations in Vietnam.[98]

As noted above, all three of these recommendations on business associations would appear in the plenum resolution. Whether this resulted from the Chamber's input is difficult to determine, but it is noteworthy that the Chamber had already started advancing these recommendations two years earlier. At a national meeting in August 2000 on improving the role and effectiveness of Vietnamese business associations, co-organized by the Chamber and the GCOP, the Chamber presented a report in which it recommended that the government develop a programme to strengthen the capacity of business associations through leadership training and support for improving information and consulting services. The Chamber also urged the government to authorize business associations to carry out various tasks of a public service nature, such as business support services, registration of trade names, and issuing professional certificates. Most significantly, the Chamber said the government should organize a study for creating a law on the organization and operation of business associations to replace outdated legal regulations that had become irrelevant. If a law could not be promulgated soon, the Chamber continued, then an ordinance or at least a government decree on business associations should be promulgated.[99] In fact, the GCOP subsequently began drafting a decree on business associations in response to a directive issued by the Prime Minister in November 2001, and it recently circulated a full draft to state agencies and business associations to solicit comments and reactions. Although it remains unclear when the document will be completed and issued by the government, the final decree is expected to include updated provisions on establishing business associations, organization and functions, the rights of members, reporting requirements, state management over the associations, and dissolution procedures.[100]

While the outcome of this decree remains a question, the Chamber was clearly satisfied with the outcome of the Fifth Plenum. On 2 April 2002, just after the Central Committee had issued the resolution, Chamber Vice President Pham Chi Lan remarked in an interview with *Lao Dong* (Labour) newspaper that the resolution was important because, through it, the Party had confirmed its viewpoint of encouraging the development of the private sector. "This has been mentioned in major resolutions," she said, "but there has still been suspicion, complications, prejudice, and discrimination in the treatment of the private sector in the actual thinking of Party members at different levels and different lines."[101] Lan also commented on the specific provisions in the resolution related to business associations and Party membership:

> For the first time ever, a Central Party resolution has emphasized the role of associations and requested a legal framework for developing their role through enhancing the capacity of associations, facilitating the involvement of associations in delivering public services, etc. This

thoughtful action will provide support for private enterprises to cooperate and unite for better development and protect the legal rights of enterprises in doing business. The resolution also mentions that Party members who are engaged in the private sector will be allowed to retain their membership as long as they comply well with state laws and regulations. This will have a strong psychological effect on private entrepreneurs and Party members who want both themselves and the country to become prosperous.[102]

Conclusion

This chapter has illustrated the increasing levels of participation by business associations in policy and law-making in Vietnam. In the early 1990s, the Chamber of Commerce and other associations began contributing policy recommendations to government appointed drafting committees, often requesting significant changes to draft legislation that would affect the business community. Subsequently, representatives of the Chamber of Commerce participated more directly in policy-making by serving as official members of the drafting committees themselves. Although precise levels of influence are difficult to measure, especially when the form of participation was verbal, specific policy recommendations made by the Chamber have consistently appeared in final versions of the laws and resolutions discussed above. What can be concluded with greater certainty is that the Chamber has acted as a firm and articulate voice for business interests over the past decade. At the same time, some municipal business associations and sectoral groups have been playing increasing policy roles within their respective spheres of operation.

Significantly, however, the Chamber and other business associations have participated in these drafting contexts because the political authorities *invited* them to do so. In this sense, the articulation of business demands has been solicited and managed from above. This form of participation is entirely consistent with the corporatist theory discussed in the introduction, which provides for the incorporation of important sectors of society into official decision-making structures. As the chapter has shown, the Vietnamese authorities clearly view "close cooperative relations" with the emerging private sector as a key ingredient in their economic plans. To promote the development of close relations with business, they sanctioned the Chamber of Commerce as the peak organization representing the national business community, encouraged other business associations to join the Chamber's membership, and facilitated the Chamber's direct participation in government policy-making. Recognizing that relations between business and labour can be conflictual in the new market economy, they also set up tripartite mechanisms (involving government, business and labour) to guide policy-making on labour relations. A recent example occurred during the drafting of the amended Labour Code, when the Chamber and the VGCL represented employers and workers, respectively, on the official drafting committee. In keeping with corporatist theory, these mechanisms seek to mitigate conflict and achieve interest group harmony by providing selected, officially sanctioned organizations with expanded opportunities to participate in policy-making.

Yet, while corporatist patterns of interest representation are emerging primarily because of political reforms implemented by the authorities, business associations and other groups, such as the VGCL, are also taking advantage of the new representative channels to advocate the bottom-up wishes of their constituencies in surprisingly strong terms. In this way, corporatist reforms from above are being reinforced by growing pressures from below—pressures resulting from new grievances being generated by the changing economic environment. For the VGCL, this enhanced representative role was exemplified in its efforts to expand worker rights during the drafting of the Labour Code in the mid-1990s, especially when it called for strikes to be included in the code as a basic right of workers, and in its efforts to increase minimum wage levels during official discussions with the government.[103] For the Chamber of Commerce, it is reflected in efforts to address serious frustrations by Vietnamese entrepreneurs over the constant and often costly interventions of state officials in their business operations. Towards this end, the Chamber has not only advanced recommendations to curb state inspections and eliminate complicated licensing procedures, but has demanded greater legal guarantees against the ultimate state intervention: the nationalization of investor assets. More generally, the Chamber also has insisted that entrepreneurs be able to carry out any business activity that is not specifically prohibited by law, as opposed to doing only what is allowed by law.

Although most of the Chamber's recommendations focus on reforming the policy environment for enterprises, they also have focused on improving the legal framework and operating conditions for business associations themselves. In making these recommendations on business associations, the Chamber is no doubt pursuing changes that promote its own interests as an organization. Yet, in many respects, the Chamber has sought to promote the interests of Vietnamese business associations generally as well. For instance, the Chamber has urged the government to support capacity-building programmes that would benefit smaller associations more than the Chamber. During the development of a draft decree on business associations, it also has called for minimal restrictions on the establishment of new associations. Of course, in an organizational context in which the Chamber is the sole representative of the national business community and the government is encouraging other business associations to join its membership structure, the growth of new associations may well enhance the Chamber's status by increasing its membership and broadening its constituency base. Looking ahead, the further development of sectoral associations, such as VINASA, should lead to increased participation by these groups in the specific policy areas in which they specialize. Barring significant reform of the policy-making process itself, however, the Chamber of Commerce can be expected to retain its privileged policy-making position when issues of broad national impact are discussed.

Notes

1 Adam Fforde, *Vietnam: Economic Commentary and Analysis*, No. 5 (Canberra: ADUKI, July 1994), pp. 7–8.

2 Howard J. Wiarda, *Corporatism and Comparative Politics: The Other Great "Ism"* (Armonk: M.E. Sharpe, 1997), pp. 6, 84–5. See also Philippe C. Schmitter, "Still the Century of Corporatism?", in *The New Corporatism: Social-Political Structures in the Iberian World*, edited by Frederick B. Pike and Thomas Stritch (Notre Dame and London: University of Notre Dame Press, 1974), pp. 85–131. Schmitter makes an important distinction between "societal corporatism" and "state corporatism": in the former, interest groups enter into bargained and consensual modes of policy-making with the state; in the latter, they operate under strict state supervision and controls.

3 Lenin referred to the mass organizations as "transmission belts" because they were meant to serve as two-way conduits between the party centre and the assigned constituency of each organization: in the top-down sense, they would mobilize the masses to carry out party policies; in the bottom-up

sense, they would articulate the rights and interests of their members to the party. In practice, however, the mobilizational role of these organizations has eclipsed their role as the representatives of grassroots interests. As Janos Kornai has written, the "mass organizations' main function ultimately becomes one of conveying the ideas and intentions of the party to 'target' sectors of society (the workers, youth, women) corresponding to the sphere of each organization". See Kornai, *The Socialist System: The Political Economy of Communism* (Princeton, N.J.: Princeton University Press, 1992), p. 40.

4 This approach to state–society relations in Vietnam draws from the model of "mobilizational authoritarianism" advanced by William S. Turley, which allows for the emergence of corporatist representation within the existing political structure. See "Party, State, People: Political Structure and Economic Prospects", in *Reinventing Vietnamese Socialism: Doi Moi in Comparative Perspective*, edited by William S. Turley and Mark Selden (Boulder: Westview Press, 1993), p. 269. For further discussion of corporatism in Vietnam and other socialist systems, see Jonathan R. Stromseth, "Reform and Response in Vietnam: State-Society Relations and the Changing Political Economy", Ph.D. diss., Columbia University, 1998, chap. 1. Corporatist labels applied to China include "communist state corporatism", "socialist societal corporatism", and simply "socialist corporatism". It is noteworthy that corporatism does not necessarily define a political system, but corporatist elements can exist in a wide variety of regimes. As described in this chapter, corporatism appears to offer important insights into institutional patterns that have been emerging in Vietnam during the reform period. On corporatism in China, see Margaret M. Pearson, *China's New Business Elite: The Political Consequences of Economic Reform* (Berkeley: University of California Press, 1997), chaps. 5–6; and Jonathan Unger and Anita Chan, "China, Corporatism, and the East Asian Model", *Australian Journal of Chinese Affairs*, no. 33 (January 1995): pp. 29–53.

5 Research for this chapter draws from primary source documents, newspaper and magazine reports, and other published materials. The author also interviewed business association officials and government bureaucrats in Vietnam in 1994–95 and again in 2000–2002.

6 Nguyen Phuong Quynh Trang and Jonathan R. Stromseth, "Business Associations in Vietnam: Status, Roles and Performance", Private Sector Discussions, no. 13. Hanoi: Mekong Project Development Facility and The Asia Foundation, August 2002, p. 1.

7 Ibid., pp. vii–viii.

8 "Statutes of Vietnam Chamber of Commerce and Industry (Amended)", passed at the 3rd National Congress and approved by the Prime Minister in Decision No. 315/TTg, dated 12 May 1997.

9 Interviews in Hanoi, 2002. For background on Doan Duy Thanh, see "Biography of President of the Chamber of Commerce and Industry of Vietnam Doan Duy Thanh", *Vietnam Foreign Trade* 33, no. 2 (1993): pp. 5–6.

10 Interviews in Hanoi, 2002.

11 The full resolution is titled "Nghi Quyet Bo Chinh Tri ve Doi Moi Chinh Sach va Co Che Quan Ly doi voi cac Co So San Xuat Thuoc Cac Thanh Phan Kinh Te Ngoai Quoc Doanh" [Politburo Resolution on Renovating the Policy and Management Mechanism for Production Units of Non-State Economic Sectors], No. 16/NQ/TW, Central Committee, Communist Party of Vietnam, 15 July 1988.

12 Interviews in Ho Chi Minh City, 1995 and 2002.

13 "Ban Sua Doi va Bo Sung Dieu Le cua Hiep Hoi Cong Thuong Thanh Pho Ho Chi Minh" [Amended Statutes of the Association of Industry and Commerce of Ho Chi Minh City], in *Dieu Le Hiep Hoi Cong Thuong Thanh Pho Ho Chi Minh, 1994–1998* [Statutes of the Association of Industry and Commerce of Ho Chi Minh City, 1994–1998], 1994, p. 14.

14 Interviews in Ho Chi Minh City, 2000 and 2002.

15 Ngo Dinh Quyen, "Non-state Firms Seek to Even the Odds", *Vietnam Investment Review* (hereafter cited as *VIR*), 20 May 1996.

16 Interviews in Hanoi, 2000–2002.

17 Interviews in Hanoi (2000) and Ho Chi Minh City (2002).

18 In August 2002, as part of administrative reforms carried out by the government, the GCOP became the Ministry of Home Affairs, and the newly established Ministry of Post and Telecommunications became the line ministry responsible for IT activities.

19 Interviews in Hanoi, 2002. For further discussion of VINASA, see "Deputy PM Praises Software Industry Body as Timely, Vital", *Vietnam News*, 29 April 2002; and "VINASA Aims to Put IT on Economic Map", *VIR*, 29 April–5 May 2002.

20 See <http://203.162.1.201/vinasa/FAQ.asp> (accessed 22 July 2002).

21 Interview in Hanoi, May 2002.

22 "VINASA Meets with the Chairman of Hanoi People's Committee" and "VINASA Attends the Second Meeting of the National Steering Committee 58" <http://203.162.1.201/vinasa/newsdetail.asp?lang=2> (accessed 22 July 2002).

23 The Office of Government is the Prime Minister's office. It serves as the secretariat to the Prime Minister and cabinet and includes technical experts and staff. It is responsible for preparing and organizing the work of the government, including inter-ministerial cooperation, and also supervises and monitors the implementation of government decisions.

[24] See "Strengthening the Organization and Activity of the Chamber of Commerce and Industry up to the Pressing Needs of Economic Life", *Vietnam Foreign Trade* 33, no. 2 (1993): pp. 11–12.

[25] Ibid., p. 11.

[26] "Nghi Quyet Hoi Nghi Hoi Dong Quan Tri Phong Thuong Mai va Cong Nghiep Viet Nam Lan Thu VI" [Resolution of the 6th Meeting of the Executive Committee of the Chamber of Commerce and Industry of Vietnam], *Dien Dan Doanh Nghiep*, 22 September–5 October 1995, p. 13.

[27] "Phong Thuong Mai da Tro Thanh Mot To Chuc Tin Cay de Tap Hop, Van Dong, Giup Do, Ho Tro va Bao Ve Loi Ich cac Doanh Nghiep trong Su Nghiep Kinh Doanh—Bai Phat Bieu cua Dong Chi Vu Oanh, Uy Vien Bo Chinh Tri Ban Chap Hanh Trung Uong Dang Cong San Viet Nam tai Hoi Nghi Hoi Dong Quan Tri Phong Thuong Mai va Cong Nghiep Viet Nam Lan Thu VI (Ngay 15 Thang 9 Nam 1995)" [The Chamber of Commerce Has Become a Reliable Organization for Gathering, Mobilizing, Assisting, and Protecting the Interests of Enterprises in Business Affairs—Speech of Vu Oanh, Member of the Politburo of the Communist Party of Vietnam at the Sixth Meeting of the Executive Committee of the Chamber of Commerce and Industry of Vietnam (15 September 1995)], *Dien Dan Doanh Nghiep*, 22 September–5 October 1995, p. 12.

[28] Ibid., p. 17.

[29] "Toi Duoc Biet Nhieu Dong Chi Chu Tich Tinh Hoan Nghenh va Ung Ho Hoat Dong VCCI (Luoc Ghi Y Kien Phat Bieu cua Dong Chi Pham The Duyet Uy Vien Bo Chinh Tri, Truong Ban Dan Van Trung Uong Dang tai Dai Hoi III VCCI)" [I Know Many Provincial Chairmen Welcome and Support the Activities of VCCI (Abridged Spoken Opinions of Pham The Duyet, Member of the Politburo and Chair of the Mass Mobilization Commission of the Central Committee, at the Third Congress of VCCI)], *Dien Dan Doanh Nghiep*, 11 April 1997, p. 2.

[30] "Pho Thu Tuong Phan Van Khai: Chinh Phu Thong Qua Phong Thuong Mai va Cong Nghiep Viet Nam de Cac Doanh Nghiep Hop Tac voi Chinh Phu Nham Day Nhanh Tien Trinh Doi Moi" [Deputy Prime Minister Phan Van Khai: The Government Approves the Chamber of Commerce and Industry of Vietnam to Cooperate with the Government to Speed up the Process of Renovation], *Dien Dan Doanh Nghiep*, 4 April 1997, p. 2.

[31] Mass organizations actually enjoyed the right to participate in law-making even before *doi moi*, as Article 86 of the 1980 Constitution empowered them to submit draft laws to the National Assembly. Nevertheless, they rarely if ever exercised this right; it was only a latent prerogative. See the 1980 Constitution in *The Constitutions of Vietnam: 1946–1959–1980–1992* (Hanoi: The Gioi Publishers, 1995), p. 122. Article 87 of the revised 1992 Constitution

also provides mass organizations with the right to submit draft laws to the National Assembly.

32 See Chapter 6 (articles 30–34) of "Quy Che Xay Dung Luat va Phap Lenh" [Statute on Drafting Laws and Ordinances], State Council, 6 August 1988, p. 6.

33 "Law on the Promulgation of Legal Documents", *Official Gazette*, no. 2 (31 January 1997), p. 16.

34 Ibid., pp. 17–18.

35 "Decision of the Government Prime Minister on Work Relations of Organs of Administration with the Chamber of Commerce and Industry of Vietnam", Government No. 310/TTg, in *Selected Documents*, pp. 18–19.

36 "Chi Thi cua Thu Tuong Chinh Phu so 16/1998/CT-TTg Ngay 31 Thang 3 1998 ve Giai Quyet Nhung Kien Nghi cua cac Doanh Nghiep" [Instruction of the Prime Minister No. 16/1998/CT-TTg. 31 March 1998 on Solving Recommendations of Enterprises].

37 "Lay Y Kien cac Van Ban Quy Pham Phap Luat" [Obtaining Comments on Legal Documents], Official Letter No. 2012/VPCP-PC, 27 May 1998.

38 Interviews in Hanoi, 1995 and 2002.

39 Interviews in Hanoi, 1994–95.

40 Interviews in Hanoi, 2002. During the drafting of the Amended Labour Code, the Chamber's Executive Vice President, Vu Tien Loc, served on the steering committee and the Director of its Employer Office, Phung Quang Huy, was a member of the drafting group.

41 These opportunities are greater for major draft laws than for other legal documents, such as ministerial-level decisions and circulars. Despite government regulations requiring ministries to obtain comments from the Chamber of Commerce before promulgating new regulations on enterprises, some ministries are still reluctant to do so (or they share draft regulations at the last minute, precluding a meaningful response).

42 Nguyen Dinh Tai, "Mot So Noi Dung Chinh cua Du Thao Luat Khuyen Khich Dau Tu trong Nuoc" [Some of the Main Contents of the Law on Promotion of Domestic Investment], *Nguoi Dai Bieu Nhan Dan*, May–June 1994, p. 1.

43 An English version of the law can be found in *Vietnam Law and Legal Forum* (September 1994), pp. 15–18. See also *Luat Khuyen Khich Dau Tu trong Nuoc* [Law on Promotion of Domestic Investment], (Hanoi: National Political Publishing House, 1994). This version is published in Vietnamese and English.

44 The report also notes that "specific provisions" will be issued "to clearly determine where capital is supplied by the budget and where capital is possessed by the enterprises themselves to prevent state enterprises from taking advantage of budget capital and turning it into their own capital in

order to receive privileges when investing". See *Tim Hieu Luat Khuyen Khich Dau Tu trong Nuoc*, pp. 22–3.

45 *Tim Hieu Luat Khuyen Khich Dau Tu trong Nuoc*, p. 12.

46 "Luat Khuyen Khich Dau Tu trong Nuoc: Huy Dong duoc Toi Da Moi Nguon Von" [Law on Promotion of Domestic Investment: Mobilizing Maximum Capital from All Sources], *Thoi Bao Kinh Te Viet Nam*, 19–25 May 1994, p. 3.

47 Phuong Thao, "Khuyen Khich Dau Tu trong Nuoc" [Promoting Domestic Investment], *Thoi Bao Kinh Te Viet Nam*, 19–25 May 1994, p. 1.

48 State Planning Committee, "Ban Giai Trinh ve Du Thao 'Luat Khuyen Khich Dau Tu trong Nuoc'" [Explanation of the Draft 'Law on Promotion of Domestic Investment'], Hanoi, 17 December 1993, 4–5. See also Tran Kim Giang, "Domestic Investment Law Expected to Unleash Flood of New Investment", *VIR*, 4 April 1994.

49 Interview in Hanoi, 1995.

50 Ibid. Information also drawn from "Ban Giai Trinh ve Du Thao", p. 5.

51 Economic and Budget Committee of the National Assembly, "Bao Cao Tham Tra ve Du An Luat Khuyen Khich Dau Tu trong Nuoc" [Examination Report on the Draft Law on Promotion of Domestic Investment], in *Ky Yeu cua Quoc Hoi Khoa IX—Ky Hop Thu Nam* [Record of the Ninth National Assembly—Session Five], May 26–June 23, 1994, vol. 4 (Hanoi: Office of the National Assembly, 1994), p. 742, hereafter cited as Examination Report.

52 "Du Thao Luat Khuyen Khich Dau Tu trong Nuoc" [Draft Law on Promotion of Domestic Investment], *Nhan Dan*, 16 April 1994.

53 Interviews in Hanoi, 1994–95, and Ho Chi Minh City, 1995.

54 Chamber of Commerce and Industry of Vietnam, "Gop Y vao Du Thao Luat Khuyen Khich Dau Tu trong Nuoc" [Recommendations to the Draft Law on Promotion of Domestic Investment], Hanoi, 10 May 1994, pp. 1–2, hereafter cited as Chamber Recommendation Report.

55 Ibid., p. 3.

56 See for example "Cu Tri Thanh Pho Ho Chi Minh Gop Y Kien vao cac Du An Luat" [Ho Chi Minh City Voters Contribute Opinions to Draft Laws], *Nhan Dan*, May 1994, p. 3.

57 "Bao Cao Tong Hop: Nhung Y Kien Chinh cua Nhan Dan ve Du An Luat Khuyen Khich Dau Tu trong Nuoc" [Summary Report: the Main Opinions of the Public on the Draft Law on Promotion of Domestic Investment], 12 May 1994, hereafter cited as Report on People's Opinions.

58 "Du Thao Luat Khuyen Khich Dau Tu trong Nuoc" [Draft Law on Promotion of Domestic Investment], Hanoi, 30 May 1994.

59 "To Trinh Quoc Hoi ve Du An Luat Khuyen Khich Dau Tu trong Nuoc" [Presentation to the National Assembly on the Draft Law on Promotion of Domestic Investment], in *Ky Yeu cua Quoc Hoi Khoa IX—Ky Hop Thu Nam*

[Record of the Ninth National Assembly—Session Five], May 26–June 23 1994, vol. 4 (Hanoi: Office of the National Assembly, 1994), pp. 724–41, hereafter cited as Presentation Report.

60 Examination Report, *Ky Yeu cua Quoc Hoi Khoa IX—Ky Hop Thu Nam.*

61 "Ngay Lam Viec Thu 10, Ky Hop Thu 5, QH Khoa IX: Thao Luan ve Du An Luat Khuyen Khich Dau Tu trong Nuoc" [The 10th Workday of the Fifth Session of the Ninth National Assembly: Debate on the Draft Law on Domestic Investment], *Nhan Dan*, 7 June 1994, pp. 1, 4; and Nguyen Tri Dung, "Domestic Investment Law Top of Assembly Agenda", *VIR*, 13–19 June 1994, p. 2.

62 "Tiep Thu Y Kien Dong Gop cua Dai Bieu Quoc Hoi ve Du Thao Luat Khuyen Khich Dau Tu trong Nuoc", Hanoi, 13 June 1994, hereafter cited as Report on the Recommendations of Deputies.

63 Tran Kim Giang, *VIR*, 4 April 1994.

64 *Nhan Dan*, 16 April 1994.

65 Chamber Recommendation Report, p. 4.

66 Article 23 of the 1992 Constitution reads: "The lawful property of individuals and organizations shall not be nationalized [paragraph break]. In cases made absolutely necessary by reason of national defense, security and the national interest, the State can make a forcible purchase of or can requisition pieces of the property of individuals or organizations against compensation taking into account current market prices [paragraph break]. The formalities of forcible purchase or requisition shall be determined by law". See *The Constitutions of Vietnam 1946–1959–1980–1992* (Hanoi: The Gioi Publishers, 1995), pp. 162–3.

67 Presentation Report, *Ky Yeu cua Quoc Hoi Khoa IX—Ky Hop Thu Nam*, pp. 730–31.

68 *Tim Hieu Luat Khuyen Khich Dau Tu trong Nuoc*, pp. 42–4.

69 Article 21 of the Foreign Investment Law reads: "The capital and assets invested in Vietnam by foreign organizations or individuals shall not be requisitioned or expropriated through administrative measures. An enterprise with foreign owned capital shall not be nationalized". See *Vietnam: A Legal Brief* (Vietnamese-English), edited by Frederick R. Burke and David Howell (Hanoi: National Political Publishing House, 1993), p. 247.

70 Article 8 of the published draft offers preferential treatment to the following types of investment projects: technical infrastructure and social infrastructure, including investment activities and development devoted to education, training, health care, and national culture (subarticle 1); production of export goods and goods for import-substitution (subarticle 2); processing of agricultural, forest, and sea products and the provision of technical services that directly supports the development of agricultural production (subarticle 3); other industrial branches that are prioritized for development in each

period, including the 5-year plans for socio-economic development (subarticle 4); afforestation, planting perennial trees on unexploited land, bare hills, and mountains; and practicing aquaculture in unexploited waters (subarticle 5). See *Nhan Dan*, 16 April 1994.

71 Chamber Recommendation Report, p. 7.

72 Report on People's Opinions, p. 3.

73 In its Presentation Report, the committee acknowledges that it made this revision to the draft law based on opinions contributed by various individuals, organizations, and National Assembly delegations. See *Ky Yeu cua Quoc Hoi Khoa IX—Ky Hop Thu Nam*, p. 734.

74 "Ngay Lam Viec Thu 11, Ky Hop Thu 5, QH Khoa IX: Tiep Tuc Thao Luan tai Hoi Truong ve Du An Luat Khuyen Khich Dau Tu trong Nuoc [The 11th Workday of the Fifth Session of the Ninth National Assembly: Continued Debate in the Assembly Hall on the Draft Law on Promotion of Domestic Investment], *Nhan Dan*, 8 June 1994, p. 3.

75 Chamber Recommendation Report, p. 4.

76 Addressing these issues in its 1995 report on the LPDI, the Ministry of Justice acknowledges that two of the most pressing problems facing Vietnam are renovating its aging technology and mitigating its unemployment problem. The ministry also asks rhetorically whether promoting the use of advanced technology conflicts with encouraging Vietnamese entrepreneurs to invest in labour-intensive enterprises. The report answers its own question in the affirmative. "Because of that", it continues somewhat confusingly, "these two requirements must be resolved together at the same time. Thus, promoting the use of advanced technology and does not conflict with promoting the use of many workers". See *Tim Hieu Luat Khuyen Khich Dau Tu trong Nuoc*, p. 66.

77 *Nhan Dan*, 7 June 1994, p. 4. Information also drawn from Report on the Recommendations of Deputies, p. 6.

78 "Phong Van Nhanh ve Luat Khuyen Khich Dau Tu trong Nuoc vua duoc Quoc Hoi Thong Qua" [Quick Interview on the Law on Promotion of Domestic Investment Just Passed by the National Assembly], *Nhan Dan*, 23 June 1994, pp. 1–3.

79 Ibid., pp. 1, 3.

80 The Chamber had pointed out in its recommendation report that the published draft did not contain "concrete measures for promoting reinvestment," adding that such measures could take the "form of a tax reimbursement or an exemption from taxes on profits that are earned from reinvestment." The AIC of Ho Chi Minh City made a similar demand in a separate recommendation report. Apparently responding to these demands, the drafting committee added a new article on reinvestment to the revised draft

issued on May 30. "In cases where investors use profit that is leftover after paying profit tax in order to reinvest," Article 11 reads, "they shall be reimbursed for the part of the profit tax that was paid on the reinvested profits."

81 "Law on Domestic Investment Promotion (Amended)", *Official Gazette*, no. 21 (31 July 1998), pp. 3–11.

82 "Law on Private Enterprises", Amended 1 July 1994, Official English Translation (Hanoi: State Committee for Co-operation and Investment and Phillips Fox, 30 September 1994); and "Law on Companies", Amended 1 July 1994, Official English Translation (Hanoi: State Committee for Co-operation and Investment and Phillips Fox, 30 September 1994).

83 Interviews in Hanoi, 2002.

84 See "Quyet Dinh cua Thu Tuong Chinh Phu ve Viec Thanh Lap Ban Chi Dao Soan Thao Luat Cong Ty (sua doi) va Luat Doanh Nghiep Tu Nhan (sua doi)" [Decision of the Government Prime Minister to Establish a Steering Committee on the Company Law (Amended) and Private Enterprise Law (Amended)], No. 37/QD-TTg, 13 January 1998; and "To Trinh ve Du An Luat Doanh Nghiep" [Presentation on the Draft Enterprise Law], in *Ky Yeu cua Ky Hop Thu Nam, Quoc Hoi Khoa X* [Record of the Fifth Session, Tenth National Assembly] (Hanoi, Office of the National Assembly, 2000), pp. 268–9.

85 Interviews in Hanoi, 2001–2002.

86 Ibid.

87 "Ban Dong Gop Y Kien vao Du An Luat Cong Ty va Doanh Nghiep Tu Nhan" [Report Contributing Opinions to the Draft Company Law and Private Enterprise Law], Hanoi Union of Associations of Industry and Commerce, 5 April 1999.

88 See Article 9.2 of the "Law on Private Enterprises" and Article 15.2 of the "Law on Companies" (both as amended 1 July 1994).

89 *Enterprise Law of Vietnam and Its Implementation Regulations* (Hanoi: Communications and Transportation Publishing House, 2001), pp. 117–19. The remaining capital requirements are stipulated in Article 6.4 of the Enterprise Law.

90 Le Dang Doanh, "Two Years' Implementation of Enterprise Law: Achievements and Remaining Problems", *UN News Vietnam* 7, no. 1 (January 2002), pp. 1–2.

91 Ibid. Information and statistics also drawn from *Vietnam Economic Monitor*, The World Bank in Vietnam, Spring 2002, pp. 11–12; *Vietnam: Country Assistance Strategy of the World Bank Group 2003–2006* (Hanoi: 5 August 2002), p. 14; and Michael Richardson, "Hanoi Faces Hard Choices on Economy", *International Herald Tribune*, 4 April 2002.

92 See Hong Vinh, "Private Sector Has Well Defined Role in National Development", *Vietnam News*, 3 April 2002; and Steve Kirby, "Vietnam Communists Can Be Capitalists: First Deputy PM", Agence France Presse, 16 March 2002. On private sector membership in the Chinese Communist Party, see Susan V. Lawrence, "The Life of the Party", *Far Eastern Economic Review* (hereafter cited as *FEER*), 18 October 2001, pp. 36–40; and Bruce Gilley, "Jiang's Turn Tempts Fate", *FEER*, 30 August 2001, pp. 18–20.

93 A number of senior Vietnamese bank officers have been jailed in recent years following accusations that they received bribes to facilitate favourable lending decisions to businesses which later became bankrupt. In general, however, these officers claimed that they did not engage in corrupt banking practices, and were simply making lending decisions in the context of an ambiguous regulatory environment. These incidents are believed to have discouraged bankers from lending to the private sector unless businesses can provide highly liquid collateral assets. Bankers and the media have therefore called for a more transparent legal framework on banking that differentiates between breaches of civil regulations (which would result in financial penalties only) and criminal offenses (which may carry jail terms or even the death penalty in serious cases). For a full text of the plenum resolution, see "Resolution of the Fifth Plenum of the Party Central Committee (IX Term) on Continuing to Renovate Mechanisms and Policies, and to Promote and Create Conditions for the Development of the Private Economy", at the official website <http://www.cpv.org.vn> of the Communist Party of Vietnam.

94 Ibid.

95 Interviews in Hanoi, 2002.

96 "Hoi Thao: Phat Trien Kinh Te Tu Nhan Thuc Trang va Giai Phap (Vai Tro cua Hiep Hoi Cong Thuong TP Ha Noi doi voi Su Phat Trien cua Khu Vuc Kinh Te Tu Nhan)" [Workshop: Situation and Solutions for Developing the Private Economy (Role of the Hanoi Union of Associations of Industry and Commerce in the Development of the Private Economic Sector)], Presentation by Vu Duy Thai, HUAIC Vice President and Secretary General, 24 October 2001.

97 Vu Duy Thai, "Co Thong Nhat Nhan Thuc va Tu Duy ve Kinh Te Tu Nhan moi Thuc Day Khu Vuc Nay Phat Trien Manh Me" [Only Achieving a Consensus on Awareness and Thinking about the Private Economy Will Encourage Development in this Sector], *Doanh Nghiep va Kinh Te Thu Do*, 1 March 2002.

98 Interviews in Hanoi, 2002.

99 "Bao Cao ve Tinh Hinh Hoat Dong va cac Giai Phap Tang Cuong Vai Tro va Nang Cao Hieu Qua Hoat Dong cua cac Hiep Hoi Doanh Nghiep o

Nuoc Ta" [Report on Activities and Solutions for Strengthening and Enhancing the Operational Effectiveness of Business Associations in Our Country], Presentation by Vu Tien Loc, Secretary General of the Chamber of Commerce and Industry of Vietnam, at a meeting on improving the role and effectiveness of business associations in Vietnam, convened on 7 August 2000 in Hanoi.

[100] Until recently, it was anticipated that the regulatory framework for business associations would be subsumed in a forthcoming law governing all associations in Vietnam (the Law on Associations, or Luat ve Hoi), with a subsequent implementing regulation being issued to cover business associations in particular. The GCOP began drafting the Law on Associations a decade ago, but key problems still need to be resolved before it can be sent to the National Assembly for discussion and approval. For further discussion of the legal status of business associations in Vietnam, see Nguyen and Stromseth, *Business Associations in Vietnam: Status, Roles and Performance*, pp. 9–15.

[101] "Nghi Quyet Hoi Nghi Lan Thu 5 cua Ban Chap Hanh Trung Uong Dang: Dong Luc Phat Trien Kinh Te Tu Nhan" [Resolution of the Fifth Plenum of the Party Central Committee: Impetus for Developing the Private Economy], *Lao Dong*, 2 April 2002.

[102] Ibid.

[103] For discussion of the VGCL's participation in policy and law-making, see Stromseth, *Reform and Response in Vietnam*, chaps. 5–6.

3

NGOs and Highland Development: A Case Study in Crafting New Roles

Michael L. Gray

For many years the role of non-government organizations (NGOs) in sociopolitical development has been described in relation to the importance of a strong civil society in fostering accountability and democratic governance. In Vietnam, until recently, the government through its mass organizations dominated the "landscape" of civil society that in most other nations is dotted with NGOs. This began to change in 1992 when the government issued Decree 35/CP allowing the formation of private, non-profit social organizations (Sidel 1995). In 1996, I interviewed about 15 organizations in Hanoi that were using the term "NGO" to describe their activities (Gray 1999). Most had used Decree 35 to register directly or indirectly under the Vietnam Union of Science and Technology Associations (VUSTA).

One of the organizations was Towards Ethnic Women (TEW), which worked with minority farmers from several highland provinces. TEW had many interesting ideas for working with minorities, including the networking of farmers from different parts of the country. But despite the innovations offered by groups like TEW, it seemed clear that NGOs in Vietnam were emerging in an environment or social space tightly controlled by the state, and their ability to offer meaningful alternatives to the state approach was very limited. I argued that the pace of growth of Vietnamese NGOs would be dictated largely by the amount of donor support, with some danger that foreign donors would expect a great deal of local NGOs, and try to push them to accomplish too much. I felt this way because in large measure the literature on NGOs and civil society talked in terms of an "independence" or even "opposition" to the state, or state structures—as if a clear dividing line could be drawn between state and society. A more accurate starting point with which to view the development of NGOs in Vietnam would be to look at civil society as a sphere or "arena" where competing ideas are debated and acted upon, as described by Ben Kerkvliet in an article on state–society relations in Vietnam (Kerkvliet 2001, pp. 239–42).

This paper will use a similar approach in looking at how TEW has grown in the past eight years. First, I will look at how TEW defines its approach and philosophy, and this will be explored further by looking at their activities in Ba Vi, where they have been trying to help a Dao community gain land-use rights in the buffer zone of the Ba Vi National Park.[1] The rapid and impressive growth of TEW indicates many of the options open to NGOs in Vietnam today. However, I stress the point that urban-based NGOs are not the same as people's organizations or social movements, and given this important fact, NGOs do not really represent a special area of sociopolitical development in Vietnam, as compared to wider issues such as labour rights, land rights, press freedom, and so forth.

NGOs and Civil Society

NGOs can be defined as private organizations established to meet some social objective, operating on a non-profit basis. Many have trustees or a board of directors that check to ensure operations are non-profit and follow the goals of the organization. Obviously, this is an incredibly broad definition that covers a wide range of organizations. Nonetheless, this is what NGOs are: a vast spectrum of organizations that are placed together only because they are non-profit and are perceived as being "non-state" or otherwise independent of formal state structures. In

Vietnam it proves very difficult to define organizations as "non-state", but in the international arena in general many NGOs might well say their independent status is the most important element of their existence, which is why the term non-government organization is used in the first place—they define themselves using a negative. Unfortunately, while this makes it clear what they are not, it leaves open the question of what they are. As a result, a whole range of professional, business and religious associations can all justifiably use the term NGO.

In the developing world, however, the term NGO is dominated by a range of private organizations that carry out charitable work to relieve poverty or develop poor communities. Although there are many types of NGOs, the non-profit development organization is so prevalent that in poor nations almost everyone thinks first of these organizations when they hear the term NGO. Norman Uphoff (1996) writes that this assumption has led some people to think that these development-oriented NGOs represent a "third sector" in the development process, as opposed to the state sector and private business. There is a general belief that these NGOs work closely with the poor and can meet the needs of the poor more directly and efficiently than state offices or the free market. Table 1 shows this basic set of assumptions; which really are like "stereotypes" of development that one can find repeated in a lot of literature.[2]

While it is probably true that small NGOs have advantages in reaching the poor, it remains difficult to argue that NGOs are a "third sector" that can be easily spliced off from the state and private business. Uphoff goes so far as to argue that NGOs are better seen as one half of the private sector, and their "clients", called beneficiaries or target groups, are similar in most respects to the customers of a private business, in that they can participate in projects if they choose, but they do not

TABLE 1

Public sector	Private sector	NGOs "Third sector"
Bureaucratic Top-down (inefficient for rural development)	Free market Profit-oriented (efficient but misses the poor)	Bottom-up Charitable (efficient and reaches the poor)

Source: derived from Uphoff 1996, pp. 23–30.

have any control over the structure or finances of the NGO. Uphoff argues that if there is any true "third sector" for development, it is a membership sector of people's organizations or independent cooperatives, which are self-help groups composed of people with common interests, who pool resources to accomplish a goal. In these organizations, the members have a say in the structure of the organization. This is shown in Table 2, which is a simplified version of the charts that appear in Uphoff's work.

As we will see, in the case of Vietnam, it is hard to lump the emerging NGOs in with private business. But Uphoff does raise an important point in stressing the difference between NGOs and people's organizations. It is important because, despite the difficulties of viewing professional, often urban-based NGOs as the "voice of the poor", they remain a focus in many countries for development funding. The rise in importance of NGOs has followed a shift in thinking among Western governments and large multilateral organizations. In the post-Cold War world it has become accepted that economic development relies in part on social and political pluralism, called a vibrant or strong civil society. For free markets to operate effectively, the argument goes, you need to foster accountability and democratic governance. Development-oriented NGOs, which at least have close contact with the poor, are seen as an important part of civil society. Funding NGOs and civil society has become such a dominant trend that many refer to it as the "new policy

TABLE 2

	Private sector		
Public sector	**Business**	**Charity**	**Membership sector**
Still bureaucratic	Customers	Beneficiaries or target groups (Both customers and beneficiaries do not manage the organization or control it)	POs and independent cooperatives (Self-help, pooled resources, members have say in management of organization)

Source: derived from Uphoff 1996, pp. 23–30.

agenda" of Western donors. It is important to note that this civil society agenda has two components: economic (to free up markets) and political (to increase pluralism).

In Vietnam, the era of market-based economic development coincided with the emergence of the new policy agenda. The 1993 decision to allow the formation of private, nonprofit "science and technology associations" that could carry out development work was made because the government was scaling back the size of the bureaucracy, and they recognized that there could be important service-delivery or other development innovations that would emerge from private organizations. By the mid-1990s, a range of organizations was emerging. While still few in total number, they could be divided roughly into the following categories, based solely on their origins: government mass organizations or other state bodies; university or hospital-based groups; and individuals not associated with earlier groups forming their own organizations, including local staff of international NGOs (Gray 1999, p. 698).

Groups that I met in 1996 that fell into the first category included the Highland Educational Development Organization (HEDO) and the Non-state Economic Development Centre (NEDCEN). In the second category, there were groups like the Centre for Natural Resource Management and Environmental Studies (CRES) and the Institute of Ecological Economy (Eco-eco). Finally, the last group included organizations like the Rural Development Services Centre (RDSC), and TEW. These organizations, formed by private individuals, were considered the "most promising" by members of the international NGO community, in terms of their potential to develop new approaches to working with the poor. A closer look at TEW, the subject of the case study in this paper, seems to bear this opinion out.

TEW Background and Approach

Towards Ethnic Women, formed in 1994, was one of the first organizations to make use of the 1993 decree on private science and technology associations. TEW registered under the Ethnology Institute, which has played little if any role in the development of the organization.[3] The director was a Ph.D. student at Hanoi University, and before that an official at the Forestry Inventory and Planning Institute. Familiar with the many problems of government programmes in the highlands, the director wanted to find new ways of working with minority people. She formed her own organization because she felt, "an NGO—in the accepted sense of the meaning as an independent body—would be the most effective vehicle for such change because it would be able to act independently of the bureaucracy of the state and therefore be more effective" (Lanh 1994, p. 4). This comment came soon after TEW was formally registered, when the director spoke at the 1994 Vietnam Update Conference in Canberra. She cautioned people, "If we understand an NGO to be an independent body not linked to Party or State, it is clear that in Vietnam there are difficulties associated with the acceptance of this definition" (ibid., p. 4).

Nonetheless, the director set up her organization to act in a manner patterned after the international NGOs she was familiar with—that is, as an organization that would work with local communities and the state offices that serve them to improve social and economic welfare. This can be verified by looking at TEW's accomplishments since 1994. Although TEW has published little about its activities, it has released several brochures that spell out its objectives, approach and philosophy, as well as one research article on its land allocation programme in Ba Vi, which will be discussed in the next section. TEW says its long-term objective is to "provide opportunities for ethnic minority communities to improve their quality of life and the ability to solve problems themselves" (TEW, n.d.). This will be done by supporting a national network of farmers who train each other in areas like natural resource management; savings and credit; and health care and herbal medicine. The TEW brochure also states that the organization will strive to "create opportunities for farmers and [government] authorities to exchange experiences and knowledge", which, in the Ba Vi case study at least, clearly looks like an incipient effort at advocacy.

TEW's objectives are evidence of a vision that does not draw very much from the approach taken by the government of Vietnam, which has relied on resettlement and other top-down programmes. The government's efforts have sometimes made matters worse for ethnic minorities, who already face enormous problems. In addition to physical isolation, there is a lack of recognition for some cultures (there are more than the 54 recognized ethnic groups, for example), and most importantly there are growing pressures on natural resources. This includes economic pressure from lowland migrants who want access to highland areas to grow coffee and other cash crops. Minorities are often not always prepared for the changes taking place around them, and women in particular have little capacity to understand the cause of many new problems—due in part to their low social status in their own cultures and communities.

TEW has responded to this situation by developing a "vision" or approach to ethnic minority development that is discussed in terms of human ecology, and gender and culture. As the TEW brochure states:

> "(The) human ecology framework strives to understand the position of communities within their natural environment and improve their lives through preserving cultural identity and improving gender relations...
>
> Participation and the human ecology approach will help to strike a balance between the needs of women as individuals, and the goals of the community as a whole."

To help accomplish these goals, TEW has developed a wide-ranging plan where it was actually at the centre of at least three levels of organizations that stretched from highland villages in Vietnam, to the Southeast Asian region and beyond. At the village and commune level, key farmers are joined in networks that are managed by field offices, which are the main project-implementing bodies. The first of these field offices was the Centre for Indigenous Knowledge Research and Development (CIRD) that was set up in Quang Binh province in 1997. By 2000, CIRD had registered as a separate NGO under the Quang Binh branch of the Vietnam Union of Science and Technology Associations (VUSTA). TEW also wanted to begin international cooperation programmes, and so in 1999 the Centre for Human Ecology Studies of Highlands (CHESH) was established. The CHESH brochure states that the impetus for international cooperation began in 1996, when TEW brought several minority farmers on a study tour to Thailand, where they worked with Thai organizations like Ethnet and Impect. (These organizations, given the Thai political environment, are inevitable more "activist" in their approach. Ethnet for example is involved in high-level research and advocacy to support land rights for highland communities.)

The multi-tiered structure therefore calls for CIRD to work directly with ethnic minority farmers in carrying out development work, while TEW will concentrate on research and advocacy at the national level, while also managing a national network of "key farmers"—the village-level coordinators who worked with CIRD and the other field offices. CHESH, meanwhile, will focus on developing regional and international cooperation programmes to promote highland development, including study tours for farmers from different countries in the region.

As of 2001, TEW had field programmes in Ba Vi commune, Son La province, Lao Cai province, and the field office CIRD, carrying out development work in 13 highland communes in Quang Binh. In addition, CHESH had a programme in two villages in Laos, managed in the field by an office of the Lao government. All of these programmes—TEW, CIRD and CHESH—are funded by the Interchurch Organization for Cooperation and Development (the Dutch acronym is ICCO), a Dutch NGO that has supported TEW since 1996. The total number of staff is now about forty, with most being recent graduates from fields such as forestry, economics and law (see TEW, CIRD brochures).

The wide-ranging and rapid growth TEW has seen since 1994 should indicate the options open to NGOs in Vietnam today—given the right financial support, of course. But the question remains whether this impressive structure can make a difference to minority peoples' lives, and help provide new models and options for highland development. The only evidence to look at here is the case study in Ba Vi, where TEW has been trying to help a Dao minority community for many years.

Ba Vi and Natural Resource Conflicts

TEW's approach to working with ethnic minorities is best illustrated by looking in some detail at how they have responded to resource conflicts in one of the communities where they work. Many would agree that conflicts over land and other natural resources are the greatest threat to highland communities in Vietnam. One of TEW's main goals has been to help highland people understand land rights and acquire land use certificates.

TEW's first published research concerns their work in Yen Son village of Ba Vi district, in the Ba Vi National Park (Lanh 2000). The Park is only about 60 km from Hanoi, and new roads have made it a popular weekend tourist destination. Yen Son village, with about 170 households, lies at the base of Ba Vi, roughly 100 metres above sea level. The village is populated by ethnic Dao farmers who originally lived on the slopes of the mountain, between 600 and 800 metres above sea level. In 1959 the government moved the Dao down to the 100 metres level and grouped them in two villages, Yen Son and Hop Nhat. Between them, the villages were given 18 hectares of wet rice paddy land. Forest enterprises were created and they started harvesting trees. During the war, much of the forest area was cleared to increase food production. Forest exploitation was so bad that in 1986 the district issued a decree to stop outsiders from cutting wood on the mountain. In 1987, the Hanoi municipal administration tried to help the Dao by initiating a major programme that involved land allocation, infrastructure development and credit for animal husbandry. Yen Son was allocated 543 hectares of land between 100 and 400 metres above sea level on the west side of the mountain.

At the same time, a small "new economic zone" (NEZ) was established at Ao Vua, a short distance from Yen Son village.[4] Some 27 households were moved to this area, and given 200 hectares for farming and growing trees. Houses were built on two sides of the pond at Ao Vua. The next year, in 1988, the Ao Vua Tourist Company was created. TEW reports that the company was given 20 hectares of the land that was originally allocated to the Dao villagers under the NEZ programme (Lanh 2000, p. 49). The company was supposed to give five per cent of all its earnings back to the villagers, to compensate for the land, plus there was an agreement between the villagers and the company to "co-manage" the land. Sensing problems, some of the villagers who did not want to deal with the company moved back to the main part of Yen Son.

The villagers who stayed were excluded from all activities related to tourism. The company built guesthouses and restaurants all along the road and, to make way for these constructions, the villagers were moved again, to the other side of the pond. Then, in 1999, a further 107 hectares of land was allocated to the Ao Vua Tourist Company, with the villagers left on a small strip of about eight hectares. In addition to their substantial loss of land, the villagers have received no earnings from the tourism facilities.

In 1989, a government programme funded by the French Programme Alimentaire Mondiale (PAM) was initiated to reforest the bare slopes above Yen Son village. The district forest department decided to plant eucalyptus, because it would grow quickly and it was thought that prices would be high because of demand at the Bai Bang paper mill. The villagers agreed with the plan, as they would receive 70 per cent of the income from the sale of the trees. Most of the 300 hectares of land up to the 400 metres level was planted with eucalyptus. Within three years, the soil around Yen Son started to deteriorate, no other plants would grow under the eucalyptus, and water levels dropped noticeably (Lanh 2000, p. 50).

The Ba Vi National Park was created in 1991, covering all the land above 100 metres. The Park took almost all the 543 hectares originally allocated to the villagers, who have since come under the administration of Ha Tay province. The villagers living above 100 metres had to move down, and the contracts signed with PAM for the eucalyptus trees were essentially cancelled. The Park argued that the area was "forest land" because it had trees on it (the eucalyptus). Eventually, in 2000, the villagers were given permission to harvest the trees. The villagers earned very little money, and in addition to the economic impact there have been many social problems and threats to the Dao cultural traditions as a result of the creation of the Ba Vi National Park. Dao culture depends a great deal on forest products such as herbal medicines, and as the TEW research puts it, "the Dao feel like thieves and criminals for doing what they have always done traditionally: their very culture has become 'against the law'" (Lanh 2000, p. 50).

Yen Son village was the first area of TEW fieldwork. The organization says its goal "has been to strengthen the Dao community so they can live permanently in the National Park's buffer zone, and participate fully in the management of the Park" (Lanh 2000, p. 50). With this goal in mind, TEW has set up a series of pilot models with the Dao farmers. This actually dates from before TEW was formally established; the director helped form a herbal medicine study group (as part of her Ph.D. research), and a garden model based on the seven households who were resettled at Ao Vua. Then, beginning in 1994 TEW tried to help the community obtain formal land rights for hill areas above the 100 metre level. This effort has had some success, as contracts (*khoan dat*) were eventually signed for land up to about 250 metres. This is not full allocation (*giao dat*) so the land remains under the control of the Park.[5] TEW feels the Park has stalled because it does not want a strong community role to hinder development plans or earning potential. As the research paper puts it, "There have been many problems with the Park administration, and TEW's ability to help the villagers has been limited largely because of the Park's role" (Lanh 2000, p. 55).

TEW, as an NGO, cannot participate directly in allocating land. That is, they can support allocation projects, but province, district and commune authorities must carry out the actual work. TEW can fund allocation and provide advice on issues like mapping and conflict resolution, but unless "invited" by the National Park, they cannot become involved. The main approach for TEW has been to lobby on behalf of the farmers and help them to contact officials at the province level and in Hanoi.

For example, TEW brokered a meeting between officials from the Ministry of Agriculture and Rural Development (MARD) in Hanoi, and four senior villagers from Yen Son. These farmers explained the situation and asked MARD to intervene. MARD did take over the land contracting process, but TEW says this had little positive impact. TEW also contacted the media in Hanoi, and newspaper journalists have interviewed the village leader and the TEW coordinator. But this type of action has had little impact on the behaviour of Park officials. Still, TEW wants to pressure the Park to re-allocate all land taken by the Ao Vua tourist company, as well as all land up to 250 metres. Also, TEW wants the Ao Vua tourist company to respect the agreement to involve the farmers by having their representative on the company board, and of course respecting the agreement to hand over five per cent of earnings. In other words TEW, has moved from implementing small garden pilot models (successfully), to a larger effort at land allocation (unsuccessfully) to a last-ditch attempt to lobby authorities in Hanoi to intervene. The most noteworthy element of the lobbying effort is that TEW tries to act as a mediator, allowing the farmers to talk for themselves.

Conclusion

As TEW describes in its paper on Ba Vi, its main approach in field work at the village level is to find "key farmers" to train in areas like herbal medicine, animal husbandry, and gardening. These farmers then re-train other members of their community. At the project and programme level, TEW sets up management boards that look similar to the "local development groups" (LDGs) discussed by Fritzen in chapter 7 of this volume, meaning a range of officials from the commune, district and province levels.

Whether TEW will be able to influence central level policy-makers in the case of Ba Vi, or other project areas, is not yet clear. Fritzen concludes from his study of a range of LDGs that project/programme size is an important factor in garnering attention at the central level. Small projects can more easily be ignored. However, projects in politically sensitive areas—such as work with ethnic minorities—will receive greater attention. That TEW is a small NGO working only on a pilot project level works against them, while the fact that their area of concern is ethnic minorities works for them, in terms of attracting attention to their efforts. As TEW begins to approach central level offices like MARD, and begins to work more closely with VUSTA,[6] it seems clear that more officials at the province and central levels will become aware of this "new voice" providing them with information and opinions on highland issues. This raises the question of how independent TEW needs to be to remain effective in helping farmers and devising new approaches to highland development. On this point, it seems clear that there is now more than enough space in Vietnam for organizations like TEW to be considered "non-government", if by this one means an ability to function autonomously from state agents and a state agenda. Particularly for TEW, financial freedom has given them a lot of room to move and test new ideas—which may not be the case for many NGOs—as the extensive survey done by Wischermann and Vinh found that few organizations in Hanoi or Ho Chi Minh City had much in the way of foreign funding (see chapter 6 in this volume). But perhaps more important than the financing, the TEW staff have been active in defining their own approach and philosophy, as shown in their brochures (and evidenced by their work in Ba Vi).

Another point to consider is what must be a changing relationship between TEW and the farmers it works with. The TEW director in 1996 said she never told farmers that her organization was an NGO, because she felt this term would have no meaning for them (Gray 1999, p. 702). But by now, the villagers in Ba Vi, such as the TEW coordinator mentioned in the research article, are obviously aware of what an NGO is. This may have importance as TEW's key farmer network expands, because farmers are meeting and discussing important issues outside the normal channels of the state (which in this case would be the Farmer's Union or the Women's Union).

Here, it would be good to return again to the views of Uphoff, and the important distinction he sees between small, private NGOs, and larger, mass-based "people's organizations" or independent cooperatives. The potential social and political significance of mass-based people's organizations should be obvious—think of Nahdlatul Ulama in Indonesia, or the National Rifle Association in America. The ability to lobby and advocate, in any political environment, depends to a large extent on numbers, and small NGOs are always at a disadvantage in this respect, when compared to people's organizations. So Uphoff is correct to stress this fact, and the lack of any independent people's organizations in Vietnam is very noticeable. However, as many of the contributions to this volume demonstrate, it does little good in Vietnam to attempt to define NGOs as one-half of the private sector, as Uphoff attempts. Clearly, many NGOs in Vietnam originated in government bodies, or are staffed by former civil servants. Thaveeporn Vasavakul writes of one such group, the Centre for Rural Communities Research and Development (CCRD), that what makes it nongovernmental is the way it applies alternative models to the locality (see chapter 2). In other words, the approach and, presumably, *results*, are more important than legal status or other technicalities. This goes along with Kerkvliet's ideas that, first, one can look within state institutions, "for evidence of struggles regarding issues of autonomy and control", (Kerkvliet 1994, p. 27) and second, and more recently, "individuals, groups, and social forces outside official channels can also affect the political system" (Kerkvliet 2001, p. 269).

This "results-based" view argues that civil society must be understood as an arena where conflicting or contrasting views and approaches come into contact. So NGOs can be lifted out of Uphoff's private sector, and dumped back into a "third sector", in this case relabelled the civil society sector. However, it remains important to look at individual actors, and not draw any sweeping conclusions regarding the democratizing potential of a strong civil society. Recent data suggest the spread of NGOs and other civic organizations across Vietnam, so there are certainly a rising number of actors to look at (Wischermann and Vinh, this volume). But, importantly, the lack of people's organizations to base their work around means that NGOs are limited to being one part of the "local development groups" that Fritzen discusses—which have numerous reasons for being successful or unsuccessful, and do not seem to depend much on autonomy or independence from existing state structures.

As for TEW, the evidence from their work in Ba Vi indicates that NGOs can now play an important role in developing new models for work with minority farmers, and their incipient efforts at advocacy—linking farmers directly with officials in Hanoi—are an important indicator of what may lie ahead. Nonetheless, there is no reason to suggest that NGOs like TEW will have any short or medium-term impact on sociopolitical developments in Vietnam. TEW is one organization, not a social movement, and there remains little contact between TEW and other Vietnamese NGOs. TEW's significance is that of a "trailblazer", offering a number of lessons on how to work with the poor in Vietnam. How long it takes for other organizations to follow and begin to speak out and band together remains to be seen.

Notes

1 The buffer zone is an area surrounding the Park where farmers are allowed to live, but under the management of strict Park rules regarding land use. The inner areas of the Park are fully protected and no one can use the land.

2 For example, in my 1999 paper on Vietnamese NGOs, I quoted an article on Grameen Bank-style microcredit programmes. The article firmly stated: "The leaders of most replications, and of the Grameen Bank itself, are convinced that governments cannot do Grameen Banking. Governments are too political—so they often cannot get the money back. Governments work through entrenched elites—so they seldom reach the poor. Government norms are too rigid and hierarchical to build the kind of village-centred, field-oriented organization required" (Todd 1996, p. 12). The author of this article later went on to praise the efforts of the Vietnam Women's Union in its "Tau Yew Mai" [sic] credit programme, funded by the international NGO, Coopération Internationale pour le Développment et la Solidarité (CIDSE). It seems the authors forgot that the Women's Union was government, not an NGO (Gibbons and Todd, in Todd 1996, pp. 77–98).

3 Under the rules of Decree 35/CP, a new organization was required to register either directly under a branch of the Vietnam Union of Science and Technology Associations, or under an organization already registered under VUSTA.

TEW chose to register under the Institute of Ethnology, given the director's existing relationship with the institute from her days as a Ph.D. student researching minority issues. It could be that TEW initially felt the need to be "sheltered" under an existing organization, rather than register directly under VUSTA. The director likely believed the organization would receive "less attention" by doing this.

4 New economic zone is the term used in Vietnam to denote new or resettled communities that are placed in an area where formerly barren land is opened up for cultivation.

5 Beginning with the 1993 Land Law, full allocation (*giao dat*) gave farmers de facto ownership of their land, with the ability to rent, mortgage, inherit and "sell" land, through a transfer of the title. A contract (*khoan dat*), however, only allows farmers certain use-rights for a set period. They have to follow a land use plan developed by the owner and cannot sell, mortgage or inherit the contract.

6 CHESH is registered directly under VUSTA, and TEW and VUSTA worked together to organize a conference on ethnic minorities, in Hanoi, in mid-2001.

References

Centre for Indigenous Knowledge Research and Development (CIRD) Brochure, n.d.

Centre for Human Ecology Studies of Highlands (CHESH). Brochure, n.d.

Gibbons, D.S. and H. Todd. "Tau Yew Mai, Vietnam". In *Cloning Grameen Bank: Replicating a Poverty-Reduction Model in India, Nepal and Vietnam*, edited by H. Todd, pp. 77–98. London: IT Press, 1996.

Gray, Michael L. "Creating Civil Society? The Emergence of NGOs in Vietnam". *Development and Change* 30, no. 4 (1999): pp. 693–713.

Kerkvliet, B. "Negotiating the State in Vietnam". *Sojourn* 16, no. 2 (2001): pp. 238–78.

———. "Politics of Society in Vietnam in the mid-1990s". Paper presented at the ANU Vietnam Update 1994 Conference, 10–11 November 1994, Canberra.

Sidel, Mark. "The Emergence of a Voluntary Sector and Philanthropy in Vietnam". In *Emerging Civil Society in the Asia Pacific Community*, edited by Tadashi Yamamoto, pp. 477–90. London: Routledge, 1995.

Todd, H. "Introduction". In *Cloning Grameen Bank: Replicating a Poverty-Reduction Model in India, Nepal and Vietnam*, edited by H. Todd, pp. 1–14. London: IT Press, 1996.

Towards Ethic Women (TEW). Brochure, n.d.

Tran Thi Lanh. "Waiting for Trees to Grow: The Dao and Resource Conflicts in Ba Vi National Park". *Indigenous Affairs* no. 4 (2000): pp. 48–55.

———. "The Role of NGOs in the Current Period". Paper presented at the ANU Vietnam Update 1994 Conference, 10–11 November 1994, Canberra.

Uphoff, Norman. "Why NGOs are Not a Third Sector". In *Beyond the Magic Bullet: NGO Performance and Accountability in the Post-Cold War World*, edited by D. Hulme and M. Edwards, pp. 23–30. West Hartford: Kumarian, 1996.

4

The Disabled and Their Organizations: The Emergence of New Paradigms

Ivo Vasiljev

Given Vietnam's war-torn history, the disabled form a sizeable community. Organized treatment of the disabled was largely in state hands until the 1980s when political reforms enabled a bigger, more proactive role for citizens to organize their own affairs. Part of this self-organization meant contact and interaction with the outside world and the input of foreign ideas and financial resources that in turn challenged the old state-dominant policy, both in terms of assumptions and in practice. In effect, there have been paradigm shifts in governance where the management of the disabled is concerned. This study looks at one such organization that grew up in a time of paradigm shifts. The details provided describe the dynamics of how NGOs relate to the state.

This paper is a study on the situation of disabled people in Vietnam that goes beyond the statistics on various kinds of disabilities and their health or rehabilitation related aspects. Some developments in the disability scene over the past two years justify the author's choice of the present subject for discussion in the context of governance. The point of departure has been the author's first-hand knowledge of a self-help group of disabled people in Hoi An, Central Vietnam, acquired during his stay there between December 1999 and July 2000. Another starting point was the author's friendship with the group's leading member, Le Nguyen Binh, and the latter's involvement with a website created for the Disability Forum, a group of foreign NGOs focusing on people with disabilities in Vietnam. Beyond this, the data is based on on-line resources and e-mail communication. The interviews targeting the Hoi An group, conducted largely by e-mail, followed the ethnographic method of M.H. Agar (Agar 1980). Most documents and data were collected from February through October 2001, without any opportunity for fieldwork. Some of the conclusions in this chapter were checked on the ground during the author's brief visit to Hanoi in December 2001.

Background

More than three decades of war in the latter half of the 20th century have produced a high rate of war disabilities in Vietnam, including long-term indirect effects after the war caused by landmines, unexploded ordnance and chemicals such as Agent Orange. When the U.S. war ended in 1975, 3 million Vietnamese had been killed and 4.4 million wounded (VNA 5 July 2001). A 1995/1996 estimate by Ministry of Health officials puts the total number of people with disabilities (PWDs) in Vietnam between 3.5 and 5 million, or 4 to 7 per cent of the population, with approximately 30 per cent of the total due to war-related injuries.[1] The latest official estimate puts the number of PWDs at "over 5 million".[2] This number may still not include all disabled people as, according to the estimate of the World Health Organization during the International Year of Disabled Persons (1981), the average number of disabled people in any country was as high as 10 per cent of the population.[3] For Vietnam, this would mean some 7.8 million persons.[4] Based on a thorough analysis of all available statistical data from the Vietnamese government as well as foreign NGO sources, a document known as the Kane Report (Kane 1999) stated in 1999 that "the range of estimates cited for the overall prevalence of disabilities in Vietnam is still quite broad (2–10 per cent, but most likely 5–7 per cent)".

The same imprecision is found in the data on war-related disabilities. According to a survey carried out by MOLISA (Ministry of Labour, War

Invalids and Social Affairs) in 1994–95 (Ho Nhu Hai, 1997), war-related disabilities accounted for 19.1 per cent of the total number of disabilities.[5] This stands in contrast to the 30 per cent estimate given by the Ministry of Health, as quoted above. In this case one can assume that, on top of all other possible reasons for statistical discrepancies (e.g., inadequate resources to collect statistics), the gap here is due to a possible difference of criteria used by MOLISA and the Ministry of Health as to what constitute war-related disabilities. Post-war landmine and unexploded ordnance related injuries may not have been included in the MOLISA statistics.

The statistical confusion suggests that the state does not seem very well informed about what must be a major social welfare problem arising from the country's war-torn history. Hence it is difficult to have a reliable understanding of the magnitude of the disability problem. On that count, governance is lacking.

In order to understand the PWD discourse in Vietnam, it is necessary to describe briefly the broad social and economic context in which PWD issues usually overlap with other social problems. These issues, especially with regard to matters of policies, funding or press coverage, are in most cases part of the problems that pertain to larger social groups. Due to this, it is often very difficult to discern people with disabilities from larger social groups in the public discourse.

The situation of war invalids (*thuong binh*) and soldiers with poor health (*benh binh*) is often discussed in the context of preferential treatment reserved for the following groups of people: revolutionary activists, resistance fighters, families of fallen combatants, Heroic Mothers (an honorific conferred on those women who lost all or some of their children in battle) and other "persons who have earned merit for the cause of revolution". All these are usually referred to as people or families "benefiting from priority policy", or in political and journalistic jargon, as "policy families" (*cac gia dinh chinh sach*).[6] Identified victims of dioxin poisoning also fall into this category, but post-war landmine and unexploded ordnance victims are not included.[7]

The term *thuong binh* does not include disabled soldiers of the pro-American southern Republic of Vietnam regime.[8] This politicized definition means "wounded soldiers who fought for our country."[9] Given this political subtext, in Vietnam, it is necessary to understand the term "war invalids" separately from the term "all individuals disabled because of war". The latter must include, on the one hand, post-war landmines and unexploded ordnance victims and, on the other hand, disabled Vietnamese soldiers who fought on the war-time enemy (ARVN) side. All these people can comfortably fit into the category of "disabled people" (*nguoi tan tat*), a comparatively new term apparently brought into the public discourse in the late 1970s. Technically speaking, the 1998 Ordinance on Disabled People may cover the veterans of the old southern regime since the act did not specifically discriminate against any group of people.[10]

Another social category in which the disabled are often included, especially when it comes to the distribution of charity funds, are poor people and "other people in difficult" or "very difficult" situations. These comprise old people with no family to support them, orphans, abandoned children, and street children, who sometimes happen to be disabled or sick, or HIV-infected.

State Policy

Equal rights of disabled people in Vietnam have, in principle, been guaranteed by the Constitutions of 1959, 1980 and 1992.[11] The 1959 Constitution guaranteed citizens basic human rights including the right to employment (Art. 30) and education (Art. 33) and disabled people were covered by this general provision without being specifically mentioned (Constitution, 1960). This is also true for the 1980 Constitution (Art. 53 and Art. 55, respectively), except that government care of orphans, solitary old people, the disabled and other "victims of war and colonialism" was specifically stipulated in Article 68 (Hien phap 1978). However, the implementation of such rights in general, not only with regard to the disabled, depended, and still does, on the capacity of the country's economy.

Nevertheless, it was not before the 1990s that a legal framework detailing specific rights of the disabled was gradually put in place. First it was the Labour Act, adopted by the National Assembly on 23 June 1994, that stipulated detailed provisions for employment of people with disabilities.[12] Then the "Ordinance on Disabled Persons" was adopted by the Standing Committee of the National Assembly on 30 July 1998.[13] It was followed by the Government Decree Detailing the Implementation of a Number of Articles of the Ordinance on the

Disabled.[14] The Architectural Barriers Act of Vietnam was prepared in 1998.[15]

These laws represent a long process of increasing awareness within the Vietnamese government of the specific problems of PWDs, a process which began in 1982 when it created a Committee for International Relations of Vietnam's Disabled to take part in the activities of the United Nations International Year of the Disabled. In 1992, the government committed itself to the Joint Declaration of Countries in the Asia-Pacific Region on Full and Equal Inclusion of People with Disabilities (On Tuan Bao 2001).[16]

However, the main impetus for more specific legislation must have come from within Vietnamese society as a result of dramatic changes in the transition from a state-controlled economy based on egalitarian distribution to a more laissez-faire market model.

Prior to the 1998 Ordinance on Disabled people, only war invalids and soldiers disabled by disease were covered by a specific piece of legislation, the Ordinance on Preferential Treatment of Revolutionary Activists, Fallen Heroes and Families of Fallen Heroes, War Invalids, Diseased Soldiers, Activists in the Wars of Resistance and Persons with Meritorious Activities in Assisting the Revolution.[17] The author was unable to find the date when this Ordinance was passed. The earliest reference to this preferential treatment was found in the draft text of the second Constitution, published in February 1978 (Art. 69). The same article stipulated also that war invalids should be assisted in recovering their ability for normal life (Hien phap, 1978). As will be seen below, some practical measures and institutions aimed at such assistance came into being during the 1960s and early 1970s.

Although the war invalids policy covers less than 20 per cent of PWDs (about one million persons), it is a convenient starting point for the discussion of several issues related to state policies on disabilities as well as to the socio-economic changes that have created a new environment for the disabled, including war invalids.

First of all, only a small number of war invalids were so severely disabled that they could not work and had to be taken care of in state-run full-time care centres, such as the one in Thuan Thanh, Bac Ninh Province, established in 1965, that caters to nearly 1,000 war invalids nationwide.[18] The more pressing need was to create jobs for those who were able and wanted to work. The best known of state-owned enterprises for war invalids seems to be the July 27 Garment Company, established in 1974 by the Department of Labour, War Invalids and Social Affairs (DOLISA) of Ha Nam Province. It is reported to have created 261 stable jobs for war invalids.[19] Some war invalids went to high schools and universities and have become teachers or other kinds of professionals.

This experience of state officials in Vietnam, especially the staff of MOLISA, with job creation for, and inclusion of, disabled servicemen must have made them rather receptive to some of the modern trends in the world disability movement as they felt that in some ways they were ahead of the times and had experience of their own to offer. These modern trends were brought to Vietnam by the United Nations and later, by foreign NGOs. Many of these NGOs were from the United States, the centre of the Disability Rights movement that was spearheaded by disabled Vietnam War veterans (Sandhu, n.d.).

Most war invalids in Vietnam stayed with their families, often doing odd jobs and receiving a special allowance from the authorities. Their income did not differ much from the wages earned in the egalitarian but generally poor society prior to the 1980s. However, the advent of market forces in the 1980s and the party's *doi moi* policy, which endorsed market reforms in 1986, brought serious strains and cracks to this society. Market prices soared, in general, ten times higher than the state-subsidized fixed prices of merchandise in the state-owned shops, and so did prices in the as yet limited free labour market. A puzzled receptionist in a state-owned hotel told me in the summer of 1985 that her one-legged husband earned ten times more with his night-time job of looking after bicycles parked on the pavement of a private coffee shop than she did doing her full day job. In no time, most government institutions organized market-oriented production activities outside working hours, totally unrelated to their day-time official duties. This was to enable their staff to survive in the new economic environment. War invalids and revolutionary activists relying on state financial assistance were also on the losing end of this growing socio-economic disparity. From the point of view of governance, this society in transition was an incredible mess although there is no denying that market reforms were needed.

The official budget to disburse aid under the preferential treatment ordinance is 3,000 billion VND (or US$214.3 million) a year.[20] This is unlikely to give recipients a decent allowance for self-sustenance. The following figures illustrate the financial plight of the seriously disabled. Under the Ordinance on Disabled Persons and related by-laws, the seriously disabled are entitled to government and public support. There are some 1.5 million seriously disabled. The seriously disabled who do not have any income and no alternative means of support are entitled to a monthly government allowance of 45,000 VND [US$3], if they are staying within the village or ward community; 100,000 VND [US$7] if they are inmates of a government-run welfare facility, or 155,000 VND [US$10] in case of serious mental patients requiring full-time institutional care (On Tuan Bao 2001). Such government allowances are not in keeping with market reality. In the labour market, a low income employee at a workshop in Hoi An is expected to earn no less than 200,000 VND dong [US$13] a month. Although seriously disabled people are also entitled to discounts for education, health and rehabilitation expenses and some other benefits, government allowances alone are not sufficient for basic living costs.

Inadequate state welfare is a source of discontent for the revolutionary activists including war invalids who have given the better part of their lives to fighting for the country. It is politically dangerous for the ruling Vietnam Communist Party to so alienate its traditional supporters. One party response to this problem is along habitual lines. It relies on mass mobilization activities organized by the Vietnam Fatherland Front to raise morale. These take the form of "gratitude activities" (*den on dap nghia*) that seem to have increased in recent years. A Gratitude Fund was established in April 1999,[21] that garnered 134 billion VND (US$9.6 million) of contributions from individuals and organizations in 2000.[22] Nevertheless, this amount added just 4.5 per cent to the government's annual budget for preferential treatment policies. "Gratitude activities" are also funded from local budgets. This includes the building of "gratitude houses" (*nha tinh nghia*), "gratitude gardens and gratitude ponds" (*vuon cay, ao ca tinh nghia*), or "gratitude wells (*gieng nuoc tinh nghia*), all essential parts of a rural household.

The main emphasis in the government policy of helping "policy families" at present is on promoting the recipients' own efforts in production and business. This is very much a feature of charity programmes of established Fatherland Front organizations such as the Trade Union and the Women's Union when they contribute to the welfare of PWDs.[23] Their contribution is important, but necessarily limited. In a recent gathering with representatives of communes and wards that have a good record of working with war invalids and priority policy beneficiaries, the speakers (who included the Deputy Prime Minister Nguyen Tan Dung and the Minister of MOLISA Nguyen Thi Hang), repeatedly referred to successful families of fallen combatants or to individual war invalids as "outstanding examples of people who surmounted difficulties and affirmed themselves to become excellent producers or businessmen/businesswomen under the market system and bettered their life" (Minister Nguyen Thi Hang).[24] Another example of this self-help emphasis is the many programmes of the Vietnam Women's Union—a member of the Vietnam Fatherland Front—that are aimed at helping "poor families, families of war invalids and fallen combatants, families in difficult situations and [preferential] policy families to *develop their family economy* in order to add to the quality of their lives."[25] MOLISA runs two vocational schools for disabled youth in the north and the south who can and want to work but have no skills to earn money. Vocational School number 1 in Son Tay (Ha Tay Province) trains students in one of the following jobs: repair of consumer electronic or electrical appliances, industrial electrical equipment, cars and motorcycles, as well as plumbing, welding, dressmaking and using computers, besides general education subjects, including basic English. Most of the graduates end up self-employed, as finding a job is difficult.[26]

Nevertheless, state efforts at promoting self-help are far from adequate. The two MOLISA vocational schools can take only a few hundred students, which is only a small fraction of disabled young people. Central Vietnam has only small private training centres. On the national scale, according to MOLISA surveys, 97.64 per cent of PWDs are unskilled. The rest who have some form of training are: 1.22 per cent from vocational schools, 0.53 per cent from technical high schools, 0.61 per cent from college or university. Unemployment among the disabled who are able and willing to work is 30.43 per cent (On Tuan Bao 2001).

These figures point to a need for more action not only by the state but also by non-state actors wanting to help the disabled. As part of its *doi moi* policy, Vietnam is opening its doors to foreign NGOs as well as allowing the growth of domestic NGOs (see chapter 6). This development has seen significant changes in the policy on PWDs. In a nutshell, the thinking on PWD welfare has experienced a paradigm shift. But these changes are not only confined to the nuts and bolts of how to improve the lot of the PWDs. Embedded in them are larger milestones of social and political changes that tell of the shifting dynamics of state–civil society relations. This raises some pertinent questions. For example, in a society that has habitually been wary of any free association of its citizens, how does the state respond to the emergence of NGOs, both foreign and domestic? How effective have these NGOs been? To excavate these issues, what follow are two case studies: one of a domestic group and its self-help philosophy and the other of a foreign-initiated forum for NGOs working on disabled welfare.

Progress of Disabled People of Hoi An Group

This case study provides an example that may be contrary to a popular view that has highlighted the difficulty of organizing representation for personal interests in a one-party dominated authoritarian polity like Vietnam. The literature on civil society in Vietnam tends to focus on the issue of whether NGOs enjoy a meaningful level of independence from the state. Linked to that issue of independence is the question of whether an NGO in Vietnam can function effectively if it is subject to state control or patronage (Nguyen Ngoc Giao 1995, p. 16; Nguyen Ngoc Truong 1994; Tran Thi Lanh 1994). That debate has not been settled yet and this study shows how an individual quite effectively organized a group of disabled people to look after their own interests within an environment where the state has not adequately provided for the disabled. Such an NGO has to work within the parameters of the Vietnamese system, negotiating issues like registration, access to information, networking with foreign organizations and the support of officialdom. In describing the growth of this organization for the disabled, this article hopes to shed some light on the possible space for NGO activities in Vietnam.

Progress of Disabled People of Hoi An (Tien Bo Nguoi Khuyet Tat Hoi An) is based in Hoi An. Hoi An with its 79,000 population is an old town in Central Vietnam that is popular with foreign backpackers. The tourist traffic generates a high demand for Internet facilities, which in turn raises locals' awareness about the English language and computer usage.

Mr Le Nguyen Binh, 37, the author's key respondent, was born in North Vietnam. His parents were both teachers and the family was much respected for their moral integrity in Hoi An, where they settled and taught upon their demobilization from the army after 1975. In 1979, at the age of 15, Binh became victim of a medical accident that left his lower body paralyzed. For the next three years, he was hospitalized. This involved much mental suffering, doubts about the meaning of human existence, and despair. At the hospital, he observed with compassion the suffering of many victims of landmines and unexploded ordnance, particularly numerous in Central Vietnam in those years. This, together with his family upbringing, his independent spirit and efforts to find answers about the meaning of life in books, gave Binh a new purpose in life. "The answer came to me as a deliverance—as something I felt was compelling me to live for, to overcome my unfortunate destiny. I hoped to do something for people who were struck with the same misfortune as myself and to find new joy in my life."[27]

The next challenge was how to be more independent of a loving family who had taken care of everything and thus excluded him from social life. He rebelled, and in 1983 went alone for a one-year tour of eight provinces in Central and South Vietnam, including several months in Ho Chi Minh City, equipped only with his identity card, a file with his medical history, and addresses of his parents' friends and relatives. Through this experience, he forged new relationships and discovered the meaning and importance of "integration" or "inclusion" (*hoa nhap*) for disabled people to become full members of society.[28]

After this self-discovery trip, Binh took evening classes to further his education, while during the day he made a living by raising and selling goldfish. He graduated from a two-year general education course and a three-year English course. He also took two six-month courses in computing in Da Nang City.[29] With his knowledge of English and access to the Internet, he acquired tools for life-long learning, making up for his lack of formal higher education. He firmly believes that life-long learning is an absolute necessity, especially for people with disabilities.[30]

Through his efforts Binh created a niche for himself. In 1997, he opened an IT training centre called Tien Bo (Progress) in his mother's house. By 2000, he was teaching as many as 70 students at a time, some of whom became his assistants.[31] In September 1999 he married Quyen, his former student, who became his closest associate in his endeavours. Through personal experience, Binh demonstrated that the more educated and skilled disabled people are, the more self-confidence they have and the better their chances to create job opportunities by and for themselves.[32] This is important in towns like Hoi An where job opportunities are limited even for young people in good health.

In 1987, together with some other enthusiasts in the local branch of the youth union, Binh started teaching groups of orphans and disabled children in the Orphans Camp of Hoi An. In 1988 an informal group, Compassion (Tinh Thuong), evolved from these activities. At first, it consisted mostly of non-impaired people.[33] Gradually, more young people with disabilities joined, organized outings and excursions, and increasingly felt that they needed an organized group to solve some common problems such as vocational training and job acquisition.

In 1998, they established themselves as a self-help group for PWDs and changed the name of the group to Progress of Disabled People of Hoi An (PDP of Hoi An), echoing the name of Binh's company.[34] The idea was to link PWDs with their peers in order that they could help each other and share experiences to improve their living and working conditions. They also set out to promote more understanding within society for the creation of accessible environments for PWDs. In 2000 the group had 15 members,[35] most of them young. Only one member of the group is a war invalid, entitled to priority treatment: the rest are children of local craftsmen, businessmen and farmers.

Between 1998 and 2000, PDP acquired 14 wheelchairs which they distributed to disabled people in the Hoi An area supplied by an Overseas Vietnamese charity, the Social Assistance Program for Vietnam (SAP-VN), a non-profit NGO in California.[36] Contributions by Overseas Vietnamese charities along with other foreign NGOs through various channels (mostly Fatherland Front organizations, or local administration bodies) have been encouraged by the Vietnamese government since the 1990s. SAP-VN has been targeting disabled people in Central Vietnam.

An impetus for a higher level of activity came in March 2000 during Le Nguyen Binh's interview for the job of Project Coordinator of the Disability Forum. The latter is an informal grouping of foreign NGOs. Though Binh did not get the job, he offered his skills to create a website for this group.[37] The website was launched on 12 September 2000.[38]

A workshop on Employment for the Disabled was jointly organized in Da Nang by MOLISA and an American NGO, the Office of Disability Technical Assistance (ODTA) of the Vietnam Assistance for the Handicapped (VNAH). The workshop was supported financially by another American NGO, the Health Volunteers Overseas (HVO). Binh was invited as representative of the PDP group, along with representatives of other PWD groups from Hanoi, Ho Chi Minh City, Da Nang and two other provinces. The workshop concluded with a number of policy recommendations, which included views expressed by the various groups of PWD.[39] In one of the PDP proposals for government agencies, Binh suggested that a larger Internet website should be created in Vietnam to connect all disability-related agencies and services and people with disabilities and their families.[40]

As a spin-off of the Da Nang workshop, the PDP group set out to "provide vocational training courses for PWDs to widen their employment opportunities and create other services that facilitate integration into the community."[41] Its first such project was a four-month course of applied IT and English for ten disabled young people from Hoi An, funded by HVO.[42] By the end of the course in October 2001, five of the participants had found employment. Two had already been working since March with a monthly wage of 450,000 VND, one in charge of a five-computer Internet centre at a local hotel and another staying with Binh's Tien Bo IT training centre.[43] One participant opened a shop at home, using e-mail and the Internet as a new tool to communicate with distant customers. The parents of the most heavily impaired participant in the class bought her a computer to do typing for customers from home. One young man works in Da Nang for a private IT services business.[44]

But the results went beyond job creation. This was a course for the disabled by the disabled. It gave the participants a feeling of extraordinary accomplishment. They saw, in fact, that computing is an activity that disabled people can do as well as people without handicaps and gained self-confidence.[45] They could also gain community recognition: one of the graduates was elected secretary of a local Youth Union branch, upon graduation.[46] There was a clear feeling that if funding were available, such courses should continue to draw students from the larger region of central Vietnam.[47] However, up to the end of 2001, no such funding was forthcoming.[48]

After the completion of the computer class, the group initiated its second project, which was a shop selling souvenirs produced by the handicapped at their homes and partly at the shop itself. An application for a licence was sent to the Hoi An Municipality's Department for Commerce and Tourism on behalf of the PDP and signed by Le Nguyen Binh on 10 March 2001.[49] He wrote: "Statistical data show that there are at least 500 disabled people of working age in Hoi An, most of whom do not have jobs or have no possibility of vocational training... It is important to create suitable jobs for them and an outlet for selling their products."[50] The authorities responded promptly, most likely because the project did not involve any controversial use of public space and because of the validity of Binh's case: the licence was issued on 20 March.[51]

The shop opened on 9 April in a small private house situated in the town's heritage area.[52] By September 2001 the revenue of this business was sufficient to cover all its operating costs including wages of four PWDs working at the site. The shop has long-term contracts with four PWD workshops from various parts of Vietnam and buys products of dozens of individuals working at home.[53] Neither the IT centre, nor the shop gets any funding from any foreign NGO or individual.

The self-help concept came to Binh and his friends as a real revelation.[54] They had previously no knowledge of such concepts as independent living, community-based rehabilitation, peer support, barrier-free environments, emphasis on abilities rather than disabilities, disabilities created and perpetuated out of prejudice, and some other contemporary ideas about disabilities. With hindsight, Binh understands that his earlier years of anguish were partly caused by the fact that there was little information in Vietnam on how PWDs can deal with their condition. That paucity of information was caused by the long years of the war and its aftermath—the U.S. trade embargo and the mistrust by the Vietnamese government of anything coming from a hostile United States. Overcoming these political hurdles has enabled groups like the PDP of Hoi An to serve as a conduit for ideas that were previously unthinkable. Such changes point to the role an NGO can play in a situation where the state has monopolized the governance of PWDs for a long time.

In actual fact, concepts such as "self-reliance" (*tu luc canh sinh*), "self-nourishment" (*tu tuc*) or "self-help" (*tu luc*) are compatible with the ideological sentiments of the Vietnamese state and have, for decades, dominated the political and economic discourse. However, these concepts had never been applied, perhaps understandably, to the severely disabled (for example, those unable to move without a wheelchair, a relatively new device, in Vietnam).

It took the severely disabled people themselves to realize that "self-help" is the only way to their inclusion into mainstream society, to their "salvation" (Binh has been usually using the term "self-salvation" (*tu cuu*), though other similar groups seem to prefer "self-help" (*tu luc*). This and other associated conceptual inventions of the American and world "disability revolution" (e.g., independent living) were imported into Vietnam and disseminated by governmental and non-governmental channels through UNESCAP and some other United Nations agencies, by foreign (including American) NGOs and by international organizations of disabled people in the 1990s, and increasingly, through the Internet.

Although established national Fatherland Front organizations (especially the Vietnam General Confederation of Labour and the Vietnam Women's Union) do much for the disabled and other underprivileged people, their focus is on charity, care and support, their contributions are important, but necessarily limited. Full inclusion of the disabled into mainstream society is impossible without their own intense and organized efforts similar to those of the PDP of Hoi An. Such organizations are, however, still a missing link in the system of social organizations in Vietnam. The total membership of active self-help groups associated with the Disability Forum, Vietnam (apart from the established Vietnam Association of the Blind with 261 local branches and 31,895 members nationwide—On Tuan Bao 2001) was 365 persons in 8 groups (5 in Hanoi and 2 in Ho Chi Minh City).[55] However, the majority of people with disabilities, more than 87 percent, reside in rural areas (Ho Nhu Hai, 1997).

What does the setting up of the PDP of Hoi An tell us about the issue of governance and NGOs? First, there was the issue of registration. PWD self-help groups in big cities like Hanoi and Ho Chi Minh acquire legal status by accepting the patronage of an existing and recognized organization, thus becoming one of its branches.[56]

An example of such an organization is the Association for Support of Disabled Children and Orphans (Hoi Bao Ho Cac Tre Em Tan Tat va Mo Coi),[57] which has branches in some localities. However, there was no such branch in Hoi An. Hoi An only has a branch of the 1969-constituted National Association of the Blind, which is a member of the Fatherland Front (On Tuan Bao 2001). But the chairman of that Hoi An association refused, apparently on the grounds that his association charter allowed only for membership of the blind, while PDP members were movement-impaired.[58] Up to the time of writing, PDP has been given no assistance either by Hoi An local government agencies or by the local branch of the Fatherland Front. The probable reason was the limited scope of public activities in the group's initial stages and the fact that the members of the group, though severely disabled, do not fit exactly into target groups of charity as their families are not poor.[59]

Thus the PDP of Hoi An has not formally constituted itself as an association. On the other hand, nobody ever stopped its members from what they were doing. PDP attends nationwide workshops where state officials are present and its credentials were never questioned by central or local authorities. There are a few explanations for this tacit acceptance of an association without bona fide credentials. First, Binh's family background or personal political history provides no a priori reason for the authorities to be suspicious of him. Second, the group evolved around a legally set up business that was providing a useful social service. Proscribing such an entity risks alienating the public. Third, the boundary between "association" and "business" in Vietnam has become rather fuzzy, as there are many businesses run by various associations. Fourth, the launching of PDP came at a time when a vast number of associations were being set up in Vietnam. Similar self-help groups for disabled people had existed in Hanoi and Ho Chi Minh City before PDP. For example, Bright Future, an 18-member group in Hanoi, was constituted in 1988 and received the required patronage of the relevant Association for Support of Disabled Children and Orphans in 1995.[60]

There are indications that central authorities may be re-considering whether the fact of being covered by an "umbrella" organization is that essential for efficient public control. A party official in a private interview with the author[61] pointed out, that the situation on the ground has become quite complicated. An "umbrella" association can now be several times removed. In local parlance, the "umbrella" association has evolved from a *hoi me* (mother association) status of being the direct overseer of an NGO to becoming a *hoi ba* (grandmother association) or even *hoi cu* (great grandmother association) as its "daughter" association becomes an "umbrella" for new associations. According to that same official, there were only three conditions for setting up an association and they were "to have an organizing/ preparatory committee, to draw a charter of the association, and to pledge that the organization would not require any state subsidy". However he added that many associations, after their approval, were not sticking to the last commitment. In the case of NGOs for PWDs, the state does not want to create more hardship for them by obstructing their work. The state, however, is concerned to see that aid money is used properly and not undermine the trust of donor organizations.[62] Taken at face value, this describes a form of minimalist governance to ensure that no financial irregularities occur. However, the official was speaking informally. While his words hold some validity, the rights of NGOs are not sufficiently institutionalized as yet, not least because many people seem not to have an exact knowledge of the boundaries between the permitted and the forbidden.

The Disability Forum

Developments in PWD welfare in the United States and elsewhere and the revolution in thinking about how the disabled can lead independent lives have had a definite impact on Vietnamese NGOs like PDP. Hence, it is essential to look at how the state regulates the relationship between foreign and domestic NGOs (For a discussion on the role of international donors, see chapter 7 in this volume). This is the reason for taking a closer look at the Disability Forum.

All foreign NGOs engaged in development or humanitarian assistance activities in Vietnam require permission from its government in the form of a "Permit for Operation, Permit for the Establishment of Project Office, or Permit for the Establishment of Representative Office".[63] To this end, Vietnam has established a Vietnam Union of Friendship Organizations (Hoi lien minh cac Hoi huu nghi Viet Nam) or VUFO[64] that oversees "issuance, extension, amendment or withdrawal" of the said permits. VUFO has established an agency Committee for Non-Governmental Organization Affairs,[65] usually referred to, in NGO parlance, as PACCOM, which stands for People's Aid Co-ordinating Committee, the name of a past organization replaced by this new Committee for NGO Affairs.

VUFO/PACCOM participates in the evaluation of NGO projects or programmes and advises the government on policies, but the job of monitoring the "implementation of approved aid" lies with the respective ministries, ministerial-level agencies, government departments, people's committees of provinces and centrally managed cities and central bodies of civic organisations in whose jurisdiction the project or programme is conducted.[66]

Partners of the NGOs implementing disabilities-related projects include MOLISA, the Ministry of Health, the Ministry of Education and Training and the individual people's committees of provinces and cities where the assistance projects are implemented.[67] Most of the projects are highly technical in nature, comprising the production and fitting of artificial limbs, improvement of rehabilitation services, training of Vietnamese rehabilitation technicians and medical staff. The funding for these projects comes both from government and private sources. The main donor behind the American NGOs is USAID's Patrick J. Leahy War Victims Fund (Kane 1999).

This arrangement seems straightforward enough but in reality, the process is compromised by delays and a lack of coordination. PACCOM's regulations stipulate that approval for projects will take 30, 60 or 90 days depending on the type of operation[68] yet the approval "can be a time-consuming and difficult process."[69] Foreign donors have also been concerned at the lack of coordination among NGOs working in different parts of the country thus leading to unnecessary replication and wastage. The data collected by the NGOs often differed from each other (Kane 1999). The NGOs themselves and the government are anxious to make sure that projects are sustainable and can multiply. The situation points to a need for better tripartite coordination between the government, NGOs, and foreign donors.

The Disability Forum grew out of this need for better coordination. Initially, the idea was to borrow the Cambodian model of setting up a Disability Action Council but skeptical Vietnamese officials dragged their feet on this. Then Larry Wolfe of Health Volunteers Overseas (HVO) found an unexpected opportunity.[70] At the VUFO-NGO Resource Centre in Hanoi, a facility provided by PACCOM for the numerous UN and other non-governmental organizations to have their meetings, there was a planned, but inactive, discussion group called the Disability Forum. Its meetings also involved government departments, mass organizations, professionals and the media. Larry Wolfe used this to invite fellow NGOs, government agencies and groups of PWDs for regular discussions.[71] The idea of the Disability Forum was endorsed, in October 1999, by the Kane Report, with its conclusion that "support should be provided to disseminate and share disability data collected by various ministries and NGOs. The NGO Disability Forum may be able to play a facilitating role in this regard" (Kane 1999).

"I had sometimes the feeling that we were moving slightly off limits," recalled Wolfe.[72] This statement can be understood as meaning that Larry Wolfe's actions, in this case, did not exactly fit the description of the initially approved project of his NGO. However, the discussions answered practical needs, generated by the overall results of assistance projects after several years of their implementation. Subsequent participation of MOLISA (discernible, for example, through the regular presence of high-ranking MOLISA officials at the Disability Forum's nationwide workshops) has shown that the innovation was not only approved by PACCOM but also fully endorsed by its government partner organizations, beginning with MOLISA and the Ministry of Health. The Disability Forum became operational in June 2000 and opened an office in August.[73]

The new Disability Forum set out to "promote co-operation, collaboration and better communication among NGOs, organizations for PWDs and relevant government ministries. The issues addressed by the Forum include rehabilitation and health services, employment, inclusive education, consciousness-raising and barrier-free access to public places. Country-wide workshops are conducted approximately every six months. Smaller meetings are held in Hanoi on an ad hoc basis."[74] The Disability Forum consists of twenty foreign NGOs and eight Vietnamese PWD groups. The primary movers behind the Disability Forum's nationwide workshops on the foreign NGO side have been, apart from HVO, the Vietnam Assistance for the Handicapped (VNAH) through its Office of Disability Technical Assistance (ODTA) and its Director John Lancaster. John Lancaster, former Coordinating Director of the U.S. President's Committee on the Employment of People with Disabilities, is also acting in a consulting role to the government.

The Disability Forum runs a website, which is useful for providing information to PWDs on the Ordinance on Disabled Persons and other legal documents and government policies related to the disabled.[75]

The Disability Forum involves organizations of Vietnamese PWDs for whom it creates, for the first time, the opportunity to learn more about the social implications of their condition and about their rights. Moreover, it provides them with a possibility to propose policies to the state that will serve their needs more effectively.

Prior to the Disability Forum, this work was done largely by the foreign HVO in the form of workshops to promote the reintegration of PWDs into society. HVO had organized these workshops in conjunction with the Ministry of Health and over a period of time, HVO had shifted the focus from talking about health issues related to PWDs to larger and more politicized topics that involved giving PWDs a greater role in shaping policies that affect them. For instance, a series of workshops starting in March 1998 with one entitled "Workshop on the Rehabilitation and Reintegration of People with Mobility Impairment and other Disabilities", made these recommendations in their final report:

- To include people with disabilities (PWDs) in the decision-making process;
- To increase the number of associations for people with disabilities and their family members;
- To form a national association of PWD to organize self-help activities and lobby the government on policies that affect PWD; and
- To have a representative of PWD in policy-making government bodies.[76]

Another HVO-sponsored workshop was to respond to the Ordinance on Disabled Persons.[77] As of June 2000, HVO transferred the responsibility for organizing the workshops to the Disability Forum. Thus the Disability Forum became a platform to encourage, step by step, the empowerment of people with disabilities and their effective inclusion into society at all levels.

This consensus between the government and the Disability Forum group of NGOs must be also seen in the context of Vietnam's 1992 commitment to the Joint Declaration of Countries in the Asia-Pacific Region on Full and Equal Inclusion of People with Disabilities (On Tuan Bao 2001).

To this end, a National Coordination Committee of Disability (NCCD) was formed in March 2001.[78] It is a government body based at MOLISA and presided by Dr Dam Huu Dac, Vice Minister of MOLISA, with Dr On Tuan Bao, a MOLISA official, serving as Director of its office. These are the same officers who represented MOLISA at a Self-Help Leadership Training Seminar for Disabled Activists in Ho Chi Minh City in August 2001, jointly organized by the Asia-Pacific Regional Council of the Disabled People's International, the NCCD and VNAH-ODTA. A document called "Recommendations Towards Full Participation and Equality of Disabled Persons" was adopted by the participants who expressed "resolve to constitute ourselves into the coordination group of majority of people with disabilities and their supporters" and called the government to "encourage and facilitate the formation of self-help organizations of women and girls, men and boys with disabilities at all levels in order to form a National Coordinating Body."[79]

The latter would be totally different from a government body. It may take time before such an organization emerges, but it seems that developments are moving towards such a goal and are quietly encouraged by MOLISA officials. At least, the NCCD enlisted several disabled activists from the Disability Forum's PWD member associations, such as Bright Future and others, featured them prominently during the December 2001 Hanoi leg of the Campaign to promote the Asian and Pacific Decade of Disabled Persons, and continued to work with them even after the event.

Conclusion

The experience of the PDP of Hoi An shows that full inclusion of PWDs into mainstream society is impossible without their own intensive and organized efforts. These can never be fully substituted by the charitable activities of other people and organizations. Thus the new, emerging paradigms, as far as Vietnam's disabled people are concerned, are an emphasis on self-help rather than charity, on action *by* the disabled rather than *for* the disabled, and on the equal participation of people with disabilities with the rest of society in all activities and sectors.

However, the scope of the Disability Forum and its activities shows that there are still too few such organizations in Vietnam. Though the Disability Forum has helped these local groups establish contacts with each other, with the government and the foreign NGOs on the national level, they are still far from having set up a solid nationwide network or a national union which they seem to perceive as one of their goals in order to better serve their specific needs. Their associations also tend to be urban-based thus neglecting the majority of PWDs who are found in rural Vietnam. Clearly, it will take many more years of efforts and enormous investment before a system of good governance over millions of Vietnam's people with disabilities and their problems can be achieved.

How do the experiences of the author's two case studies relate to the issue of governance in Vietnam in general? Both the locally-initiated Progress of Disabled People and the foreign-sponsored Disability Forum do not suffer from long-abiding differences with the Vietnamese state to make a working relationship impossible. On the contrary, the working relationship gets better with time and the NGOs enjoy progressively greater space. This is not to say that state–NGO dynamics always run smoothly. The relationship requires initiative and some patience on the part of the NGOs. It is also a complementary relationship. While professing to provide for the welfare of PWDs, existing state institutions lack the resources to do an adequate job. In that sense, governance has its shortcomings and requires the supplementary effort of civic organizations, both foreign and local. In order for these civic organizations to be effective, the state has to be more accommodating of their initiatives. These developments have taken place against a background of the country's political leadership re-examining its old paradigms of governance. It has spawned a climate of reforms within which many sectors of society can also seek out new paradigms of operation. The PWD community is no exception. It has made use of the more open climate of *doi moi* to engage the outside world, absorb new ideas and lobby for policy improvements. In that sense, NGOs that have spearheaded these changes for PWD welfare have, first, been able to exert themselves in matters of governance and second, contributed to better governance.

Notes

The writer wishes to thank the following for their valuable assistance in preparing this article: Mr and Mrs Le Nguyen Binh of Hoi An; Mrs Pham Hoai Giang, Director of Department for International Cooperation, Vietnam Women's Union in Hanoi, and her staff; and Ms Nguyen Hong Ha, Programme Coordinator, Disability Forum, Vietnam, in Hanoi.

1 Le Ngoc Trung, Nguyen Thi Hoai Thu and Dr Nguyen Xuan Nghien, speaking at the Workshop on Rehabilitation and Reintegration of People with Mobility Impairments and Other Disabilities, Hanoi, 23–25 March 1998. Quoted in: Landmines Report 2000 (henceforth, Landmines Report 2000) at <www.icbl.org/lm>, website of the International Campaign to Ban Landmines.

2 "Ca nuoc co tren 5 trieu nguoi tan tat", Lao Dong on-line, Thoi su, October 13, 2001, <www.laodong.com>.

3 Quoted in: Funding proposal for the project "Personal Assistance for Independent Living" by the People Awareness on Disability Issues Agency (South Africa), 1995, Paper distributed by the Disabled Peoples' International. Le Nguyen Binh, personal archive.

4 The 10 per cent ratio, however, should be checked against actual figures acknowledged by individual countries. For example, the gap between 10 per cent and the actual estimate of 1 per cent of the total population (220,000 out of over 22 million) given by the government of Malaysia is too wide to make the high per country estimate of the world body sound credible enough. See Kementerian Sumber Manusia. *Kod Amalan Penggajian Orang Kurang Upaya di Sektor Swasta*, Kuala Lumpur: KSM, 2001, p. 1.

5 Landmines Report 2000.

6 "Khai mac hoi nghi xa, phuong lam tot cong tac thuong binh, liet si va nguoi co cong cac tinh, thanh pho mien trung va Tay Nguyen" (Declaring open the meeting of communes and wards of central Vietnam and Western Highlands provinces and cities who carry out effectively the work of caring for war invalids, fallen combatants and people who have contributed [to the cause of revolution]. Nhan Dan on-line, Thoi su, July 18, 2001 at <www.vietnamnews.com>. See also the Ordinance on Disabled persons (No. 06/1998/PL-UBTVQH10 of July 30, 1998) at <www.disabilityforum.f2s.com/publications/onlineresources/disabilityordinance>.

7 Landmines Report 2000.

8 This is just one small part of the disastrous humanitarian fall-out of the consistent policy of successive French and U.S. administrations from 1946 through 1975 to win the war in Vietnam by "politicizing" it in order to change the anti-colonial war of resistance started by the Democratic Republic of Vietnam in December 1946 into a "civil war". Thus a "State of Vietnam" under former emperor Bao Dai with its armed forces was set up in June 1948 and succeeded by the Republic of Vietnam under president Ngo Dinh Diem with its army (the ARVN) in October 1955. The latter was founded with the

view to pre-empt the unification of Vietnam through general elections to be held in July 1956 as foreseen by the Geneva Agreements of July 1954. However, the DRV (later re-named the SRV) always regarded the war as one of liberation against foreign aggression and the "nationalist forces" as "puppet troops" in the service of the enemy of the Fatherland.

9 The term is used to confer honour and is part of a larger ongoing campaign to remember people and their families who have contributed to the resistance wars against France and the United States. In reality, being recognized as a *thuong binh* does not translate into generous welfare from the state. Until the end of the 1980s disabilities, whether caused by war or not, were not amongst the priorities of Vietnamese health administration. Resources were concentrated on constructing hospitals and dispensaries throughout the country and general disease prevention.

10 The only mention of ARVN invalids was found as part of the Veterans Vietnam Restoration Project (VVRP)—started in 1989 under the 1988 bilateral agreement between the governments of Vietnam and the United States—when its 8th team in March 1994 constructed a housing unit for ARVN amputees in Thu Duc, Ho Chi Minh City. VVRP works with MOLISA (see <www.vvrp.org/completedprojects.htm>). Former ARVN servicemen (most of whom are not disabled) are still a sensitive subject. It is, for example, rumoured that some of them are trying to buy "liberation veteran" status from corrupt local government officials, which is looked upon, in certain quarters of the political establishment, with great suspicion. Such considerations may someday be a stumbling bloc in the development of the disability movement.

11 Bai phat bieu khai mac cua Thu truong Dr Dam Huu Dac, Bo LDTBXH, tai lop tap huan, "Nang cao nang luc lanh dao cho Nguoi tan tat" (Opening remarks of Vice-Minister Dam Huu Dac of MOLISA at the DPI-APRC Self-help Leadership Training Seminar), Ho Chi Minh City, 20–21 Aug, 2001. Le Nguyen Binh, personal archive.

12 <www.laodong.com/trangchu/luat/boluatlaodongvn.htm>.

13 Ordinance on Disabled Persons, No. 06/1998/PL-UBTVQH10 of July 30, 1998. <http://forum.wso.net/publications/onlinedocuments/ordinance.htm>.

14 Decree No. 55/1999/ND-CP of July 10, 1999, published in the Official Gazette No. 31 of 22 August, 1999. At <http://forum.wso.net/publications/onlinedocuments/decree.htm>.

15 At <http://forum.wso.net/publications/onlinedocuments/barriersact.htm>.

16 See also n. 1.

17 Quoted in Article 2 of the Ordinance on Disabled Persons.

18 "Party Leader Meets War Invalids". *The People* (Nhan Dan), on-line News, 26 July, 2001 at <www.vietnamnews.com>.

[19] Ibid.

[20] "*Khai mac hoi nghi xa, phuong...* As above, n. 6.

[21] "350 ty dong Quy den on, dap nghia" [VND350 billion for the Gratitude Fund]. Nhan Dan online, Thoi su, 26 July, 2001 at <www.vietnamnews.com>.

[22] "Ca nuoc dong gop hon 134 ty dong xay dung Quy den on, dap nghia (Gratitude Fund draws VND134 billion nationwide). Nhan Dan on-line, Thoi su, 17 July, 2001. <www.vietnamnews.com>.

[23] These organizations support or organize other activities that are meaningful for PWDs, especially those who are young. Such activities include sporting events and art competitions.

[24] *Khai mac hoi nghi xa, phuong....* As above, n. 6.

[25] *Cac hoat dong cua Hoi Lien hiep Phu nu Viet Nam nham thuc hien Phap lenh ve Nguoi tan tat* [Activities of the Vietnam Women's Union for the Implementation of the Ordinance on Disabled Persons]. Paper prepared by the Department for International Cooperation, Vietnam Women's Union, for this author in September 2001.

[26] Author emphasis. Information from the headmaster, Doan Quang Trinh during a visit to the school by some participants of the Campaign 2001 to promote the Asian and Pacific Decade of Disabled Persons.

[27] Le Nguyen Binh, interview 29 March, 2001.

[28] Ibid.

[29] Le Nguyen Binh, letter of 29 December, 2001.

[30] Ibid.

[31] Contribution of the Hoi An Group Progress of Disabled People; Workshop on Employment for People with Disabilities, Da Nang 10–11 August, 2000. Le Nguyen Binh, personal archive.

[32] Ibid.

[33] Le Nguyen Binh, letter of 30 October, 2001.

[34] Ibid.

[35] <www.disabilityforum.f2s.com/general/ppdhoian.htm>.

[36] SAP-VN was founded in 1992 by "a group of young and caring professionals" <www.sap-vn.org/aboutsap-vn.htm>, all apparently overseas Vietnamese. Its primary objective is "to provide direct relief to poor and needy people, especially orphans and handicapped people". Through one of their many projects, the "Gift of Mobility" wheelchair project they were able to deliver 174 wheelchairs or tricycles in 1997–2000. <www.sap-vn.org/wheelchairproject.htm>.

[37] Le Nguyen Binh, letter of 18 March, 2001.

[38] Le Nguyen Binh, interview 29 October, 2001. The website: <www.disabilityforum.f2s.com>, in August 2001 moved to <http://forum.wso.net>.

39 Bao cao ket qua Hoi thao viec lam cua nguoi tan tat [Report on results of the Workshop on employment of disabled people], Da Nang 10–11 August, 2000. Le Nguyen Binh, personal archive.

40 Contribution of the Hoi An Group... As above, n. 31.

41 <www.disabilityforum.f2s.com/general/ppdhoian.htm>.

42 <www.disabilityforum.f2s.com/vnpages12/vnevent12.htm>.

43 Le Nguyen Binh, interview 19 May, 2001.

44 Le Nguyen Binh, letter of 29 October, 2001.

45 Le Nguyen Binh, interview 19 May, 2001.

46 Huynh Thi Nhung. "Nguoi tu dung day, va diu moi nguoi cung dung day bang hai banh xe lan" [A man who has stood up by his own efforts and helped others to stand up on their wheels], made available by the author, October 2001.

47 Le Nguyen Binh, interview 19 May, 2001.

48 Le Nguyen Binh, letter 24 October, 2001.

49 To trinh v/v mo co so san xuat kinh doanh hang thu cong my nghe cua nhom Nguoi khuyet tat Hoi An [Application for licence to open a souvenir production and business shop by the Hoi An Group of Disabled People]. Le Nguyen Binh, personal archive.

50 Ibid.

51 Le Nguyen Binh, interview 19 May, 2001. By the time Binh opened his IT centre in 1997, there had been hundreds of private shops and workshops, licensed by Hoi An municipality. So for an application to be approved in 2001 was relatively easy.

52 Ibid.

53 Le Nguyen Binh, letter 6 October, 2001.

54 Le Nguyen Binh, letter 24 October, 2001.

55 See <www.disabilityforum.f2s.com/general/partner2a.htm>.

56 Such organizations providing official patronage for other new organizations are usually referred to in English as "umbrella" organizations. The corresponding expression in Vietnamese is *hoi me* or "mother organization".

57 See <www.disabilityforum.f2s.com/general/partner2a.htm>.

58 Le Nguyen Binh, personal meeting on 15 December, 2001.

59 Le Nguyen Binh, interviews on 18 August, 2001 and 19 May, 2001.

60 See <www.disabilityforum.f2s.com/general/partner2a.htm>.

61 Held on 12 December, 2001 in Hanoi.

62 Ibid.

63 "Regulations on the Operation of Foreign Non-Governmental Organizations in Vietnam" (Promulgated in accordance with Decision no 340/TTg dated 24 May, 1996 of the Prime Minister). Article 1. Unofficial translation by PACCOM. A handout by PACCOM.

[64] "Decision of the Prime Minister of the Government on the Issuance of the Regulation on the Management and Utilisation of Aid from International Non-Governmental Organizations", no. 64/2001/QD-TTg, Ha Noi 26 April 2001, Article 13. Unofficial translation by PACCOM. A handout by PACCOM.

[65] Regulations…, Article 5.

[66] Decision of the Prime Minister…, Article 16.

[67] See <www.disabilityforum.f2s.com/partners&projects.htm>.

[68] Regulations…, Article 8.

[69] Landmines Report 2000.

[70] Larry Wolfe is Project Director of Health Volunteers Overseas (HVO), an American NGO funded by USAID. HVO has worked with Vietnam's Ministry of Health since 1992.

[71] Interview with Larry Wolfe in Hanoi, 15 December 2001.

[72] Ibid.

[73] Nguyen Hong Ha. Disability Forum and People with Disabilities in Vietnam, at <http://forum.wso.net>.

[74] The NGO Forums/Sector and Working Groups, The Disability Forum at <www.ngocentre.netnam.vn/ngores_E/forfr.htm>.

[75] Ibid.

[76] Ibid.

[77] *Hoa Nhap* [Integration], a newsletter by and for the members of the DYA (Disabled Youth Association), Ho Chi Minh City. no 33, December 2000–January 2001, at <www.disabilityworld.org/01-02_01/contents.htm>.

[78] See <www.disabilityforum.f2s.com/partners&projects.htm>.

[79] See <www.disabilityforum.f2s.com/partners/vnself-helpgroups.htm>.

References

Agar, M.H. *The Professional Stranger: An Informal Introduction to Ethnography.* Orlando: Academic Press, 1980.

Constitution de la République Démocratique du Vietnam. Hanoi Editions en Langues Étrangères, 1960.

Hien phap nuoc Cong Hoa Xa Hoi Chu Nghia Viet-Nam (du thao). [Constitution of the Socialist Republic of Vietnam, draft text, Hanoi, Central Office Press, completed in February 1978]. Hanoi Xuong in Van phong trung uong. Xong thang 2 nam, 1978.

Ho Nhu Hai. "Disabled People in Rural Areas of Vietnam [1]". <www.fao.org/waicent/FAOINFO/SUSTDEV/Ppdirect/Ppre.0063.htm>.

Kane T. "Disability in Vietnam in 1999: A Meta-Analysis of the Data" [the Kane Report]. The United States Agency for International Development, Displaced Children and Orphans Fund and Patrick J. Leahy War Victims

Fund (October 1999) at <www.usaid.gov/pop_health/dcofwv/reports/evals/wvvietnamdisabilitydata99.html>.

Nguyen Ngoc Giao. "Media va Xa hoi cong dan trong qua trinh doi moi o Viet Nam" [Media and Civil Society in the Process of Doi Moi in Vietnam]. *Dien Dan* so 37(1995): 16–20.

Nguyen Ngoc Truong. "Grassroots Organizations in Rural and Urban Vietnam during Market Reform: An Overview of their Emergence and Relationship to the State". Paper presented at the Vietnam Update conference, Doi Moi, The State and Civil Society. The Australian National University, 10–11 November, 1994, Canberra.

On Tuan Bao. "Tong quan tinh hinh Nguoi tan tat Viet Nam va su ho tro cua chinh phu". Speech [of the Director of the NCCD Office] at the DPI-APRC Self-help Leadership Training Seminar), Ho Chi Minh City, 20–21 Aug, 2001. Le Nguyen Binh, personal archive.

Sandhu, J.S. "From Dusty Documents to Common Practice. A Brief History of Mainstreaming". <www.design-for-all.org/magazine2/main_from_dusty_documents.html>, n.d.

Tran Thi Lanh. "The Role of Vietnamese NGOs in the Current Period". Paper presented at the Vietnam Update conference, Doi Moi, The State and Civil Society. The Australian National University, 10–11 November, 1994, Canberra.

VNA (Vietnam News Agency). "Vietnam, United States to Jointly Research on Agent Orange". *Nhan Dan* on-line news. <www.vietnamnews.com> (accessed 5 July 2001).

5

Authoritarian Governance and Labour: The VGCL and the Party-State in Economic Renovation

Eva Hansson

Economic liberalization and industrialization have brought rapid changes to Vietnam's labour scene in recent years. Cheap and disciplined labour attracts foreign investors and the party-state has been anxious to maintain control over labour by restricting autonomous workers' organizations.[1] Simultaneously, the industrial labour force in this predominantly agricultural country is growing and the number of conflicts in the labour market has remained at a high level all through the 1990s. This article looks at the impact of economic liberalization on the regulation and organization of labour and discusses what possible political consequences these developments may have on the wider political structures.

My point of entry into the issue of trade unionism is the rising number of labour conflicts, which leads to questions concerning the role of the Vietnam General Confederation of Labour (VGCL or Tong Lien Doan Lao Dong Viet Nam) and its relations with the party-state and how these relations have changed. In Vietnam's authoritarian political structure, the VGCL, the only officially recognized trade union organization, is part of the one-party system. Its organizational size in combination with its potential role in accommodating labour–capital conflicts in a market economy makes the VGCL important for political stability. I will argue that the VGCL has failed to carry out the reforms needed to respond to the concerns of workers in the emerging market economy. This has led to a situation where workers are left with no or very limited protection. In order to defend themselves, they organize outside the formal party-state structures, primarily, through illegal strikes (but also through "study groups", "labour councils", etc.). I argue that this development challenges the role, legitimacy and organizational monopoly of the VGCL and has also put pressure on the relations between the party-state and the VGCL. Consequently a process of de-authoritarianization of power relations from below is taking place.[2]

Challenges to Authoritarianism

Understanding Vietnamese trade unions requires taking note of the restrictive environment in which they operate. Most aspects of civil society are controlled, limited by law and restricted in practice by the party-state. Vasavakul has commented that the party leadership "has been tolerant of popular associations focusing on economic and social affairs, [while] it has been less tolerant of political, intellectual and religious groups that expressed disagreement with the leadership's policies" (2001, p. 398). A plethora of NGOs often supported by international donors have been flourishing, especially since the late 1990s, dealing primarily with "development issues" such as poverty-reduction, education, clean water and other matters that might normally be regarded as the duties of a state.[3] At the same time, organizations with clearly stated political concerns—for example, human rights groups or labour watch groups—that can be found in most other Southeast Asian countries are not permitted to operate despite the widely-recognized problems in the labour market. The only organization permitted by law to work in the field of labour rights is the VGCL. In 2000, it was reported that the government "censored targeted persons' mail, confiscated packages, and monitored telephone, electronic mail, and facsimile transmissions" and although Internet subscribers were up from around 40,000 in 1999 to 120,000,[4] the system is only available behind firewalls. Only international hotels, top officials, foreigners, and the press are permitted to have satellite television. According to a government decree, beginning in 2000, all singers, musicians and dancers must have special permits to perform live.[5] All news media are subject to censorship: meetings are held on a weekly basis between the editor and officials belonging to the VCP Ideology Department (Heng 2001, p. 227).[6] Civil society in Vietnam is further restrained by the lack of academic freedom. Most research, especially on political and social change, is commissioned by state-party organizations, which has resulted in a lack of knowledge of important issues related to the new market economy. This was acknowledged in a report by the VGCL in 1998, which suggests that many theoretical and practical questions remain, such as "labour relations, the role and position of the Vietnamese working class, the relations between trade union organizations and party and administrative bodies at each level."[7]

In an authoritarian system, a particular ruling group—a certain party or the military, or sometimes a coalition of groups—controls the state and often exercises hegemonic control over most political and civic organizations. Authoritarian governance lacks popular control and transparency and is often plagued by corruption and inefficiency. Organizing activities are strictly controlled by the state through co-option and/or repression. Challenges to authoritarianism can occur at many levels in varied ways. They may sometimes be intentional as when an organization, individual, or group demonstrates or agitates against a certain regime. Other actions may be less overt and not necessarily targeted at political authority but at other power relations in society such as those at a workplace or between genders. Viewed individually, such actions provide little understanding of their political impact at a macro level. In my study, the focus is on instances where such contestations occur in collective form through the organization of strikes or labour disputes. When the system fails to address and resolve such conflicts within its institutional framework, it loses relevance and a consequence may be the gradual erosion of the authoritarian system itself.

Yet another dimension is added to this process through the growth of civil society. Civil society theory may provide us with tools for understanding these wider implications. The scholarly discourse on civil society has to grapple with a concept that is complex and ambiguous. Despite the definition problems, scholars try to refine the concept and develop frameworks for understanding and analyzing civil society in relation to democratization, political liberalization and challenges of authoritarianism (Cohen and Arato 1995; Keane 1998; Luckham and White 1996). "Civil society" is here understood in the Walzer sense, as a metaphor for the "space" of "uncoerced human association and [...] the set of relational networks [exemplified by Walzer as unions, churches, political parties and movements, co-operatives, neighbourhoods, schools of thought, etc.]—formed for the sake of family, faith, interest and ideology—that fill this space" (Walzer 1992, p. 89–90). In other words, it may be understood as dealing with agents, discourses and actions. Communication in civil society is multidimensional and may be both confrontational or cooperative, although this chapter takes an interest in the more conflictual aspects of civil society, with an emphasis on the political. Essentially, this places the focus on civil society as an autonomous sphere in which "political forces of interests in society [may] contest state power"; "a site of conflict, struggle and strife, as well as of negotiation and agreement" (Hewison 1996, p. 75). While the varied groups in civil society may have dissimilar agendas in terms of the issues they engage (e.g., health services, gender equity, poverty alleviation), they share a common interest to defend political rights such as freedom of association and expression needed for them to function effectively. These rights underline the political nature of civil society and relate to central arguments in the civil society discourse on organizational autonomy. Some groups would be inclined to work with power structures, which may also be a strategy for change from within, while others may challenge them and strive towards more autonomous relations.

Is such a struggle for autonomy evident in the Vietnamese trade union movement? Is it reasonable to understand the conflicts in the labour market in terms of a challenge to the authoritarian political system? These issues are addressed through more specific questions regarding the relations between the party-state and the VGCL and how these relations have changed during the course of economic liberalization. VGCL claims it has to reform itself in order to meet the new reality of the market economy. But has it done so?

VGCL Modus Operandi

Structure of the Movement

Trade union relations with the party-state in Vietnam are a part of the authoritarian system under the control of the VCP. The VGCL is officially defined as the socio-political institution, a component of the party-state system, supposed to "grasp thoroughly the class character in all activities...and at the same time represent the majority of workers."[8] Formally, the VGCL is organized under the Vietnam Fatherland Front (Mat Tran To Quoc Viet Nam), an umbrella organization that includes all mass organizations in Vietnam. The VGCL may not question the leading role of the party. Informants at the central level of VGCL claimed that the VGCL waits until top-level party officials decide the proper way to go before it acts.[9]

The VGCL is the largest of Vietnamese mass organizations. In 1999, it had about 3,632,626 members.[10] At the national or central level, it is headed by a presidium which comprises a president, four vice presidents and other office bearers at the national and provincial levels.[11] The VGCL gathers together 17 component industrial unions of about 500,000 members.[12] These national industrial unions represent various industries or professions.[13] Organized parallel to the national industrial unions are 53 province or city federations[14] with a total of 2,800,000 members.[15] At the *grassroots level* (i.e., the union within each enterprise) there are about 46,230 unions. These grassroots level unions may belong either to an industrial union or to a province or city federation or in some cases both to a province or city federation *and* to a national industrial union. According to the official organizational scheme, the unions at the different levels cooperate with the party and government institutions at that corresponding level. For example, the VGCL of Ho Chi Minh City is supposed to work closely with the Ho Chi Minh People's Committee and the city branch of the Ministry of Labour, Social Affairs and War Invalids (MOLISA). In practice, the organizational structure is unclear. A union at the grassroots level may work with both its corresponding province/city level VGCL *and* one of the 17 national level trade/profession unions it is affiliated with. There were also examples of grassroots unions in which the leaders claimed they were organized directly under the local People's Committee.

In practice, the links between the trade union and party-state institutions are complex and based on personal as well as formal relations. The same complexity also applies to the relations between the VGCL at central level and its provincial/district and grassroots level organizations. Local power configurations seem to be of more importance when evaluating the position of the trade union within the party-state system. In my fieldwork, I find that the VGCL at provincial level might in some cases behave in a more autonomous manner vis à vis the party-state institutions while in other cases they may be totally intertwined and inseparable.[16] A similar variation is found when observing how assertive VGCL branches are with employers.

Laws and Regulations

The role of the VGCL and its relations with the party-state are regulated by the country's laws, primarily the Constitution, the Labour Code and the Trade Union Law. For instance, the VGCL as a component of the party-state structure is cited in Article 10 of the Constitution, which defines its functions as a *political* and *social* organization under the leadership of the VCP. The organization is expected to participate in state administration and in "social management."[17] The Constitution also states the dual role of the VGCL according to which it is expected both to protect the rights and interests of the workers as well as to promote production and create jobs.[18] The dual role and also its participation in state management are also expressed in Article 2 of the 1990 Trade Union Law. The Trade Union Law stipulates the rights of the President of the VGCL to attend cabinet meetings as well as to attend meetings of government agencies and organizations when discussing matters relating to "the rights, obligations and interests of workers."[19] The Trade Union Law gives the VGCL the right to submit "draft laws and ordinances to the National Assembly and the State" in matters of concern for workers.

A crucial development was the enactment of the new Labour Code by the National Assembly in June 1994, the implementation of which started in 1995. This was Vietnam's first coherent labour law.[20] Prior to the Labour Code, decisions had been based on state laws passed by the standing committee of the National Assembly, circulars by MOLISA, or decrees issued by the government or the party. Institutional practices, however, continue to a high degree as before and circulars, decrees and other provisions are thus constantly added to the Labour Code provisions.

Although the Labour Code was welcomed by most parties, it also met with some criticism. According to Dinh Ngoc Vuong, who worked in the Law Commission for the Labour Code[21] prior to *doi moi* (between 1980 and 1985), a general problem was that, since the Code was adopted in a period of transition, some parts would be outdated even before they were implemented.[22] He suggested that the role of the trade union might have to be redefined to emphasize protection of labour rights including the right to organize strikes. The regulation of trade unions was one area that stirred most discussions in the commission and the final result offered some possibilities for workers to form their own unions.[23] There were also discussions on how to deal with those cases where the trade union did not have the support of the workers. This resulted in the provision that if a union (at enterprise level) has fewer members than half of the workforce, it is not allowed to be the only representative of the workers who may then choose their own representative. In this case they can form a "representative commission" which the local People's Committee must recognize as the representative of the workers. This means that technically speaking, the Labour Code has provisions for forming unions independently. The Labour Code also re-conceptualized relations in the labour market. One intention behind the new code was to make a clear distinction between "employer" and "employee". In earlier regulations all had been referred to as "working people", a vague concept that included both employers and employees. It may also be said that the idea behind the Labour Code was to separate trade unions from management. Another issue that stirred much debate both in the Labour Law Commission (Hansson 1995) and the National Assembly[24] was the right to strike. Little, if any, disagreement had earlier been voiced in this regard.[25] The right to strike was finally granted in the Labour Code and in the newly amended Labour Code (*Labour Code of Socialist Republic of Vietnam, as amended 2 April 2002*) it is stipulated in Chapter XIV, Resolution of Labour Disputes.[26]

Economic Liberalization and the Changing Role of Trade Unions

Even though the initial steps towards economic liberalization were taken in the late 1970s and market reforms were endorsed by the 1986 VCP Sixth Congress with its adoption of the *doi moi* policy, it was only in the mid-1990s that economic changes such as private enterprises and joint ventures with foreign investors were seriously affecting VGCL's operations. The economic reforms of *doi moi* have seen an inflow of foreign investment, attempts at privatization and the closing down of many state-owned enterprises (SOEs). From 1990 to 1992, the number of SOEs was reduced from 12,000 to 6,000, resulting in the retrenchment of about 1.1 million workers (Quan Xuan Dinh 2000, p. 362). Vietnam's industrial structure has changed to one in which "half or less of the output (comes) from the foreign-invested sector, slightly more than a quarter from the state sector, and slightly less than a quarter from the non-state sector" (Fforde 2002, p. 369). This economic trend has necessitated changes in the party-state's policies on labour as well as changes in the role of the VGCL.

The VGCL is supposed to have a dual function of protecting workers' interests and promoting production. In theory it has to work as the old Leninist model of a "transmission belt" between the party-state and workers (see p. 99 n.3) which means serving, on the one hand, as a channel for official propaganda and implementation of state-party policies, and on the other, as a channel for workers' discontent. In the pre-reform system the duties and roles of trade unions were quite comprehensively defined and implemented. Together with party officials, trade union leaders participated in management at the workplace.[27] In my interviews with trade union representatives in the state sector in the mid-1990s, they claimed that their role in the workplace was primarily to provide input in the setting of production targets and to implement the production plan.[28] However, this old arrangement has undergone extensive changes as SOEs become progressively marketized, thus reducing the role of the unions and marginalizing them.[29]

In the pre-reform system, one of the main tasks of the trade union at the workplace had been to participate in the setting and implementation of production targets.[30] Union representatives sat on management boards. From the mid-1990s, however, economic restructuring started to have consequences for the everyday operations of the SOEs. The old system of "collective management" which included representation of the trade union, the party, the youth union, and the directors changed. Managers were to be held responsible for the results of their production unit and the obligation to consult with the other parties was abolished. In the mid-1990s, local branches of the VGCL were increasingly locked out of the management deliberations, which prevented the unions from taking an active part in decisions concerning the workers (Hansson 1995). According to many union officials, what remains of the union's role is to help implement production policies, which they no longer have an effective role in setting. Union leaders organize production teams and arrange competitions among workers through which individual workers or teams are rewarded for their skills and productivity.

In the pre-reform economy, trade unions also played an important role in workers' social security, including housing allocation, schools and kindergartens for children, management of pensions, unemployment benefits and medical benefits. They also arranged social activities such as vacations, and buying gifts for birthdays and weddings benefits. To be able to enjoy these social welfare benefits, workers had to become members of the trade union. In theory, workers could choose not to be a member of the union but, since it was only through such membership that they gained access to social security, it was not a viable option.[31] Union membership was open to all fully employed workers who had not committed serious crimes.

Trade unions in Vietnam do not normally negotiate wages. Officially, the market regulates wages only for a small part of the working population, mainly those in highly qualified positions. There is, however, a formal wage system that affects a great number of people where wages are set by the government and not by the employers in negotiations with the union or with the employees.[32] Wages stipulated for indigenous private companies and SOEs are different from those stipulated for foreign-owned companies and joint ventures. In 1999, the minimum wage in the foreign sector was set at US$45,[33] while in the state sector the same year it was as low as US$15,[34] which is not sufficient to keep a family at subsistence level. Furthermore, the minimum wage system allows for quite wide regional differences. In areas with lower growth, wage levels can be considerably lower than those with higher growth, especially the big cities. There are no reliable statistics on wages in most sectors. In general, the situation points to the trade unions' lack of influence in the wage-setting process.

Although reforming the VGCL is on the *doi moi* agenda, the labour movement has hardly felt any of its impact. The situation of many SOE workers is a case in point. As market reforms gained momentum, thousands of SOEs had to be closed down because they were not economically viable. This led to massive retrenchments (Nørlund 1997).

According to the VGCL, labour conflicts had been rare and when they occurred, the parties involved would normally work out a consensus since they all "had the same goals and interests". The VGCL response to this development was to initiate international contacts with trade unions in order to learn how to function in a market economy. The changes in the labour market pushed the VGCL to search for new roles. With the developing market economy came also the need for new labour laws. The implementation of the Labour Code, however, is still weak. Many workers, and even trade union officials, are not aware of their rights (and obligations) under the Labour Code.[35] A new role of the VGCL is to be responsible for checking the implementation of the Labour Code at the local level in collaboration with the local People's Committee.

In practice, the VGCL struggles to adapt to the changing logic of the new system. There is still little understanding of a trade union's role in a market economy. Labour disputes and strikes are becoming more frequent and VGCL has no organizational structure to handle such conflicts. There are also uncertainties within the VCP, and consequently within the VGCL, on how to deal with this situation. Trade unions at the grassroots level dare not deal with problems nor do they have the competence to resolve conflicts. In most cases when a strike broke out, officials from the central VGCL headquarters in Hanoi or from the provincial or city federations or from the local People's Committee tried to negotiate between the workers and employers or to persuade the workers to get back to work. However, there is some confusion regarding the mediation process. As will be seen below, mediation in Vietnam generally involves workers, employers, union representatives and local government; the specific composition of actors can vary. Conflicts are largely dealt with in an ad hoc manner.

Labour Conflicts

The perception in official circles is that labour conflicts and strikes have been on the rise since the policies of *doi moi* started to affect people's lives.[36] Already in 1993 the problem of strikes was recognized by the VGCL. In a statement to the Seventh VGCL National Congress, Nguyen Van Tu, then president of the Confederation, expressed concern:

> In several places, conflicts between employers and workers have arisen. Since 1992, dozens of collective reaction against management misconduct have been accompanied by claims for pay rise and democratic

> behaviour from the employers at private businesses, joint ventures with foreigners, and even at SOEs.[37]

This statement was made before the right to strike was sanctioned by law, thus, strikes have to be termed "collective reactions". Strikes pose a challenge to the VGCL's role as the sole labour organizer. The Confederation takes the threat of strikes seriously, being primarily concerned with their implication for political and social stability. A report was prepared by the Law Department of the VGCL on the "Real Situation: Strikes 1995–1998".[38] From 1995 (when the implementation of the new Labour Code started) to 1998 there had been a total of 222 officially recorded strikes. On average about 20 per cent of the strikes took place in SOEs, between 50 and 60 per cent in foreign-invested enterprises, and about 30 per cent in the indigenous private sector. According to the official statistics, Dong Nai and Song Be/Binh Duong and the greater Ho Chi Minh City region were where most of the strikes occurred. These were areas that experienced the most intensive economic liberalization.[39] In 1997 and 1998, 77 per cent and 71 per cent respectively of the total number of recorded strikes occurred in Ho Chi Minh City area.[40] All the strikes were considered illegal because they did not follow the procedures stipulated by law. In none of the cases had the local trade union branch played an active role in organizing the strike. The unions generally characterized strikes as "spontaneous reactions", denying the possibility of organization behind them. In some cases the strikes involved thousands of workers making it reasonable to assume that some organizing among the workers outside the framework of the VGCL had taken place, e.g., the one reported on 3 January 1999 involved some 2,000 workers for 7 days (Tran Thanh Ha 1999). Informal labour organizations could be behind the strikes. This adds to VGCL's legitimacy claims. In the process of resolving a strike, management, trade union, and the local People's Committee will send representatives. At the same time, a representative of the striking workers will also be part of this process. If others have organized the strike, it is unlikely that workers will readily accept a trade union official as their spokesperson.

According to a VGCL report, most strikes in foreign-invested enterprises occur where grassroots trade unions have not been established and where there are no collective agreements. In the course of this study, visits to workplaces that had recently experienced strikes show that the presence or absence of a formal trade union had little impact on whether or not a labour dispute would result in a strike. In factories where a strike had occurred, the trade union had nothing to do with its organization.[41] A VGCL report states that "regarding the scope of strikes, the number of workers joining strikes are on the rise. Since 1989 there has been a visible rise in the number of strikes reported" (Tran Thanh Ha 1999). This increase has followed the development of the market economy and the liberalization programme. Another interesting trend is an increase in strikes at SOEs. According to official rhetoric, this sector is characterized by consensual management where there is little reason for workers to strike since workers have the same interests as their managers. Since all SOEs have trade unions, it also suggests that the trade unions' capacity for resolving conflict is limited. The VGCL tends to give priority to containing and preventing strikes in the joint venture and foreign invested sector, thus leaning towards promoting production by focusing on creating a stable environment for foreign investors.[42]

The reasons behind strike actions vary. While the reasons for strikes in the mid-1990s were described as "cultural misunderstandings" they are now identified in terms of poor working conditions such as low wages and long working hours. This may partly reflect a change in the VGCL's perception of strikes, regarding the latter as something more acceptable and even normal in a market economy.

Wage disputes can involve a company failing to pay wages that were already fixed by agreement or the minimum stipulated by the law. This was the case at the Gafain Enterprise IneXim Co, a joint venture in Tan Hung, Ho Chi Minh City, where the workers went on strike in August 1999. The company had paid sub-standard wages that had been further reduced without informing the workers.[43] Another common problem is the failure to pay the Tet (Lunar New Year) bonus. This is an important part of the Vietnamese wage system whereby a bonus (normally one extra month's wage) is paid to all employees to celebrate Tet. A report on strikes in the Ho Chi Minh City area in 1999 shows that the strikes were mostly caused by low wages, failure to pay the legal minimum wage, no compensation for overtime, long working hours, and other labour law-related problems. In some cases the causes were illegal or inhumane punishment of workers. In two cases, the cause of the strike was that workers had been beaten, as in the Taiwanese-owned company Shenyee in the Viet Hung Industrial Zone in Binh Duong.[44] In addition to these labour law-related strikes, the VGCL also recognizes the occurrence of politically motivated strikes. This refers to strikes that arise from workers wishing to exercise freedom of association in setting up a trade union. Between 1995 and 1998, the VGCL suggests that the fourth most frequent cause of strikes was related to the right to set up a trade union or to issues related to the election procedures of a local branch executive committee.

All conflicts, according to the VGCL official view, are settled through mediation and negotiation. When a strike occurs, representatives of the VGCL at the factory or at provincial/city level, the provincial/city branch of the Ministry of Labour, the Ministry for Planning and Investment, and local police officers will collect information from the workers. They will negotiate with the employers and ask the employers to observe stipulations in the law. The mediation process is characterized by organizational weakness, and lack of knowledge of roles and responsibilities. This was identified in a report by the central level VGCL (Tran Thanh Ha 1999), which says that the local union branches remain weak in handling the grievances involved in the strikes. The conflict resolution process itself is weak and the functions and duties of each party are, according to the report, insufficiently defined. This is supported by my field interviews. The Hoc Mon case, discussed below, is only one of many similar cases where the workplace union had no role in organizing the strike or resolving the conflict. In cases where a solution was reached, arbitration had been carried out by different actors depending on the local power structure, including the trade union, the People's Committee, and the Ministry of Labour at province or city level. The report claims that grassroots trade unions are passive and appear embarrassed in the face of a strike; they are inefficient in addressing the problem that caused the strike; and that they are "under different types of pressures" that make them weak; for example, they are limited by the "economic or administrative pressure of employers" (Tran Thanh Ha 1999). In addition, they do not show their ability to organize legal strikes or knowledge of their right to do so.

Institutions Dealing with Labour Problems

In addition to the VGCL, new institutions with an emphasis on labour protection and the resolution of labour conflicts are taking shape. Two examples are the new labour court system[45] and labour inspection committees. It is difficult to be precise about the structure of institutions dealing with labour and how they should be placed in relation to each other and the labour management system as a whole. The system is in transition and the relations, responsibilities and roles are often not clear to the actors themselves. Informants and official documents thus often give contradictory information. This also adds to the general picture of a system still grappling with problems in an ad hoc manner. Still it is important to note new developments such as the labour inspection committee of Ho Chi Minh City set up by the Ho Chi Minh City People's Committee. The task of this inspection committee is to visit companies and check if they are complying with current labour laws. From what has been said about the role of the VGCL, this should be a duty of its grassroots trade unions. The committee inspects all types of companies: domestic, which includes both state-owned and private ones, as well as foreign. In total, during the first seven months of 1999, 473 companies operating in Ho Chi Minh City were inspected (of which 35 were SOEs). One of the committee's reports concludes that violations related to the signing of labour contracts, working hours and rest time, overtime payment and the payment of social insurance,[46] are "big and common problem[s]" mainly in private enterprises. The findings were submitted to the Ministry of Labour branch office in Ho Chi Minh City.[47] It is interesting that the inspections are organized by the People's Committee but the reports go to the Ministry of Labour branch for action because the latter has the power to issue a fine. This institutional arrangement implies the complexity of a bureaucracy where inspection is done by one institution and action taken by another. The reports only mention trade unions as one of the inspection criteria, i.e., does the company inspected have a trade union? One report states that only one of the 473 inspected companies did not have a trade union. Referring to breaches of the labour law, the report stated that in almost all cases the inspectors found it necessary to "communicate the Labour Code's provisions" to the workers and sometimes to the management. Viewed critically, these findings by the inspection committee underline the fact that despite their overwhelming presence at places of work, trade unions play a very limited role in checking on compliance with labour laws and protecting the interests of workers. Another detail in the report illustrated this point when individual workers themselves, and not the trade unions, petitioned the inspectors about poor working conditions.

The report says that 45 of the inspected companies were fined by the city branch of the Ministry of Labour for violating the labour laws. It would seem the operating brief of the inspection committee was to refer cases to the Ministry. No court action was initiated by the committee. What follows is a case where a group of workers, not represented by any trade union, resorted to litigation to resolve a labour dispute.

The Hoc Mon Case

In Hoc Mon district, Ho Chi Minh City, 43 workers in a Taiwanese garment factory went on strike. Eight of the workers who arranged the strike and the trade union officials in Hoc Mon who were responsible for dealing with the conflict were interviewed during my fieldwork. The conflict is interesting because the workers, under the leadership of one of the seamstresses, brought the case to court. In this instance, as in many other cases investigated, the cause of the conflict was both abuse of workers and problems regarding payment of wages. The trade union branch at the workplace had not acted in any way to protect the workers' welfare. The workers explained that they worked six days a week from seven o'clock in the morning to nine in the evening with very little food.[48] In the evenings only porridge (rice and water) was served when it was necessary to work overtime. Discipline was harsh in the factory. The workers spoke of the rule of "no talking". They were only allowed two toilet visits in one day and the factory had toilet guards to police the rule. If any rule was broken the workers were punished through reduced wages. For example, talking meant reductions of VND 5,000, not wearing a name tag VND 5,000, and being late VND 10,000. The factory compound had only one tree which provided little shade and the workers had to walk around in the full heat of the sun during their lunch break. The factory had no clean drinking water which caused many workers to fall ill. Each production line had to fulfil a set quota. One of the workers explained:

> ...for example, initially we had to meet the quota of 800 pieces a day and we could stop work at 4.30 p.m. when we fulfilled the quota. The following day, the quota was raised to 1,000. Whenever we managed to finish on time they constantly raised the quota. They just moved the

> limit. The quota was moved forward all the time, it was very hard work with very little food. Soon some of the workers fell down unconscious because the quota was raised higher and higher and we could not work harder…

The workers sent a written complaint to the management about the working conditions and the low wages not complying with the minimum wage stipulated by the government. The management did not reply. That was when plans were made to go on strike. Despite the strike, the workers had no reply from the manager. When the strike was called off and they tried to return to work, they were at first not allowed into the compound. So they decided to sit outside the front gate as an act of protest. According to the workers, in the end they were allowed in because the management was afraid that a crowd outside the factory gates would attract too much attention. The manager came out of the factory with his bodyguards and a list of names. He read out the names of the 43 workers and gave orders that they were not allowed to return to work. The guards informed the workers that they were fired but they were not allowed to leave the compound and rouse public attention in the neighbourhood. Some of the workers tried to run into the factory in order to inform other workers what was going on. They were chased by guards equipped with electrical batons. One of the women, however, managed to escape through a hole in the fence and contacted the district trade union of Hoc Mon. They came and talked to the manager and the workers were finally released. The manager promised to pay them the compensation the company owed them according to the labour law since they were fired but he never fulfilled the promise. I asked the workers if they had a trade union at their workplace and one of them replied that "…there is a trade union but we don't know much about it. Maybe it is because of the manager, but the trade union has very little activities…"

The Hoc Mon Trade Union representatives suggested in interviews that it was never a question of a strike in the first place because the "workers had voluntarily agreed to stay home that day…to oppose the manager, to raise their wages and to show their disappointment." The trade union official explained that since they were fired without receiving their compensation the managers broke the law. In the interviews, the VGCL representatives were more interested in discussing the legal aspects of the problems in the factory rather than the failings of the trade union.[49] One of the women workers fought to get the case to court. Eventually she was helped by the Hoc Mon trade union. The court summoned the manager several times but he never showed up. Finally, the company was convicted in absentia and ordered to pay the compensation it owed the workers. But the workers did not receive the money. The manager had gone back to Taiwan and the company claimed he was personally responsible for the problems at the factory. The new manager had no intention of paying the workers their compensation.

This case illustrates several problems with labour related institutions and the bureaucracy in Vietnam. The problems the workers describe could have been solved by an active trade unionism involving proper negotiations over wages and working conditions in the factory. In the absence of such a union the only solution seen by the workers was to organize a strike. There was a trade union at this company but the workers did not know much about it or what kind of support they could demand of it. Even when the conflict had turned into a strike, the union at the workplace did not get involved. It was the VGCL at district level that tried to defuse the tension.

Evidently the VGCL representatives and the workers they were supposed to represent had different accounts of the dispute and its causes. The union officials did not recognize the workers' action as a strike. The workers, on their part, felt they had to take matters in their own hands. As the conflict was about to be brought to court they were helped by the Hoc Mon trade union to present their case. But, in fact, during the interviews, union officials showed little understanding of the procedures concerning strikes and about the right to strike in general. The bureaucratic weakness of the system is furthered illustrated by the inability of the system to enforce a legal verdict.

Conflicting Perceptions of the Right to Strike in the VGCL

One of the reasons behind the weak organizational capacities of the current institutions in dealing with labour disputes is the conflicting perceptions of the right to strike. Officials in the VGCL involved in conflict resolution or in analysis and policy-making hold different views.

Some tended to deny that strikes occurred at all, suggesting either that they were very out of touch or that strikes were something that should not be discussed with a foreign student.[50] Their position was that there is a consensual way to solve problems at the workplace, which means that strikes are never necessary and that conflicts were always solved in discussions between the managers and the employees. If those at the enterprise level were not able to reach an agreement, the VGCL at provincial, city, or central level would step in as a mediator to help. This might have been the case in the SOEs during the years before market reforms when the trade union had a significant role in the management of a production unit. Another explanation of some official's position could be the fact that the strikes did not follow the "proper procedures" and were thus not strikes, technically speaking.

Most officials interviewed at the VGCL in 1999, however, held a more open attitude towards strikes and labour disputes. Some admitted that strikes were officially illegal because workers had not followed the procedures stipulated by the law. But they also felt that it was demanding too much of workers, who sometimes had little education and no trade union at their workplace, to know of the new labour law and the correct strike procedure. Some admitted that strikes are a normal, albeit undesirable, part of a market economy. One expert in the legal department at the VGCL claimed that all the strikes were illegal and that the control of strikes must become stricter. The VGCL, according to this interviewee, was working on an amendment to the 1995 Labour Code that would tighten the regulation on the right to strike and limit labour disputes. "We must create an environment for foreign investments and so strikes have to be stopped."[51] All informants agreed on one thing, the VGCL had never been involved in or helped workers to arrange a strike. Their obvious knowledge about the situation in the labour market in combination with the sort of arguments presented and passive role in strikes indicate that there is a state-imposed agenda embraced by the VGCL which makes it very reluctant to use strikes as a legitimate means to redress workers' grievances, even when they were acute. This forces workers to rely on their own resources to settle their disputes with employers, in the course of which they sometimes violate the Labour Code, which is not widely disseminated in a country where the rule of law is still weak. In many such instances, the VGCL is seen by workers as not representing their interests.

In 1999, a VGCL document suggested that those who attend or organize illegal strikes should not be punished in view of workers' ignorance of the relevant provisions.[52] Its solution was to increase labour inspections, suggesting at the same time that those in charge of labour issues such as inspecting and monitoring the implementation of the labour code had too little resources. The problem was aggravated by the weakness of grassroots trade unions and the weakness in the cooperation between related organizations and state officials. The VGCL tends to take the view that the challenge against it would diminish if only it could ensure that the Labour Code was more efficiently implemented. The report concluded, "to stop illegal strikes would require comprehensive measures, including knowledge, organization, co-operative mechanisms and strong and continuous influence on both employers and employees."[53] The paper recommends a research project to be developed on "Realizing the Right to Strike". The aim was to propose an amendment to the Labour Code so as to simplify the process for handling labour conflicts. The recognition of the occurrence of strikes and the decision not to punish the workers involved suggest that there are forces within the VGCL who are prepared to work for reforms that may help to transform the organization into more of a trade union and less of a state department of labour. The VGCL obviously wants to protect workers when it can, thus leading to a situation where it seems like it is just muddling through with no clear vision of what it should do for the workers it claims to represent.

Challenges to the Organizational Monopoly of the VGCL

The challenge seen by the VGCL was in increasing its membership in the growing sector of companies with foreign investments. As mentioned above, all companies with more than ten employees must, according to the law, have a trade union in place at the latest six months after starting operations.[54] In the case of workers forming their own union they have to apply for recognition by the VGCL. If they fail to do so, the union will be considered illegal. The law was introduced in response to the difficulties of recruiting new members in the new private companies, particularly foreign-owned and joint venture companies. The possibility for workers to form a representative commission, as discussed above, in cases where the union, for one reason or another, is not considered by workers as their representative, may also in effect challenge the organizational monopoly of the VGCL: in 1999 the VGCL officially announced that one of the most important tasks was to increase activities in this sector.[55] This sector was already a target for membership recruitment in 1994.[56] There are many reasons for the lack of progress in VGCL's membership drive in this sector as well as within the export processing zones. Workers may not be sufficiently aware of labour laws and their rights. Their confidence in the VGCL may be low. Many trade union officials talk of their difficulties when trying to gain access to the factories. One informant within the VGCL said that the latter had only managed to establish branches in joint venture companies when the companies were compelled by contracts to retain staff from former SOEs. This meant that a trade union was already in place that could work from within. In some companies in southern Vietnam the failure of the VGCL in attracting members in this new sector has led to employees setting up their own informal organizations, dealing with issues normally considered trade union activities such as negotiating with employers and organizing strikes. These organizations are autonomous from the VGCL. It is difficult to know if they are independent because they do not want to be associated with the official union as a matter of principle or for other reasons. These new informal "trade unions" may in the long run pose a challenge to the monopoly of the VGCL. It may be worth noting that the initial steps towards autonomous trade unions in Indonesia came from this kind of informal organizing.[57]

The 1998 VGCL Political Report—Critique of Relations with the Party

The 1998 political report of the VGCL criticizes the movement's relationship with the VCP in harsh terms. It writes that there is a "shortage of measures to detect and prevent incidents of bureaucratism, arbitrariness, corruption and bribery among trade union members who are public officials and employees in the state apparatus and agencies of authority and have responsibility in handling civic affairs." It further suggests that "party and state have failed to come up with comprehensive solutions or create conditions and mechanisms [that allows] the trade union [to] carry…out [their] lawful roles." In the view of VGCL, workers' influence in management remain largely nominal and the state is too slow to issue the documents and directives necessary for the implementation of laws as for example in the field of social policies: "[m]any social welfare policies...on housing, rest and children's day care and a number of policies on women labourers remain inappropriate and are slow to change despite trade union recommendations."[58] Trade union complaints are not resolved although they have been considered by the appropriate state authorities and managers fail to develop a proper understanding of the lawful role of trade unions.

The VGCL report goes into the causes for the failures. It is clear that the VGCL is dissatisfied with the current relations between the trade union movement and the party-state. It suggests that "[t]rade union organizations have not taken initiatives in working out effective measures for their own operations and their handling of relations with authorities at all levels"[59] and that unions are not allowed to perform their full constitutional and lawful role. Many plans and programmes have been initiated but only few are properly supervised, appraised and reviewed. Red tape is still commonplace and implementation work lacks resolve, focus and efficiency.[60] Another strain on the relations between the party-state and the VGCL is caused by the diminishing state budget allocations for the trade union,[61] which in effect compels it to seek other ways of financing large parts of its operations, either through membership fees and/or through international cooperation with foreign trade unions and international organizations. The political report generally points out that the VGCL in practice has increasingly been barred from participation in policy and implementation as guaranteed by law.

Concluding Remarks

In theory, the mass organizations of the Vietnamese party-state are intended to ensure representation of a range of social-economic-political interests. They are supposed to work as "transmission belts" between their constituency and the party-state, thus performing the dual role of promoting production as well as protecting, supporting and representing workers' interests. This would make autonomous organizing of interest representation unnecessary or rather state-sponsored agencies are expected to take care of problems. Given this ideological starting point, it is not surprising that legally, it is difficult, if not impossible, for groups to organize independently of the state. In practice, the VGCL finds it hard to reconcile the duality of roles. The contradictions it has to grapple with between the state's economic agenda and workers' interests have increased with market reforms. What can be said of its actual performance in this respect?

At the central level of the VGCL there are encouraging signs of an awareness about the problems within the existing trade union structure. In the Political Report to the Eight National Congress of the VGCL in 1998 the shortcomings of the VGCL were discussed, acknowledging that the efficiency of protecting the interests and rights of workers had been low.[62] The report also recognized the Confederation's failure to "promote the collective wisdom of their members". At the central level it had not been effective in intervening with state agencies in "drafting, complementing and amending regimes, policies and legal bills relating to the obligations, rights and interests of the workers". According to the report, the VGCL did not exercise well its functions in "controlling and supervising the observance of regimes, policies and laws". In addition to this, organizational reforms had not been pursued effectively. The failure to function as a proper trade union in the market economy is seen as a failure of organizational renewal.

> ...[the] trade union organizations in the non-state sectors, especially in private and foreign invested enterprises are having trouble defining the content and methods of their activities. The role of the trade union organizations at these enterprises is not well played, resulting in failures to promptly intervene and recommend solutions to workers' collective complaints and let them eventually grow into strikes.[63]

There is no doubt the VGCL has identified problems in general and at the grassroots level. Where the latter is concerned, it admits that a number of "trade union organizations are virtually inoperative and fail to provide a backing for labourers". The frank critique does indicate, up to a point, that the VGCL would like to assume a more conventional trade unionist role that will lean more towards protecting the interests of its members than promoting production.

However, the VGCL has already had more than fifteen years to adjust to the challenges of market economics and has failed to do so adequately. There is confusion regarding the delegation of duties and leadership among different levels of the trade union. It has failed to be of support to workers in negotiating wages, addressing poor working conditions, the implementation of labour laws, to name just three conventional functions expected of a trade union movement. This inability has led to a stage where even minor problems may turn into strikes. There are no institutional channels for workers' grievances and demands. The current institutional structure is outdated and cannot deal with the "new" situation and problems. Thus, conflicts occur outside the formal structures of the party-state and are still dealt with in an ad hoc manner largely depending on the local power configurations where the conflict takes place. As was demonstrated by the Hoc Mon strike, grassroots trade unions were not at all involved in the process leading up to strike, nor were they involved in its resolution. It was only when the case was about to be presented in court that a higher level trade union came in to support the workers.

These seemingly intractable operational problems of the VGCL should be viewed in the larger context of governance within an authoritarian polity. With an authoritarian political structure still in place and its own position as part of the party-state, the VGCL is not able to move beyond existing parameters; thus its ineffectual attempts at addressing specific problems. However mounting events on the ground are forcing changes upon the old out-dated dynamics of governance, which the VGCL represents. This is evident in regions such as the Ho Chi Minh City area where growth in the market economy is the fastest and strongest. An increasing number of workers are resorting to organizing themselves rather than relying on moribund VGCL grassroots unions. The organization of big strikes with several thousand participants without support from the VGCL indicates that workers are seeking independent forms of organization, which by their very existence challenge authoritarian habits. Furthermore, strikes are not always about rectifying poor working conditions. The VGCL is aware of the existence of politically motivated strikes concerning issues of organizational freedom. Such developments weaken the hitherto VGCL monopoly on trade unionism, forcing it to acknowledge that it cannot take its legitimacy among Vietnam's workers for granted. This changing reality means that the authoritarian system regulating the labour market has to be fundamentally re-examined. Within the VGCL establishment, different perceptions of the legitimacy of strikes indicate a plurality of views on policy options for the future.

However, the changes go far beyond just the VGCL reforming its institutional structure and leadership appointments. The current institutions have not been able to handle the conflicts within the system, partly because the resistance and protests have occurred outside the formal structures. Individually these strikes are not targeted at the VCP or the VGCL. They are aggrieved workers reacting against unfair power relations at a particular workplace. Nevertheless, when these incidents are viewed collectively, we can begin to understand how they are shaping industrial relations in Vietnamese society. These developments together with the growing problems of corruption and other abuses of power among the élite erode the authoritarian system. In a nutshell, a process of de-authoritarianization is taking place. As these broad-based changes percolate through the system, a more autonomous civil society may be emerging.

Notes

1 Vietnam has a one party system whereby the Vietnam Communist Party (VCP) is, by the country's constitution, the only legal political party. "Party-state" refers to this situation where the VCP and the state intertwine, not only as a constitutional provision, but at all practical levels of administration. In such a system, party and government institutions run parallel to each other with overlapping functions and unclear divisions of power. For this paper there is no need to differentiate between the state and the party. For a further discussion of this typology see, for example, Cohen and Arato's discussion on "party-state" and "authoritarian state socialism" (Cohen and Arato 1995, p. 446–7).

2 This chapter is primarily based on material that was collected during several field trips to Vietnam beginning in 1994 and especially during 1999 and 2002. The data gathered included interviews with workers who had been involved in recent strikes, trade union officials and state officials as well as observations from visits to workplaces. The fieldwork was conducted as part of the work for my ongoing Ph.D. project at the Department of Political Science, Stockholm University, and was financed by the Swedish International Development Agency (Sida)/Swedish Agency for Research Co-operation (SAREC). This text should be considered a work in progress.

3 These organizations are mainly foreign-funded and bear little resemblance to the type of grassroots civil society organizations that are often pictured in the academic literature on civil society and democratization. Some of them are primarily consultancy firms, hired by international aid organizations to implement various aid projects or research related subjects. These organizations are of little threat to the authoritarian political system.

They complement the state in areas where the state institutions lack competence or resources.

4 BBC Monitoring World Media, January 22, 2001.

5 "Freedom in the World, 2000–2001: Vietnam, Freedom House", <www.freedomhouse.org>.

6 At these meetings, officials inform editors what the taboo issues are, i.e. not for press reporting and what they would like to see highlighted, e.g., the authorities "declared that economic data such as money supply, state reserves…and inflation are state secrets." (Adrian Edwards, "Vietnam—A Different Kind of Freedom", *Far Eastern Economic Review*, 29 March, 2001).

7 VGCL, "Shortcomings, Weaknesses and their Causes, Vietnam General Confederation of Labour Central Executive Committee Political Report to the Eighth National Congress, Hanoi, November 5–6, 1998" (unofficial translation), p. 18.

8 *Vietnamese Experience—The Trade Union Movement in Vietnam*, Hanoi: Foreign Languages Publishing House and Vietnam Federation of Trade Unions. 1988, p. 26.

9 Various discussions with VGCL officials, Hanoi, 1999.

10 "Trade Union Organization Determined to Increase Membership in Economic Sector", Hanoi, September 2, 1999, Vietnam News Agency.

11 Other members of the presidium are the directors of departments within the headquarters such as the directors of the International, Women's, Financial, Personnel, and Education and Information departments, together with the presidents of some of the large National Industrial Unions such as the National Union of Building Workers and the National Union of Educational and Training Workers, as well as some of the province or city-level federation presidents.

12 It is difficult to assess membership numbers due to unclear and divergent practices regarding who is considered a trade union member and due to the differing numbers presented in different documents. In some cases, workers are automatically counted as members while in other cases trade union membership requires that a worker actively join a union. The VGCL being a complex structure from national through regional down to the shopfloor level may also double count its membership in some instances. For instance, in the case where a trade union at the grassroots level organizes both under the branch/industry organization but *also* under the provincial/city federation organization and, thus, its members are counted twice. Further, inflating its membership numbers may also be in the strategic interest of the VGCL.

13 The 17 National Industrial Unions are the National Unions of Building Workers, Workers in Agriculture and Rural Development, Educational

and Training Workers, Aviation Workers, Bank Workers, Commercial Workers, Health Workers, Industrial Workers, Railway Workers, Oil and Gas Workers, Transport and Communication Workers, Printing Workers, Public Sector Employees, Fishery Workers, workers in National Defence, Maritime Workers, and Workers in the People's Police. The membership in these National Industrial Unions varies from only about 574 in the National Union of Health Workers up to around 74,000 members in the large National Unions of the Building Workers and that of the Public Sector Employees.

14 The cities with federations are Ho Chi Minh City, Hanoi, Hai Phong and Thanh Hoa. These are industrial centres and their federations have the largest memberships: Ho Chi Minh City Federation at about 420,000, Hanoi 220,000 and Hai Phong and Thanh Hoa at about 100,000 each.

15 These are official figures provided by the VGCL. If the 500,000 membership of the industrial federations is added to the provincial/city membership of 2.8 million, the total is 3.3 million. In other official documents the VGCL claims to have around 3.6 million members. The discrepancy may be explained by double counting (see n. 12).

16 Although the officially stated ambition of the party and VGCL is that they should be institutionally separate, I have observed several cases in which a trade union representative and the party cell leader at a workplace were one and the same person (in one instance, the leader of the SOE was also the trade union representative as well as the leader of the enterprise party cell). It should be noted, however, that the central VGCL officials I interviewed considered this to be a problem. This problem is also highlighted in Nørlund's discussion of the membership structure of trade unions in foreign and private companies where she points out that "the share of managers in the unions is surprisingly high" and that "the tendency is that supervisors are an important membership group, which might have relation to the fact that supervisors often are trade union representatives." (Nørlund 1999, p. 87–8). Nørlund´s study shows that the problem is not isolated to the SOE sector.

17 *The Constitution of the Socialist Republic of Vietnam*, 1992, The Gioi, Foreign Languages Publishing House, Hanoi.

18 This model is usually referred to as the "classic Leninist dualism" and was the result of a compromise in Russia in the late 1920s (see *Trade Unions in Communist States*, edited by Pravda and Ruble, 1986).

19 Article 2, *The Trade Union Law of the Socialist Republic of Vietnam*, 1990.

20 On the new Labour Code of the Socialist Republic of Vietnam the process leading up to it, see Hansson, "Trade Unions and Doi Moi", 1995.

21 The Law Commission was a group within the National Assembly working on the drafts of the Labour Code.

22 Interview with Dinh Ngoc Vuong, Scholar Council Secretary, National Center for Social Sciences and the Humanities (Hanoi), 1 July, 1994.

23 If ten or more workers at an enterprise want to form a trade union, it has to be accepted by the management. The union must then gain recognition from the central level of the VGCL.

24 *Vietnam Investment Review*, 30 May–5 June, 1994.

25 Interview with Phan Trung Ly, Vice Director of the Department of Law at the Office of the National Assembly of S.R. Vietnam, Hanoi, July, 1994.

26 For a discussion of this process and the right to strike, see Hansson 1995.

27 This is what is referred to as the "collective leadership".

28 For more on the pre-reform role of the VGCL, see Hansson, "The Vietnam Railway Trade Union", in *Vietnam—Reform and Transformation*, edited by Beckman, Hansson and Romàn 1996, p. 179–86.

29 All information on the duties and roles of the trade unions comes from interviews from 1994 to 1999 with trade union officials at workplaces and at VGCL offices of different levels.

30 Interviews with officials of the Vietnam Railway Trade Union, Hanoi, 1994.

31 It is difficult to assess whether the choice not to join a union existed in practice. There were different opinions on the issue in my interviews. VGCL officials at central levels always claimed that workers were free to join or not while at some workplaces there were clear indications that workers were automatically regarded as members. A problem in the mid-1990s was the increased use of temporary labour who could not join the union and thus were excluded from social security benefits.

32 There is of course also an informal wage system in which wages are set at a considerably lower level than the minimum wage levels set by the government.

33 The minimum wage in the foreign-owned sector did not change much during the 1990s. In 1994 it was even lowered from US$55 to US$45 in order to attract investors. In practice, however, many companies are exempted from the minimum wage provision. In remote or comparatively underdeveloped areas, the minimum wage stipulation is hard to police. VGCL reports often suggest that many companies refuse to pay the minimum wage. Without a functioning union there is not much that can be done to ensure that companies abide by the law.

34 According to a MOLISA official in Hanoi, 1999.

35 See, for example, "Project on Women Workers' Rights", Vietnam General Confederation of Labour, Women's Department, 1998.

36 For example, in an interview with MOLISA Vice Minister Le Duy Dong, Hanoi, August, 1999.

37 Nguyen Van Tu, "On the Renovation of Trade Unions' Organization and Activity in Order to Build and Defend the Fatherland and Care for and Protect Workers' Interests", 1993, p. 6.

38 VGCL Law Department, *Tinh Hinh Dinh Cong Cua Nguoi Lao Dong Trong Cac Nam 1995–1998, Va Mot So Kien Nghi, Giai Phap* [The Real Situation on Strikes in the Years 1995–1998, Proposals and Solutions], 27 April 1999.

39 See, for example, "Investment by Province as of February 10, 1998." *Vietnam Investment Review*, no. 332, 23 February–1 March, 1998.

40 Interviews indicate that there is more openness in the Ho Chi Minh City area regarding the strikes and their causes and how to deal with them. Therefore the numbers for other regions may be higher than shown in the statistics.

41 This was emphasized by trade union officials I interviewed in 1999 at companies where there had been a strike.

42 All VGCL reports on strikes and other labour disputes that I have accessed during this research exclude the SOEs in their discussions. If this sector is mentioned it is only very briefly and in general terms. None of the interviewees in the central VGCL organization has identified the strikes in SOEs as a pressing issue.

43 Only between VND 186,000 and 236,000 (about US$13–16) per month for 25–30 working days when the minimum wage is US$45.

44 *Strikes in 1999*, VGCL of Ho Chi Minh City.

45 The Labour Court system is a new and not yet well established institution in the labour management system. The labour court system and its workings were the focus of my fieldwork in Vietnam in late 2002 and will be discussed further in my forthcoming thesis.

46 The social insurance policy came into effect in 1994 and it is stated in the Labour Code that the employer and the employee are responsible for paying 15 per cent and 5 per cent respectively of the employee's wage to the Social Insurance Fund.

47 Inspection Report on the Labour Code Implementation in the Enterprises Located in the City During the First Seven Months of 1999. Ho Chi Minh City People's Committee, Labour Code Implementation Inspection Delegation, No: 1897/SLD/KTBLLD, Ho Chi Minh City, 25 August, 1999.

48 All quotes come from interviews with eight of the striking workers in Hoc Mon, 1999. It is not the purpose of this paper to evaluate the veracity of the workers' alleged grievances. My objective is to examine how the VGCL responds to such a situation.

49 There were problems in the factory concerning labour contracts, which according to the law must be signed between the employer and the employee after three months. In this factory the managers had only signed contracts with the employees working in the office and for the chief of each production line.

50 Since strikes are frequently reported in the local media, VGCL officials have no basis for saying that do not exist.

[51] Interview with Tran Thanh Ha, Legal Expert in the Legal Department of the VGCL, 15 September, 1999.

[52] *Tinh Hinh Dinh Cong Cua Nguoi Lao Dong Trong Cac Nam 1995–1998.*

[53] Ibid.

[54] Chapter XIII, Articles 153–156 in the *Labour Code* (1994, as amended 2 April, 2002) on the rights, duties and obligations of trade unions.

[55] "Trade Union Organization Determined to Increase Membership in Economic Sector". VNA, Hanoi, September 2, 1999.

[56] Interviews with VGCL officials in Hanoi in 1994.

[57] See, for example, Vedi R. Hadiz, *Workers and the State in New Order Indonesia*, 1997.

[58] VGCL Central Executive Committee, "Political Report to the Eighth National Congress: Shortcomings, Weaknesses and their Causes", p. 19–20.

[59] Ibid.

[60] Ibid.

[61] Discussions with VGCL officials in Hanoi, August, 1999.

[62] VGCL Central Executive Committee, *Political Report to the Eighth National Congress.*

[63] Ibid.

References

BBC Monitoring World Media, January 22, 2001.

Beckman, Björn, Eva Hansson and Lisa Romàn (eds). *Vietnam: Reform and Transformation.* Stockholm: Center for Pacific Asia Studies, Stockholm University, 1996.

Beckman, Björn, Eva Hansson, and Anders Sjögren (eds). *Civil Society and Authoritarianism in the Third World.* Stockholm: Politics of Development Group (PODSU), 2001.

Bernhard, Michael. "Civil Society and Democratic Transition in East Central Europe". *Political Science Quarterly* 108, no. 2 (1993).

Bring, Ove, Christer Gunnarsson and Anders Mellborn. *Vietnam—Demokrati och mänskliga rättigheter. En rapport på uppdrag av sida.* [Vietnam—Democracy and Human Rights]. Stockholm: Utrikespolitiska Institutet, 1998.

Cohen, Jean and Andrew Arato. *Civil Society and Political Theory.* Cambridge, Massachusetts and London: MIT Press, 1995.

Edwards, Andrew. "A Different Kind of Freedom". *Far Eastern Economic Review,* March 29, 2001.

Fforde, Adam. "Light Within the ASEAN Gloom? Vietnam's Economy since the Asian Financial Crisis". In *Southeast Asian Affairs 2002,* edited by Daljit Singh and Anthony Smith. Singapore: ISEAS, 2002.

The Constitution of the Socialist Republic of Vietnam. Hanoi: The Gioi, Foreign Languages Publishing House, 1992.

Freedom House. "Freedom of the World, 2000–2001, Vietnam", <www. freedomhouse. org>.

Hadiz, Vedi R. *Workers and the State in New Order Indonesia*. London: Routledge, 1997.

Hansson Eva. "Trade Unions and Doi Moi—The Changing Role of Trade Unions in the Era of Economic Liberalisation in Vietnam". Politics of Development Group, PODSU, no. 2 (1995).

———. "The Vietnam Railway Trade Union". In *Vietnam: Reform and Transformation*, edited by Björn Beckman, Eva Hassan and Anders Sjögren. Stockholm: Center for Pacific Asia Studies, Stockholm University, 1996.

Heng, Russell Hiang-Khng. "Media Negotiating the State: In the Name of the Law in Anticipation". In *Negotiating the State*, (Special Issue), *Sojourn* 16, no. 2 (October, 2001): 213–37.

Hewison, Kevin. "Political Opposition and Regime Change in Thailand." In *Political Opposition in Industrialising Asia*, edited by G. Rodan. London: Routledge, 1996.

Ho Chi Minh City Labour Federation, Board of Organisation. *Summary of Labour Disputes, 1995 and 1996*.

———, *Summary of Strikes in Ho Chi Minh City 1997*.

Ho Chi Minh City People's Committee, Labour Code Implementation Inspection Delegation. *Inspection Report on the Labour Code Implementation in the Enterprises Located in the City During the First Seven Months of 1999*, No: 1897/SLD/ KTBLLD, Ho Chi Minh City, 25 August 1999.

———, *Inspection Report on the Labour Code Implementation in the Enterprises Located in the City During the First Seven Months of 1999*, Ho Chi Minh City, 28 June, 1999.

Keane, John. *Civil Society: Old Images, New Visions*. Cambridge: Polity Press, 1998.

Kerkvliet, Benedict J. "An Approach for Analysing State-Society Relations in Vietnam", *Negotiating the State in Vietnam*, (Special Issue), *Sojourn* 16, no. 2 (October, 2001): 238–78.

Koh, David. "Negotiating the Socialist State in Vietnam through Local Administrators: The Case of *Karaoke* Shops". In *Negotiating the State* (Special Issue), *Sojourn* 16, no. 2 (2001): 279–305.

Labour Code of the Socialist Republic of Vietnam, 1994.

Labour Code of the Socialist Republic of Vietnam, 1994 (as amended 2 April 2002 and effective as of 1 January 2003).

Luckham, Robin and Gordon White. *Democratization in the South: The Jagged Wave*, Manchester and New York: Manchester University Press, 1996.

Nguyen Van Tu, "On the Renovation of Trade Unions' Organisation and Activity in Order to Building and Defending the Fatherland and to Caring for and Protecting Workers' Interests". In *The Report of the Executive Committee of the VGCL to the VII National Congress of Vietnamese Trade Unions*, (Official English translation by the VGCL), 1993.

Nørlund, Irene, "Democracy and Trade Unions in Vietnam: Driving a Honda in Slow Speed." Paper presented at the 48th meeting of American Association of Asian Studies, Chicago, March 13–16, 1997.

———, Survey of Working, Living and Trade Union Conditions in Foreign and Private Companies in Ho Chi Minh City and Da Nang. Textile Garment and Shoe Industries in Vietnam, Draft Report, Project between Vietnam General Confederation of Labour and the Norwegian Confederation of Trade Unions, Nordic Institute of Asian Studies, Copenhagen, 1999.

Pravda, Alex and Blair Ruble (eds). *Trade Unions in Communist States*. Sydney: Allen and Unwin, 1986.

Quan Xuan Dinh. "The Political Economy of Vietnam's Transformation Process". *Contemporary Southeast Asia* 22, no. 2 (2000): 360–88.

Rodan, Garry (ed.). *Political Opposition in Industrialising Asia*. London: Routledge, 1996.

The Trade Union Law of the Socialist Republic of Vietnam, 1990.

Tran Thanh Ha, *Nhinh Lai, Cac Cuoc Tranh ChapLao Dong Tap The—Dinh Cong Trong Cac Doan Nghiep Co Von Dau Tu Nuoc Ngoai Nhung Kien Nghi Va Giai Phap* [Review on Collective Labour Conflicts—Strikes in Foreign Invested Enterprises: Proposals and Solutions], Vietnam General Confederation of Labour, Hanoi, 1999.

U.S. Department of State. *1999 Country Reports on Human Rights Practices*. The Bureau of Democracy, Human Rights and Labour, U.S. Department of State, February 25, 2000.

Vasavakul, Thaveeporn. "Vietnam: *Doi Moi* Difficulties". In John Funston (ed.) *Government and Politics in Southeast Asia*. Singapore: ISEAS, 2001.

Vietnamese Experience—The Trade Union Movement in Vietnam. Hanoi: Foreign Languages Publishing House and Vietnam Federation of Trade Unions, 1988.

Vietnam General Confederation of Labour. "Shortcomings, Weaknesses and their Causes". Vietnam General Confederation of Labour Central Executive Committee Political Report to the Eighth National Congress, Hanoi, November 5–6, 1998, (unofficial translation).

———. "Political Report to the Eighth National Congress". Hanoi, November 5–6, 1998, (unofficial translation).

———. *Phu Luc III: Doan Vien Cong Doan Va Cong Doan Co So Nghiep Doan Den Thang 6 Nam 1999* [Trade Union Membership and Vocational Grassroots Trade Unions up to June 1999].

———. "View Exchange Sheet on Training Trade Union Officers in the Non-state Economic Sector", 1999.

———. *Tong Hop Dinh Cong 9 Thang Dau Nam 1999* [Statistics on Strikes First 9 Months of 1999], 1999.

Vietnam General Confederation of Labour, Law Department. *Tinh Hinh Dinh Cong Cua Nguoi Lao Dong Trong Cac Nam 1995–1998, Va Mot So Kien Nghi, Giai Phap* [The Real Situation on Strikes in Years 1995–1998, Proposals and Solutions], Tham luan cua Ban Phap luat TLDLDVN, 27/4/1999 [A Reference Note by the VGCL Law Department, 27 April, 1999].

Vietnam General Confederation of Labour, Women's Department. *Project on Women Workers' Rights*, 1998.

Vietnam General Confederation of Labour in Ho Chi Minh City. *Strikes in 1999*.

———. *Tong Hop Dinh Cong 9 Thang Dau Nam 1999* [Statistics on Strikes First 9 Months 1999].

Vietnam Investment Review, 30 May–5 June, 1994.

Vietnam Investment Review, 25 February–1 March, 1998.

VNA. "Trade Union Organisation Determined to Increase Membership in Economic Sector", Hanoi, 2 September, 1999.

Walzer, Michael. "The Civil Society Argument". In *Dimensions of Radical Democracy: Pluralism, Citizenship, Community*, edited by Chantal Mouffe. London and New York: Verso, 1992.

6

The Relationship between Civic and Governmental Organizations in Vietnam: Selected Findings

Joerg Wischermann and
Nguyen Quang Vinh

For many years it was quite common, in the analysis of the Vietnamese political system, for American and European political scientists to presuppose a mono-organizational model of state–society relations. This model is not or no longer appropriate. Current research on Vietnam indicates "that a multiplicity of changes is underway in this country" (Thayer 1995, p. 59). We do not want to discuss whether such models ever were appropriate for analyzing Vietnam's socio-political development. Nor do we want to speculate on whether there was much more local activity and scope for "everyday politics" in Vietnam in the 1960s and the 1970s than previously imagined, as Thayer put it (ibid., p. 59). Instead, we would like to offer some empirical evidence for the thesis that a remarkable diversification of social, political, and economic practices has taken place in Vietnam since the official start of the "policy of reform" (*doi moi*) in 1986. One of these is an impressive variety of different types of what we call Civic Organizations. In Spring 2000, our research team identified more than 700 Civic Organizations in Hanoi and Ho Chi Minh City.[1]

We use the label Civic Organizations as a general term for a heterogeneous ensemble of non-state, voluntary, non-profit-oriented societal organizations (See also chapter 1). Within this set, we differentiate between Mass Organizations, Professionals' Associations, Issue-Oriented Organizations, and Associations of Businessmen/women.[2] We include even such organizations that many scholars call "Government-Run-and-Inspired Non-governmental Organizations" (GRINGOS), and hybrid organizations that function in a dual mode and are "amphibious", to use Ding's term, (Ding 1994, p. 298).[3] We do not presuppose specific relationships between these Civic Organizations and Governmental Organizations, but leave this issue open for discovery in the process of our empirical research. The organizations we analyze are "civic" in their concern for articulating interests and affecting policy (Diamond 1999, p. 265), but they are not necessarily "civic" in the way Putnam puts it.[4] All of them enjoy at least some leeway in pursuing their respective activities. Box 1 in the appendix provides an impression of the variety of Civic Organizations in Hanoi and Ho Chi Minh City. This box also includes examples of our classification of these organizations.

Our understanding and classification of Civic Organizations in Vietnam is based on a taxonomy reached using empirical and inductive methods as well as on the results of our own research, which began a couple of years ago.[5] Its focal point is research seeking to answer the following questions: Why and how do Civic Organizations in Vietnam come into being? What are their structural characteristics? How do Governmental Organizations react to the emergence of Civic Organizations and how do Governmental Organizations and Civic Organizations interact? What are the different modes in the relationships between Governmental Organizations and Civic Organizations and what are the various roles that have developed within these relationships? Upon which factors do modes of interaction between Civic Organizations and Governmental Organizations depend on? The empirical stage of the research was organized in two phases: after the identification of 706 Civic Organizations, two teams of Vietnamese interviewers under the guidance of Prof. Bui The Cuong (National

Centre for Social Sciences and Humanities, Institute of Sociology, Hanoi), Mr Nguyen Quang Vinh, Sociologist (then head of the Centre for Sociology and Development at the National Centre for Social Sciences and Humanities, Institute of Social Sciences in Ho Chi Minh City) and Dr Joerg Wischermann (Freie Universitaet Berlin), carried out standardized interviews with 257 representatives of different sorts of Civic Organizations in Hanoi (133 organizations) and Ho Chi Minh City (124 organizations) between June and August 2000.[6] In the second phase of the empirical research, in-depth interviews with 50 representatives of selected Civic Organizations and Governmental Organizations were carried out between April and June 2001. In addition, in March 2002 two workshops were held in Hanoi and Ho Chi Minh City. These workshops focused on the presentation of the most important empirical findings of the project and the discussion of the results with Vietnamese scholars and representatives of Vietnamese Civic Organizations.

Our research approach is inspired by different theories, with particular consideration for so-called mid-range theories, which are put into use at different levels:

- On *a macro-sociological level* we refer to general patterns of societal change and we make use of selected parts of "Modernization Theory". We will elaborate further on this theory.
- On a *meso-level* we focus on the impact of political-administrative institutions, specific policies, informal procedures and strategies. Besides this, we ask about the importance and availability of resources such as trained personnel and funding for collective action. Here our analysis is inspired by mid-range theories such as "Political Opportunity Structures Approach" and "Resource Mobilization Approach", respectively. We will also elaborate on such approaches.
- On a *micro-level* we analyze the importance of individual motivations and reasons, and pertinent orientations and attitudes of different actors for establishing Civic Organizations, and their relationships with Governmental Organizations and officials. Here we refer to various socio-psychological and other concepts that focus on processes of changes in values (in the broadest sense). But this part of our research is still in its initial stages. Our next project will concentrate on such questions.

The single components of the different approaches we apply to our research are mutually supportive of each other. In our view their combination offers a noteworthy explanatory capacity.

Due to space limitations further explanations are offered below only in respect to some of the basic assumptions of our research and as regards three of the theoretical approaches used on the macro and the meso-levels, respectively, of our study.

Part and parcel of our research approach is the assumption that the emergence and development of Civic Organizations in Vietnam, as in other countries undergoing processes of transition, are closely interwoven with processes of social structural change. We use selected parts of different strands of Modernization Theory as a general frame of reference to analyze and assess the influence of patterns of societal change on the birth and continuing existence of Civic Organizations. Our basic assumption is that Vietnam has been going through a fundamental process of societal change since the mid-1980s, triggered by economic change. Societal changes go along with processes of socio-political differentiation, manifesting themselves in socio-cultural changes (for example processes of "individualization" and a "change in values") *and* are linked with the appearance of new societal actors as well as with the search by well-established actors for new roles and tasks. The most important actors seem to be professionals and members of the intelligentsia. Concurrent with, and connected to, processes of social differentiation, the relationship between state and society changes, and new as well as old or well-established societal actors get (at least) some leeway for their respective purposes. We conceptualize Civic Organizations and their activities as well as their activists as protagonists of processes of societal, political and cultural change. Analyzing the successes they achieve, the obstacles they face, and studying concrete patterns in their relationships with Governmental Organizations, give us insight into some patterns in the overall change in the relationship between state and society. How this relationship develops in turn is an essential factor in the further economic, political and cultural development of Vietnam.

To analyze the impact of some of the political conditions, we focus on a comparatively small set of properties of the political-administrative system: its *formal structure* and its *informal institutional structure,* and *informal procedures and strategies.*[7] Concerning the *formal structure* for example, we assumed that an examination of the impact of "signals" (to use Tarrow's term) is useful. Signals are information expressing the degree of openness of the formal system; for example, laws, decrees and other legal provisions issued by the central and/or local Government may encourage professionals and members of the intelligentsia to establish specific groups. In addition, an appraisal of the state's policy-implementation capacity is necessary and instructive. Finally we take into account the impact of "state tradition" (i.e. how central a role the state should play and which areas of life are the state's responsibility). All things considered, we have come up with the assumption that in the case of Vietnam, there is on the one hand a strong tradition of "statism", especially in the North (seen here as a specific form of state tradition). But, on the other hand, the Vietnamese state neither had nor has had unrestrained capacity to implement policies for much of the period after 1945. Since policy-implementation capacity may vary not only over a period of time, but also in respect to regional and other differences, this constellation might be responsible for different relationships between (different types of) Civic Organizations and Governmental Organizations in different parts or regions of the country.

Besides "opportunities" they can make use of, Civic Organizations need at least a minimum of organization and they need resources to develop collective action and to pursue their goals. Resources can be money, engaged and trained personnel, time or other useful sorts of "input". Here it is not necessary to go into the details of the Resource Mobilization Approach that we are referring to here.[8] It is sufficient to assume that organizational capacity and resources are supportive to the development of Civic Organizations, and decisive for their relationship with Governmental Organizations.

Main Findings

The Variety of Civic Organizations

As mentioned above, we identified more than 700 Civic Organizations in both cities in Spring 2000. For the purpose of carrying out standardized interviews (the first stage of our survey) random samples were drawn out of all the subgroups in Hanoi and out of the subgroup of the Issue-Oriented Organizations based in Ho Chi Minh City (for how the random samples were drawn, see Box 2 in the appendix). Since the number of representatives of Mass Organizations, Professionals' Organizations and

Associations of Businessmen/women based in Ho Chi Minh City was not too big, all representatives of these organizations could be interviewed there. For the additional 50 in-depth interviews (the second stage of our survey) representatives of 50 Civic Organizations were drawn randomly out of the total of the 257 Civic Organizations interviewed during the first stage of our research. All interviewed representatives of Civic Organizations were presidents, directors, chairpersons or at least deputies of these top officials. Table 1 in the appendix shows how the different sorts of Civic Organizations are distributed within the total of all organizations.

The distribution of the different kinds of Civic Organizations shows that in Hanoi there are more Mass Organizations and Professionals' Associations and less Issue-Oriented Organizations than in Ho Chi Minh City. In Ho Chi Minh City the proportion of Issue-Oriented Organizations is not only remarkably high, but it is only here that we were able to unearth a small but important group of Organizations of Businessmen/women.[9] The different distribution of various types of organizations, within as well as between the subgroups, might be seen as a first indication of some fundamental differences between the Civic Organizations in Hanoi and those in Ho Chi Minh City.

Timing and Motivations for Establishing Civic Organizations

The timing of establishment of Civic Organizations and the different reasons given by the interviewees for establishment reflect not only socio-political development after 1975 in general but also some major socio-political issues that developed in both cities after the start of the policy of reform. The motivations of the founders point towards political and professional interests, but also to very personal reasons. Furthermore, differences in timing of establishment exist between Hanoi and Ho Chi Minh City, and these differences point to key issues.

After the start of *doi moi* in 1986, Hanoi lagged behind Ho Chi Minh City in the establishment of new Civic Organizations, with a remarkable delay of at least 2–3 years (see the two histograms in the appendix, Figure 2). In Ho Chi Minh City more than four-fifths of all Civic Organizations existing in 2000 were set up after 1985. Closer examination of the foundation year shows different cycles in which different organizations were brought into being. First came the Mass Organizations, established to play a specific role in the newly established political system in the South. By the end of the 1980s nearly all Mass Organizations existed. On the other hand, most of the Professionals' Organizations sprang up between 1985 and 1995 (see appendix, Figure 3). One might conclude that their establishment was possible only after the basic structures of the new political system in the south, with the Mass Organizations as its major components, had taken shape.

Up to the point when the policy of *doi moi* became the official policy of the VCP (1986), Issue-Oriented Organizations hardly existed in the south. Nevertheless, the founders of these organizations obviously reacted slowly to the proclamation of a new policy; afterall, the "boom" of newly founded Issue-Oriented Organizations took place between 1990 and 2000. After a cautious beginning between 1985 and 1990, 50 new organizations sprang up in the 1990s, more in the first half of the decade than in the second half (see appendix, Figure 4).

The organizers of the Associations of Businessmen/women in Ho Chi Minh City were even more cautious than the founders of Issue-Oriented Organizations: most of these organizations were founded in the late 1990s. Under the existing political circumstances, the initiative to establish such organizations is commonly left to governmental agencies, which in this case (generally and after a while) reacted positively to pleas put forward by businessmen/women and (by and large and later) supported such foundations. Besides, the fact that such organizations came into existence relatively late may indicate a wait-and-see stance pursued by these professionals towards the government's economic policies.

In Hanoi, nearly a quarter of all (interviewed) Civic Organizations already existed before 1975. A bit less than half of all Mass Organizations and less than a third of all the Professionals' Organizations existed before the re-unification. Until 1986, no single Issue-Oriented Organization existed in Hanoi.[10] Similar to counterparts in Ho Chi Minh City, the founders of Issue-Oriented Organizations in Hanoi waited until the beginning of the 1990s before they cautiously began to establish new groups. But even then, the pace in Hanoi was slower than that in Ho Chi Minh City: most of the Issue-Oriented Organizations in Hanoi were founded after 1995 (see appendix, Figure 5). The rate of establishment of new Civic Organizations in Hanoi accelerated in the 1990s. Most of them were founded in the last five years of the twentieth century, with nearly a third of all Professionals' Organizations coming into existence between 1995 and 2000 (see appendix, Figure 6). During this period even new (branches of) Mass Organizations were founded on a significant scale.[11]

If the foregoing indicates that political conditions are important factors for establishment of Civic Organisations, then the interviews indicate otherwise. Only one-third of the representatives of Issue-Oriented Organizations in Hanoi and less than one-fifth of the representatives of such organizations in Ho Chi Minh City indicated that the economic, political and cultural conditions were favourable for what they intended to do. Why do representatives of the Issue-Oriented Organizations (especially those in the south), organizations that have been established mainly in the years of the *doi moi*, more or less deny that the political situation has been favourable for the establishment of such organizations and for what they intended to do?

- A first answer can be found in the high rates of assent found on this item by the Mass Organizations (in Hanoi) and the Professionals' Associations (in Hanoi and Ho Chi Minh City).[12] This bespeaks the fact that the political-administrative system, despite the reform policies, still works very much in favour of "established" organizations.
- Besides this, we have to take into account that up to the mid-1990s many of these organizations, especially those working in politically difficult fields, such as the fight against HIV/AIDS, faced a lot of difficulties. They had to spend a lot of time and effort endeavouring to convince authorities to give up outdated positions, and instead support the proposed agenda. In general it was not until the mid-1990s that the situation for the Issue-Oriented Organizations significantly improved, and this process came about slowly.
- A third explanation could be found by accepting a counter-assumption that "favourable conditions" are not decisive for up to 77.6 per cent of the founders of Issue-Oriented Organizations. Many strongly motivated, energetic and determined persons, regardless of whether the political circumstances were favourable, how long it took and how complicated the procedures were, established many of the southern small, welfare-oriented organizations. Other Issue-Oriented Organizations, especially those in research and consulting based in Hanoi, are obviously

more dependent on favourable conditions or they react more strongly to encouraging "signals" from the state, or both. We will return to this point in our conclusion.

As regards the *reasons and motivations* for establishing Civic Organizations, in Hanoi as well as in Ho Chi Minh City, a majority of organizations point to their wish to participate in solving urgent social problems as the most important reason for establishing their respective organization.[13] But beyond this common ground there are more differences that are partly a result of the differentiation in tasks and functions among Civic Organizations. But there is one distinguishing feature which has nothing to do with such differences—it seems to be that the founders of Civic Organizations in Hanoi are more interested in influencing and changing policies than their Ho Chi Minh City counterparts. With this key difference, it could be said that the Civic Organizations in Hanoi are more politically motivated than their counterparts in the south. This conclusion can be drawn from the following facts.

- In the standardized interviews, the representatives of the Mass Organizations in Hanoi indicate that they were more or less politically motivated and oriented towards an improvement of the conditions of their members when they established their organization. In stark contrast, the representatives of the same organizations in Ho Chi Minh City point to other reasons motivating them to establish their organizations, such as improving cooperation between governmental organizations and Civic Organizations, and assisting those who need help.
- According to the data from the standardized interviews, the representatives of the Professionals' Associations in Hanoi point more strongly to political reasons for the foundation of their organization (an important reason for them was, for example, to offer alternatives to the existing policies) whereas their counterparts in Ho Chi Minh City seem to be less politically motivated, more socially minded. In addition they seem to be more in favour of a stronger promotion of their membership's interests than their northern counterparts. Besides this, in the in-depth interviews, the representatives of Professionals' Associations in both cities point to "classic reasons" for the foundation of such organizations.

They want to foster and protect the respective interests of their members; they want to change policies that are not favourable for the members of their organizations or for the organizations themselves; and they want support for their businesses (as far as business-related associations are concerned).

- Taking into consideration the results of the standardized interviews, the southern Issue-Oriented Organizations seem to be far less politically motivated. More or less politically motivated reasons appear and rank after reasons of public-spiritedness. In additional in-depth interviews with representatives of such organizations in the south, the founders of Issue-Oriented Organizations often refer to very personal reasons and experiences as the most important reasons for establishing an Issue-Oriented Organization (for example the experience of a difficult childhood). As an expression of such personal experiences, they want to contribute to the improvement of living conditions of a specific group of disadvantaged people (for example street children) or they want to contribute to a general improvement in social welfare. In sharp contrast, founders of such organizations in Hanoi point to policy interests (for example, the implementation of an energy saving policy by installing wind energy plants), and professional interests (professionals seeking to continue specific professional activities after retirement). Only after that (or in combination with the above-mentioned reasons) comes the intention to contribute something useful to the whole society or a particular group. For the representatives of Issue-Oriented Organizations in Ho Chi Minh City, an engagement in social welfare seems to be more of a practical and personal matter than a political issue.

We had earlier noted one particular common motivation for establishment of Civic Organizations was "to participate in solving urgent social problems" (found in the standardized interviews). The Association of Businessmen/women in Ho Chi Minh City, however, put more weight on other motivations. For them the most important reasons were the wish to offer alternatives to the existing policies and to see urgent problems solved. It does not seem to be far-fetched to assume that by "urgent" problems the interviewees mean economic problems. The Associations of Businessmen/women in Ho Chi Minh City offer a clear-cut and reasonable bundle of motivations that universal organizers of such organizations commonly have. Their emergence can be seen as related to *doi moi* policy, which allowed private businesses and exposed business people to economic management problems. Accordingly, nearly half of the interviewed representatives of the organizations of businessmen and businesswomen indicated that economic, political and cultural circumstances were favourable for what they intended to do.

Organizational Structure and Funding Sources

Civic Organizations based in Hanoi tend to operate nationwide as well as at the city level. The Civic Organizations in Ho Chi Minh City are predominantly locally active organizations. The number of Civic Organizations in Ho Chi Minh City may be large, but their respective sizes, however, are not. Civic Organizations in Ho Chi Minh City, especially the Issue-Oriented Organizations, tend to be closely connected to grassroots-level initiatives by ordinary people and members of the intelligentsia. These organizations, especially those established in the 1990s, are flexible, dynamic and small, and they restrict their activities to Ho Chi Minh City (or the different political-administrative levels that determine the geographical scope of their activities).

In both cities, all types of Civic Organizations have a high percentage of full-time staff members, but the organizations based in Hanoi have a much higher percentage of full-time staff members than those in Ho Chi Minh City (75.6 per cent compared to 59.4 per cent). A very interesting comparison is that in Ho Chi Minh City many more Civic Organizations have volunteer staff members than in Hanoi (26.9 per cent compared to 12.7 per cent). As regards the social background of staff members in Civic Organizations, the number of people coming from the state apparatus is relatively high in Mass Organizations in both cities (an average of 21.9 persons per unit in Hanoi; 17.1 persons per unit in Ho Chi Minh City). The existence of professional or semi-professional social workers in the structure of staff members has a very important meaning in terms of the capabilities of Civic Organizations to mobilize social capital for developmental works. On average, each Civic Organization in Ho Chi Minh City has two staff members with this specific social background (the respective data in Hanoi is 0.2) (see appendix, Table 2).

Many staff members of the Vietnamese Civic Organizations are members of the "intelligentsia". When asked, an average of 9.42 staff members per organization in Hanoi and 8.24 staff members per organisation in Ho Chi Minh City indicate that they are part of the "intelligentsia". Working for Civic Organizations seems to be especially attractive for academics. For example, social scientists in Hanoi like to work for Issue-Oriented Organizations, and natural scientists in Ho Chi Minh City like to work for Professionals' Associations.

Figures referring to the age structure of staff members disclose that in general those working for Civic Organizations in Hanoi are younger than those working for such organizations in Ho Chi Minh City. In Hanoi, staff members who are 30 years old and under make up 28.9 per cent of the total, while in Ho Chi Minh City they constitute only 16.1 per cent. And this trend is even stronger in the next subgroup, which is the group of staff members between 31 and 49 years of age (in Ho Chi Minh City 54.6 per cent of the staff members are in this age group, in Hanoi only 40.3 per cent). In Ho Chi Minh City's Mass Organizations, as much as 66.3 per cent of the staff members are in this category.

As regards the question of sex/gender of the staff members, our figures show that women play a relatively important role. The general proportion of men/women as staff members of Civic Organizations is 47.2 to 52.8 per cent in Hanoi, whereas in Ho Chi Minh City the respective percentages are 53.2 to 46.8 per cent. Female staff members also make up the majority in the Issue-Oriented Organizations in Hanoi (62.5 per cent) and in Ho Chi Minh City (57.3 per cent). However, men dominate the staff structure in the other subgroups namely Professionals' Associations in both cities (Hanoi: 63.6 per cent; Ho Chi Minh City: 78.3 per cent), in the Mass Organizations (60.2 per cent) and in the Associations of Businessmen/women of Ho Chi Minh City (77.0 per cent).

In both cities, Civic Organizations that have registered members account for more than 60.0 per cent of the total (Hanoi: 63.6 per cent; Ho Chi Minh City: 61.7 per cent). An overwhelming majority of these organizations accept only "selected people" as registered members. Those organizations have their own criteria for selecting (and sometimes putting on probation) people who share the objectives of the organization and apply to join the unit. However, some 46.0 per cent of Ho Chi Minh City's Issue-Oriented Organizations accept "everybody" who wants to participate as an ordinary member. This phenomenon may reflect a certain open-mindedness of the people leading these organizations, a participatory approach in respect to the broader public as well as to the target groups—an approach suitable for tackling the difficult problems in the field of charity work and in the fight against social vices.

The examination of internal decision-making unveils specifics concerning the influence the membership, the staff and the target groups have in the making of various decisions. In the case of Civic Organizations based in Hanoi, the board has a very important role (45.9 per cent) and after that the chairperson (32.3 per cent) has a say in major decisions. The general assembly of the organizations in Hanoi is also relatively important (Professionals' Associations: 25.0 per cent; Mass Organizations: 20.0 per cent). In Ho Chi Minh City's Civic Organizations, the chairman/woman has a greater say than the board (39.8 per cent compared with 28.5 per cent). The board, however, has a dominant voice in the Associations of Businessmen/women (80 per cent). Our assumption is that the decisions made by this kind of association are closely and directly related to and aimed at the furthering of the (mainly economic) interests of businessmen and women. The chairperson must share his/her decision-power with the board, which is elected by all the members.

A certain diversification of the process of decision-making can be observed in the case of Ho Chi Minh City-based Issue-Oriented Organizations. Only in these organizations does the staff have a certain say in decision-making. The extent "differ(s) as the case arises" and "decisions arise out of general discussion and debate". Having to deal with complicated social problems, the decision-making processes of these organizations have to be more flexible, more adapted to difficult societal conditions and adequate for complex problem structures. Thus, decision-making processes are rather horizontal in nature. The counterparts of this group in the north show a similar pattern of diversification.

Funding and maintaining an annual budget is very important not only for the operation and the development of the Civic Organization, but also for the consolidation of its independence and the possibility of its exerting power as a societal actor. Our findings show that an overwhelming majority (Hanoi: 81.2 per cent; Ho Chi Minh City: 97.6 per cent) of Civic Organizations have their own annual budgets, which are collected from different sources. Where does the money and other kinds of funding come from? In Hanoi, the Civic Organizations first indicate membership fees (60.2 per cent), then sponsorship by government agencies (57.9 per cent), followed by fees for services provided (47.4 per cent), funding from foreign partners (41.4 per cent), with donations from domestic sources coming last (35.8 per cent). In Ho Chi Minh City the funding structure is a different one: fees for services provided is at first place (41.4 per cent), then come the donations from domestic sources (37.9 per cent), followed by sponsorship by government agencies (36.3 per cent), membership fees (35.3 per cent), and funding from foreign partners coming in last (29.0 per cent). Although the distribution of these different sources differs somewhat in respect to the various types of organizations in both cities, we would make an off-hand assessment that the scheme of the distribution indicates a certain balance between different sources. "Balance" means that most or even all kinds of sources of funding have been mobilized. In our survey, the data show that all types of organizations mobilize support from diverse sources.[14]

Many authors have criticized the fact that many Civic Organizations in "developing countries" are dependent on financial resources from the "developed countries". In Vietnam however the situation is different. Only one type of organization in one city—the Issue-Oriented Organizations in Ho Chi Minh City—indicates that financial sources from foreign donors are the most important funding resource. But these Issue-Oriented Organizations in Ho Chi Minh City nevertheless evidence a structure of resources that is well-balanced between private donors, foreign partners, governmental sponsorship, and fees for services. One can assume that it may be seen as a first step towards what Hudock calls a "sustainable financing strategy", which should give such organizations a greater autonomy over their programs (Hudock 1999, p. 98).

The figures in the category "most important funding resources" of Civic Organizations show that governmental sponsorship and fees for services provided are at the top of the list for Mass Organizations (see appendix, Table 3).[15] These two sources are also the most important sources for the Professionals' Associations. A very interesting difference in respect to the most important funding sources can be observed in the case of the Issue-Oriented Organizations in the two cities. In Hanoi, these organizations indicate that their most important resources are "fees" and (less important) "funding from foreign partners". The clear-cut priorities seem to indicate a certain dependence on fees for services provided. There is a certain danger of commercialization here, but according to our recent in-depth interviews, this danger has not manifested itself. As mentioned above, Issue-Oriented Organizations in Ho Chi Minh City have a more diversified pattern. The different extent to which the different types of organizations (are able to) make use of different resources leads us to the thesis that these differences indicate the respectively different opportunity structures are available to a given type of organization. For example, Ho Chi Minh City based Issue-Oriented Organizations can take more advantage of certain traditions such as that of private donations to either charities or other social welfare organizations.

The Relationship between Civic and Governmental Organizations

General Assessment

As mentioned in the introduction, the form and content of interaction between Civic Organizations and Governmental Organizations may demonstrate how the relationship between state and society in Vietnam is undergoing change. Civic Organizations can be seen as protagonists in the process of social, political and cultural change. But before we examine the general findings concerning this relationship we have to refer to some quite remarkable differences concerning the different levels of this interaction.

We have mentioned that Civic Organizations in Ho Chi Minh City prefer to work on the local level, in contrast to their counterparts in Hanoi, who prefer to work on the national level. It is no wonder that almost no Civic Organizations in the former city indicate that they have contacts with governmental agencies at the national level, and that about two-thirds of them have contacts with governmental agencies at the municipal level. The Civic Organizations in Ho Chi Minh City obviously concentrate their activities on local problems and issues, and accordingly confine their contacts with governmental agencies to those of the city. About one-third have contacts with governmental organizations at district or ward level. In Hanoi, 50.4 per cent of the Civic Organizations have contact with governmental agencies at the national level, less than one-fourth of them interact with Governmental Organizations at the municipal level, and less than a fifth communicate with state agencies at the district or ward level.

In general the representatives of interviewed organizations in both cities tend to assess their relationships with Governmental Organizations as being unproblematic rather than as being burdened with conflict. More than half of the interviewed representatives in Hanoi and two-thirds in Ho Chi Minh City classify their relationships with Governmental Organizations as "easy". Only a quarter of interviewees in Ho Chi Minh City and a third of interviewees in Hanoi indicate having problems with Governmental Organizations. While we may not compare the Business Organizations in Ho Chi Minh City with Business Organizations in Hanoi, it is worth mentioning that nearly two-thirds of the interviewed Businessmen/women Associations' representatives classify the relationships between their organizations and the Governmental Organizations as "easy" (see appendix, Table 4).

The Mass Organizations, the Professionals' Organizations and the Issue-Oriented Organizations indicate to different extents the ease in working with governmental agencies. The Mass Organizations indicate the highest percentage (Hanoi: 68.6 per cent; Ho Chi Minh City: 84.6 per cent), while Issue-Oriented Organizations indicate the lowest percentage (Hanoi: 37.0 per cent; Ho Chi Minh City: 60.0 per cent). Professionals' Associations are somewhere in between (Hanoi: 67.3 per cent; Ho Chi Minh City: 70 per cent). Because Mass Organizations are considered important organizations within the political system of the country, they take a particular position towards Governmental Organizations and have advantages as regards their work with governmental agencies. The same can be said in respect to major parts of the Professionals' Associations.

The Civic Organizations that say "sometimes there are problems" with Governmental Organizations hardly make up more than a fourth of the total in Ho Chi Minh City, and over a third in Hanoi. These data indicate that although sometimes there are difficult relationships between Civic and Governmental Organizations, the main tendency of these relationships is not a negative one. This general context should be kept in mind when the respective data concerning the Issue-Oriented Organizations are further examined. The Issue-Oriented Organizations of both cities indicate their having more problems with Governmental Organizations than with other types of Civic Organizations: 35.7 per cent of the Issue-oriented Organizations in Ho Chi Minh City and 52.0 per cent of these organizations in Hanoi indicate that "sometimes there are problems" in their relationships with Governmental Organizations.

There are multiple reasons for the emergence of "problems" between Civic Organizations and Governmental Organizations. Working in a sensitive field seems to be one reason. If we single out those Issue-Oriented Organizations of Ho Chi Minh City engaged in sensitive fields such as the fight against "social vices", we can easily detect that these organizations have more "problems" with Governmental Organizations than other organizations of the same type. Almost every second one of these organizations refers to problems with Governmental Organizations (41.4 per cent)—in comparison: this percentage is one and a half times the percentage of all Civic Organizations in the city that indicate they "have problems" within this relationship.

In Hanoi the percentage of Civic Organizations that indicate having "problems" in their interaction with Governmental Organizations is even higher than in Ho Chi Minh City. Again it is the group of Issue-Oriented Organizations, which has problems with Governmental Organizations, but in this specific case it is not the organizations engaged in the fight against "social vices". On the contrary, the subgroups of Issue-Oriented Organizations (56.5 per cent), which offer a whole variety of services, indicate relatively more trouble. What explanations might be given for the high degree of problems in the relationship between this specific cluster of Civic Organizations and Governmental Organizations in Hanoi? We will return to this question in a general way in the next section of our paper, but we would like to mention here some assumptions based on psychological, social psychological and cultural postulations that have arisen out of discussions among the researchers as well as between the researchers and representatives of Civic Organizations:[16]

- It could be assumed that in general staff members in Hanoi tend to react more sensitively to problems within these relationships. Many of them are members of the intelligentsia. They enjoy a high social status and they are used to getting things done according to their wishes and aspirations. They may react with much disappointment and embarrassment when obstacles stand in their way. In addition, they might tend to have high expectations regarding the possibilities and means of the state to solve social and other problems.
- A further explanation could be seen in our assumption that a certain number of state officials in Hanoi are a bit less flexible due

to their experiences within the state apparatus, that they are less familiar with one or another new (social) problems arising out of the emergence of a market-oriented society, and less familiar with new ways to tackle those problems.

Major Modes of Relationships

In general the majority (Hanoi: 55.6 per cent; Ho Chi Minh City: 65.0 per cent) of the representatives of the Civic Organizations in both cities indicate a relatively high degree of independence. Less than a quarter indicate controlling and guiding of activities. Direct intervention in planned or ongoing activities is rare (less than 3 per cent). Data from interviews, however, indicate a general trend towards more controlling and guidance of the activities of Civic Organizations by Governmental Organizations in Hanoi. On the other hand, in Ho Chi Minh City the trend is towards more "independence" for Civic Organizations and less trouble between them and governmental agencies (see appendix, Table 5).

The empirical data disclose that Mass Organizations and Professionals' Associations enjoy a relatively high degree of independence (in the case of Mass Organizations in Hanoi: 48.6 per cent; in Ho Chi Minh City: 61.5 per cent), although a small number of them do indicate being subjected to guidance and control. Issue-Oriented Organizations enjoy quite a high degree of independence in their activities (52.2 per cent in Hanoi and 62.9 per cent in Ho Chi Minh City). However, when we examine (again) the subgroups among Issue-Oriented Organizations engaged in the fight against "social vices" in Ho Chi Minh City, we find that their representatives indicate a bit less independence than representatives of other Issue-Oriented Organizations in this city. The same pattern is also obvious in Hanoi when we analyze the subgroups of Issue-Oriented Organizations that offer services. They also claim less "independence" than others (only 47.8 per cent can work independently), and indicate a higher degree of "no pattern in the mode of relationships" (26.1 per cent). This remarkably high proportion of "no pattern in the mode of relationships" could be understood as an indicator for "less independence" if we work on the following assumption: if the representatives of such organizations cannot detect a clear pattern in the actions or reactions of the authorities, they may tend to refrain, at least temporarily, from certain activities. Insofar as a (self-imposed) restriction in respect to certain activities takes place, the organizations may actually enjoy, at least temporarily, "less independence" than other organizations of the same type. In any case, both sub-types of organizations seem to have more "problems" in their relationships with Governmental Organizations *and* they seem to attract Governmental Organization's attention to a degree.

In conclusion, we would like to put forward the thesis that there seems to be a tendency towards "easy" relationships between Civic Organizations and Governmental Organizations. Furthermore, the former enjoy a certain degree of independence that is curbed by the latter if there are sensitive issues implied or if other problems arise. We will return to such problems in the next section of our paper.

The Roles of Civic Organizations

Comparing the different roles that the representatives of Civic Organizations indicate they play, we come up with a somewhat surprising result. The responses do not indicate many differences in the roles indicated. Nor are the differences between the two cities deeply marked. In general the responses indicate a common understanding of the roles the Civic Organizations play within the political system. In both cities the role of "coordinator" comes first, second that of "implementer", third the (more political) role of "intermediary" (as reflector of societal concerns to political institutions) and fourth the role of "networker". At position five various forms of "partnership" dominate responses from Hanoi, whereas in Ho Chi Minh City "others" dominate this position. The response of various forms of "partnership" is convincing, as it goes together with that of "intermediary". The response of "supervisor" is at position six in both cities. The role of "innovator" is at seventh place in Ho Chi Minh City and at eighth place in Hanoi. The role of "advocate" (initiator of administrative or legislative reforms) takes last place in Ho Chi Minh City and next to the last in Hanoi (see appendix, Table 6).

Some other regional differences are worth mentioning. In general the understanding of the roles Civic Organizations play or have to play is slightly more uniform in the north. There it does not matter very much which type of organization the interviewees represent, for the frequencies and the order in which they put the respective roles do not differ significantly. The Mass Organizations and the Professionals'

Organizations share a very similar comprehension of their respective roles. Nor do the Issue-Oriented Organizations in the north fundamentally differ. In the south, differences are a bit more frequent. One of the most striking is the small number of Ho Chi Minh City-based Issue-Oriented Organizations claiming the role of "advocate". Only 1 out of 68 organizations in Ho Chi Minh City wants to play or sees itself playing this role. In Hanoi there is the quite remarkable number of 10 Issue-Oriented Organizations (out of 46) that indicate likewise. In comparison to their southern counterparts, a significant number of the Issue-Oriented Organizations in Hanoi seem to cling to a more political understanding of their work and they seem to prefer a more active role with a certain political dimension ("supervisor", "advocate"). In addition, nearly a quarter of the Issue-Oriented-Organizations in Hanoi also consider themselves to be "innovators". This understanding seems to be closely related to the original reason for the foundation of many Issue-Oriented Organizations in Hanoi, according to the data of the standardized interviews, many of them indicated that one reason for their establishment was to present alternative solutions for certain issues and problems.

In contrast, in Ho Chi Minh City more than 90 per cent of the Issue-Oriented Organizations repudiate such an understanding of their role. These organizations cling to their roles of "implementer" (38.8 per cent), "coordinator" (34.3 per cent) or "intermediary" (33.8 per cent). Rather than implying an overt stance to political issues, they prefer a conflict-minimizing, pragmatic interpretation of the activities, tasks and functions of their organizations. Such an understanding fits well with the down-to-earth interpretations of the problems such organizations face in the different fields of social welfare. In avoiding political predicaments, these organizations make it possible for themselves to tackle other problems even in sensitive areas.

Factors Affecting the Relationship

The following enumeration of factors that affect the relationship between Civic and Governmental Organizations does not pretend to summarize comprehensively the analysis above. Not listed in ranking order, these seven important factors (*objectives; activities; key persons; political connections; resources; issue-culture; state traditions*) emerge out of the different methods that we applied to our research. The first five factors are the outcome of the statistical analysis of the data of the standardized interviews with 257 interviewees; the other two factors could be found in the answers 50 interviewees gave in the second phase of the survey.

In general, from the practitioner's perspective, *objectives, activities, key persons,* and *political connections* are decisive factors for the development of the relationship between Civic Organizations and Governmental Organizations. But each of these four factors also impacts on different types of Civic Organizations in different ways. Take, for example, the factors, "connections to persons who bear high responsibility" and "key persons in the own organization". Both the Issue-Oriented Organizations and the Associations of Businessmen/women in Ho Chi Minh City indicated these factors as not being important. Their assessment reflects a certain distance of these organizations from Governmental Organizations in this city. This detachment may be a consequence of the fact that, in a hierarchical society, one must be a high-ranking person in order to have connections to persons who bear high responsibility. Neither of these two organizations has chairpersons who bear "high responsibility" either in the party or in the state administration. Thus, their opportunities to approach influential persons in the party or the state are limited. In contrast, the existence of "key persons in the own organization" has great importance for all the various organizations in Hanoi, even for the Issue-Oriented Organizations.

With respect to degree of easiness or difficulty, which type of relationship is correlated with which factor? Statistical methods give us some clues, but only with regard to the Mass Organizations and (to a certain degree) with respect to the Professionals' Associations. With respect to the Mass Organizations, in most cases all four factors are correlated with "easy" relationships. As regards the Professionals' Associations in many cases, the four factors are linked with "easy" relationships, but there are also some cases where factors like "key persons" and "activities" are associated with problematic relationships. One could state that "easy" relationships between Governmental Organizations and Mass Organizations and at least many Professionals' Organizations are supported by a common understanding of their objectives and activities, and fostered by good relations between state officials and leading personnel of the Mass Organizations and Professionals' Associations.

As regards the Issue-Oriented Organizations, at least from a statistician's point of view, the picture remains rather unclear (only in Ho Chi Minh City are the factors "activities" and "objectives" correlated with "easy" relationships). In respect to the Associations of Businessmen/women in Ho Chi Minh City, the analysis of data does not provide us with any clues about the impact the above-mentioned factors have on the relationship between these organizations and Governmental Organizations. Nevertheless, we would like to use these meagre results as a first hint supporting a thesis we will elaborate on later; that is, "easy" relationships between the Ho Chi Minh City-based Issue-Oriented Organizations and Governmental Organizations might be fostered by a common understanding or at least a tacit acknowledgement of the objectives and activities of such organizations by the state agencies. In Hanoi there seems to be a lack of such a common understanding at least with respect to the Issue-Oriented Organizations. This may cause problems in relationships between Governmental Organizations and Issue-Oriented Organizations. Not even the existence of "key persons" in such Issue-Oriented Organizations in Hanoi may help to overcome problems within these relationships. We will return to this thesis later on.

Despite the practitioners' claim that resources have no significant direct impact on the relationships with Governmental Organizations, we would argue that the availability of different resources has at least an indirect influence on the different roles taken by Civic Organizations and Governmental Organizations in relation to each other, and also on the modes of relationships that emerge. This conclusion of indirect influence can be drawn from two examples.

Let us first take the case of those Issue-Oriented Organizations in Hanoi (31 cases) that concentrate on various services (research, consulting, counselling, social welfare measures, charity, etc.) and have the organizational structure of "Centres". Most of them came into existence during a "boom" around the mid-1990s. Their relationship with Governmental Organizations is more strained than is the case with other Issue-Oriented Organizations. The modes of the relationships differ from other organizations in this group. These "Centres" are not allowed to work as freely and the percentage of those that indicate that the Governmental Organizations do not support some of their plan, is higher than is the case for other organizations of this type. Nevertheless these organizations see themselves more strongly than others in this group as "implementers", even as "partners" of Governmental Organizations, as "networkers", and as "innovators". These organizations also have the self-confidence to claim for themselves a bit more strongly than others the role of "advocate". If these "Centres" portray themselves as self-confident partners of governmental organizations, the basis of this self-confidence seems to be the resources they can rely on (even if the balance of different sources of funding is a very shaky one), which are the fees for the variety of services they provide. Or, as one interviewee put it when he elaborated on the reasons why his "Centre" can work independently: "We do not depend on anyone in funding!"[17] We tend to think that these "Centres" benefited from a certain phase of the reform policy, when it was possible to earn money and to get funded by providing a variety of services. These organizations thus enjoy more room to manoeuvre and hence are able to work as partners and "implementers" of governmental programmes and programmes funded by foreign agencies. These specific modes of funding are indispensable for this clearly stated, politically motivated self-understanding on the part of representatives of the "Centres".

A different case is a subgroup of Professionals' Associations in Hanoi (18 cases). They promote the interests of specific societal groups, or foster harmony with, and promote the efficiency of, governmental programmes (in which these specific Professionals' Associations are probably involved), or both.[18] As regards the most important resources, these Professionals' Associations rely heavily upon governmental sponsorship. Noteworthy is the fact that these Hanoi-based organizations have more problems than many other Professionals' Associations in their relationships with Governmental Organizations. Representatives of these organizations lament that they are significantly less independent in their work and are heavily controlled and guided in their activities by the Governmental Organizations. When they indicate playing the role of "implementers" and "networkers", these organizations seem to be in a more subordinated position and to be following "suggestions" from above. Most of them shy away from the role of "initiator of political reforms", but cling to the role of "intermediary"—even though there is strong evidence for the assumption that these organizations are limited in their ability to play this role adequately. In spite of the interviewees strongly denying the importance of the resources they are not in command of, or that they cannot mobilize, we would assume that this very factor is the most important in the respective relationship: these Professionals' Associations rely heavily on governmental sponsorship; they have no balance in the different sorts of funding resources.

It is mainly from the in-depth interviews that we have gained insight into the importance of the following two factors for the relationships between Civic Organizations and Governmental Organizations: *Issue–culture* (i.e., the dominant ways to deal with, for example, social problems) and *state tradition* (i.e., how central a role the state should play and which areas of life are the state's responsibility).

Issue-culture refers to different traditions and different experiences that bound city administrators when they handle governance issues. One important example can be found in the realm of social work. In Ho Chi Minh City "modern" or "westernized" practices and theories of social work are comparatively well known. In the 1950s, 1960s and 1970s, French and American programmes educated, trained, and influenced many groups and individuals (Sidel 1995, p. 3). The "tradition" of "modern" social work was kept alive through all the years after 1975, even at times when—officially—other ways of tackling social problems were preferred. It may be that this social work tradition has strengthened a certain public understanding of different or even alternative ways to tackle social problems. In addition, it might have helped state officials gain an adequate understanding of social problems. The north neither has such a tradition nor a similar widespread understanding of practices and methods of modern social work as a tool to deal with societal problems. We assume that such "traditions" and "experiences" may help to ease problems between societal and governmental organizations. Their absence may lead to more strained relations.

State traditions are a major factor in precipitating strained relations between both Issue-Oriented Organizations and Professionals' Organizations on the one hand and the Governmental Organizations on the other. This is especially so in Hanoi. The indication of there being a bias against non-state ("private") activities on the part of governmental officials, Governmental Organizations and Mass

Organizations runs through all interviews with the representatives of Hanoi-based Issue-Oriented Organizations like a thick red thread. (Representatives of Professionals' Associations from Hanoi report similar experiences.) Some interviewees indicate a general "lack of understanding", even a "prejudice" against their organization and its activities (not only at the time of founding, but also later on). Some point to the "ignorance" government officials show as regards Issue-Oriented Organizations and their activities, and some others criticize the unconcealed attitude of "non-cooperation" manifested in words or deeds by state officials. Other representatives of such organizations in Hanoi even report some nasty incidents when contacting government officials. Some indicate an unjustified preference for state organizations and state-owned enterprises when their organizations wanted to participate in biddings (for "Overseas Development Aid" or similar funded programmes and projects). Some state agencies and state-owned enterprises seem to perceive Issue-Oriented Organizations as competitors who need to be kept out of competition or at least kept under their thumb. Last, but not least, some of the interviewed representatives claim that there are state agencies that do not realize that some Civic Organizations are already conducting activities that should actually be carried out by Governmental Organizations. The idea that many government officials contribute to problems in the relationships between Governmental Organizations and Civic Organizations might be gathered from the following. In interviews, officials acknowledge that it took a long time before they understood not only the objectives of some Civic Organizations and the sense of some of their activities, but also the real power and the direction of some of these organizations.

Our impression is that even today many state officials neither clearly understand the activities of such organizations nor are they capable of appraising, for example, the new approaches some of these organizations are applying to their work. Nevertheless, state officials insist upon directing, guiding and controlling societal organizations. They insist on their right to approve any activity undertaken by organizations under their administration. Besides this, many officials seem to perceive Civic Organizations (especially those they are in direct control of) as an integral part of the implementation of state-led programmes and policies, incorporated into the state's administration and meant to fulfil specific tasks, administered by Governmental Organizations. Even more, Civic Organizations are seen as only temporarily necessary. This view of Civic Organizations is put in a nutshell by a People's Committee chairwoman (in Ho Chi Minh City). In her view, for example, poverty alleviation is a duty of the state and a problem which will be solved mainly by state-administered programmes at a given time: "The operation of societal organizations is just temporarily urgent!"

Despite the last quotation, "statism" seems to be less of a problem for Professionals' Associations and Issue-Oriented Organizations in Ho Chi Minh City. It is noteworthy that the representatives of such organizations ask for the state's financial and organizational support. They do insist on and point to the necessity of clear-cut roles and a common understanding of the tasks both "partners" have to carry out and they ask for regulations that are "in favour of Civic Organizations". But, compared to the Issue-Oriented Organizations, they do not ask as strongly for appreciation of their work and their organization by state organizations. Business Associations as well as Professionals' Associations report "easy" relations with Governmental Organizations due to a proper, reasonable and functional acknowledgment by the latter of their organizations and the activities they are undertaking. But problems arise if an association has difficulty defining its own role, identifying proper tasks to perform, organizing its work and internal procedures, or sorting out leadership problems. Under such circumstances, the relationships between State and Civic Organizations tend to sour. Most of the Issue-Oriented Organizations that have an "easy" relationship with Governmental Organizations have a similar clear-cut, but rather traditional, definition of the role they are meant to play, which this remark from one former representative of such an organization shows: "As long as we do charity work or our work is understood as charity work by the authorities, there is no problem."

Problems Faced by Civic Organizations

Here we would like to draw attention to the findings concerning the final question of the questionnaire used in the first phase of our survey. In this question we asked for a general assessment of achievements of the respective organizations as well as of the obstacles they have faced or still face. We were surprised upon analysis of the data at how many of the respondents had used this question as an opportunity to explain in full detail mainly the obstacles their organization face. Noteworthy is the sombre style in which the enumeration of problems was put forward as well as the concrete and positive mode of criticism in respect to unfavourable patterns in the relationship between Civic Organizations and Governmental Organizations. The main results are the following:

- Representatives of all different types of Civic Organizations indicate a lack of funding. Representatives of all different types of Civic Organizations indicate insufficient or no financial support for activities and salaries. In some cases the lack of funding is described as due to lack of access to additional funding resources. As a result of such a lack of financial means, the Professionals' Associations in Hanoi in particular indicate the existence of three "nos": "We have no telephone, no office space and no money to pay the staff!" In addition they lament their dependence on voluntary staff members to keep things going. Related to the problem of a shortage of funds seem to be that representatives of Professionals' Associations and Issue-Oriented Organizations (in both cities) lack office equipment, and reading material, training, and communication tools such as computers and faxes. In Hanoi, representatives of Professionals' Organizations and Issue-Oriented Organizations express their wish for basic support of their activities from the state.
- The interviewees indicate feeling a widespread lack of well-trained and experienced professionals ("cadres") to run the operations of the Civic Organizations, to plan further activities, and to develop new fields of activities. Possibilities for (additional) training and education for staff members would be highly appreciated by all types of Civic Organizations. Representatives of Issue-Oriented Organizations in Hanoi criticize state agencies for offering additional or further training and education classes mainly to cadres of Mass Organizations, State-Owned Enterprises and Governmental Organizations. Representatives of Mass Organizations in Hanoi specified that many of their cadres are not specialized enough for the assigned

task, that the field they have to work in is too all-encompassing, and that many of the cadres are too old.

- Representatives of the Mass Organizations also mention a difficulty in attracting new and young members (under 30 years of age).
- Representatives of Professionals' Associations in Ho Chi Minh City criticize their own members for a lack of "consciousness". They indicate that a significant number have no clear idea of their Association's mission, its problems, and its potential for ameliorating the situation of its members.
- Professionals' Associations and Issue-Oriented Organizations especially indicate problems with the existing legal provisions regulating their work. On the one hand there is a lack of regulations, on the other hand there are too many regulations. In addition there are problems with the implementation of existing regulations.
- (a) As one representative of an Issue-Oriented Organization in Hanoi put it: "The state takes too much time to change its policy. Up to now there has not been a comprehensive regulation system that lets Civic Organizations take part more and more in solving problems, a need in reality."
- (b) Representatives of Ho Chi Minh City-based Professionals' Associations criticize that the administrative procedures for obtaining permission to receive and use funds from abroad are too complicated and are a waste of time and personnel for small organizations.
- Many representatives of Professionals' Organizations and of Issue-Oriented Organizations in both cities indicate a lack of recognition by Governmental Organizations of their activities and the missions they fulfil. This lack of recognition is not only a problem articulated by "newcomers" coming from the ranks of the Issue-Oriented Organizations, but is also strongly pointed out by well-established Professionals' Organizations such as the Association of the Blind, the Association of Linguistics and the Association of the Lawyers (all based in Hanoi). An insufficient appreciation of their work by the broader public is indicated by a representative of an Issue-Oriented Organization (in Hanoi).
- With the exception of the Mass Organizations, the varied roles that different types of Civic Organizations can play within the

political-administrative system are not properly and clearly defined. This fuzziness correlates with the above-mentioned problem of recognition, but that is not all. In particular, some Professionals' Organizations have difficulties determining their distinctive tasks and functions or developing a proper internal organizational structure. Concomitant with these problems of the exact definition of their own role is a deterioration in performance and a dissatisfaction within the membership, causing members to leave the organization and making it difficult to attract new ones. But this is also a familiar problem among the Associations of Businessmen/women in Ho Chi Minh City: "Most of the (business-related) Unions do not have a clear operational system or a identifiable role, functions and tasks," indicates one representative of an Association of Businessmen/women.

There is another problem that can be easily detected by analyzing the statistics of newly founded Issue-Oriented Organizations in both cities. In 2000/2001 there was a steep decline in such organizations. This downturn could be related to a trend characterized by the tendency of especially young, well-educated people to join the ranks of the well-established Vietnam branches of international agencies such as the World Bank, Asian Development Bank, and United Nations Development Program, instead of founding organizations of their own. This is in no way surprising, since such organizations offer much better working conditions, higher salaries, certain social security standards and, if all goes well, even chances of being promoted to higher ranks and better jobs.

Conclusion

At present, Vietnam has a whole variety of different types of Civic Organizations. Besides well-known Mass Organizations and Professionals' Associations, Issue-Oriented Organizations and Associations of Businessmen/women also exist. Their large number and variety are empirical evidence for the thesis of an increasing diversification of social, economic and political practices in Vietnam. The different modes and roles arising out of the relationships between Civic Organizations and Governmental Organizations are also understandable as a first and preliminary verification of two of our basic assumptions. First, the "modernization" of Vietnamese society and the ongoing processes of societal change are resulting in the emergence of new social actors and the renewal of existing ones. Both can be seen as protagonists of these processes of change. Second, the complex process of societal change implies an opening of some political space that the Civic Organizations can make use of.

The following conclusions should shed some light on the relationship between societal change and the emergence and development of Civic Organizations in Vietnam. In addition, we would like to review the impact of political conditions on the nature of the relationships between Civic and Governmental Organizations.

First, the main objectives pursued by the different types of Civic Organizations in both cities show that these organizations respond to a variety of societal problems. Their fight against social problems, the use of social work practices combating domestic violence, the offer of training and education classes free of charge, the establishment of public health care projects, the creation of jobs and income for poor people and especially for women by credit and savings groups, and many other activities, all point to the fact that there is a widening gap between desperate societal needs and what the state and the economy can provide. Civic Organizations fill this gap and they are filling it in very specific ways. With some characteristic differences between the contributions of Civic Organizations in Hanoi and those in Ho Chi Minh City.

Second, among the most striking findings of the survey are the differences between Civic Organizations based in Hanoi and those in Ho Chi Minh City. These differences exist in and between the different types of organizations and their subgroups, in both cities. We put forward the thesis that these organizations express the particular economic, political and cultural conditions prevailing in each of the two cities. These conditions reflect the recent history of these cities. They bespeak the varying social, cultural, economic and political practices that have continued, notwithstanding different political systems.

Third, there is an obvious concurrence of the founding years of different types of Civic Organizations and "reform policy". This correlation may not be mere coincidence. Taking into account the empirical findings, the substantiation for such a cause-effect thesis exists, but only with the following qualification. Various policy reforms open "windows of opportunity", but the final outcome as to which actors and which organizations can make use of them, and how they react and what might be the result of these activities depends on a whole variety of different factors. These factors include the type of organization, the resources the actors are in command of, the objectives of the actors, and the activities they take part in. The policy of reforms does not have the same impact on all Civic Organizations.

Fourth, besides societal change as well as the continued existence of different economic, political and cultural conditions, some political-administrative institutions, specific policies, informal procedures and strategies have an impact on the emergence of certain types of Civic Organizations, and on their roles and activities and their relationships with Governmental Organizations. Here we would like to mention only one example. For those, who wanted to found Issue-Oriented Organizations that are engaged in the field of research, consulting and related services, two legal documents issued in January and November 1992 were positive "signals" (to use Tarrow's term) allowing the establishment of new organizations.[19] Thus, favourable legal provisions precipitated the first boom of such organizations in Hanoi during the mid-1990s. No such similar positive "signal" was given to those who wanted to found Issue-Oriented Organizations in the field of social work, public welfare, etc. at that time. In fact, most of the founders of such organizations, and here again we think of the founders of such organizations in Ho Chi Minh City, had to rely on their strengths: personal motivation, endurance and energy, and various kinds of resources (for example money and trained and educated staff members and supporters). Therefore it could be said that in respect to the "political opportunity structures" the policy of reform offers different conditions even for the establishment of the same type of Civic Organizations.[20]

But it is also possible that some Issue-Oriented Organizations, especially those in the south and especially those working in the field of social welfare, are not dependent on such conditions.[21] Their "independence" of political opportunities might be seen as a function of their general orientation ("charity"), their organizational structure (small, flexible, grassroots-oriented), how they perceive the structure of the problems their activity is focused on, and how they deal with these problems.

Fifth, there is a lack of common understanding of a proper division of work between Governmental and Civic Organizations. Some or even many state officials have no real understanding of what certain types of Civic Organizations are actually doing, which tasks could be carried out or are already being carried out by (which) Civic Organizations, which roles such organizations could play or are already playing, and which modes of relationships between Governmental Organizations and Civic Organizations are suitable so that such organizations can carry out their respective tasks and play their respective roles. We would like to put forward the thesis that there is a linkage between this lack of knowledge or comprehension and a still persistent statism. "Statism" and other "state traditions" are important factors, which might very well cause strained relations between some Civic Organizations and Governmental Organizations.

To put such a finding and its interpretation into a more practical and constructive perspective, we would like to refer to the recommendation most recently proposed by the World Bank in its Report, *Vietnam 2010: Entering the 21st Century*. The report highlights that, besides the importance of a "Law on Associations" and the issue of NGOs, "sensitization and capacity building of government officials that interact...with associations...need to be stepped up significantly, if these organizations are to fulfil their potential as partners to Government". There is also a need to build up the capacities of the Civic Organizations "in terms of organization, human capital, physical capital and financial resources in order to make the participation of society and communities effective", adds the report. We would like to suggest that the topic of a proper division of work between State and Civic Organizations and the form and content of fruitful cooperation between these two partners be included in any programme focusing on this "sensitization and capacity building of government officials".

Sixth, under the specific circumstances of a Vietnam in transition, the political context is of considerable importance for the mediation of processes of societal change—at least to a certain degree. In short, policies matter. Some of these policies encouraged the foundation of Civic Organizations and were much awaited by many of the founders of at least certain types of Civic Organizations. Some of the policies adopted were biased against certain types of Civic Organizations; other policies ignored the motivations and intentions of many founders of Civic Organizations. Nevertheless, many of these organizations did come into existence. But in many such cases the relationships between societal and state organizations became problematic.

In the light of this last observation we would like to close with the hope that further improvements of policies regulating the setting up and running of Civic Organizations will be aimed at facilitating the emergence of a full-fledged and diversified ensemble of Civic Organizations. Thus, cooperation between State and Civic Organizations would be strengthened and Civic Organizations would be able to contribute even more to the development of an equitable, fair, democratic, and civilized society in Vietnam.

Notes

We are grateful to Prof. David Marr and Dr David Koh for their comments on previous versions of this article. Additionally we would like to thank the Volkswagen Foundation. Without their generous financial support this research would not have been possible.

1 The 706 Civic Organizations were identified and located in different ways. In the case of Hanoi the research team could make use of such varied sources such as:

- lists (undated) from different state agencies which register or are responsible for different organizations (lists from the Ministry of Science, Technology and Environment, from the City's Department of Science, Technology and Environment, from the Bureau of the City's People Committee) and lists from Civic Organizations such as the "Union of Science and Technology Associations" and from various Mass Organizations;
- a list (undated) of local partners at the "NGO Resource Centre" in Hanoi, which contains organizations cooperating with the World Bank, UNDP and UNICEF;
- information from local newspapers (1998–99);
- information from local Civic Organizations (resource persons), and
- last, but not least, the (year 2000) telephone book of Hanoi proved to be an additional source of information, at least in order to locate an identified Civic Organization and check the information.

In the case of Ho Chi Minh City, there was only one list available for the research team, a list (date unknown) from the City's Department of

Labour, Invalids and Social Affairs, providing information in respect to those Civic Organizations cooperating with this department. A directory of societal organizations working in the field of social work (1999) provided by a centre of social workers proved to be very helpful. Besides these sources, the team in Ho Chi Minh City used the "snowball technique" to gather further information. Since both research teams have extensive knowledge of, and are familiar with, many of the Civic Organizations, the process of identification and location of such organizations proceeded smoothly.

The information provided by the research teams on the activities of most of the organizations in both cities as well as additional information gathered from other Vietnamese experts on the respective issues helped us to come up with the classification of Civic Organisations used in our survey.

The team in Hanoi had seven members: Prof. Bui The Cuong (head), Duong Chi Thien, Le Phuong, Dang Viet Phuong, Nguyen Thi Phuong, Dang Bao Khanh, and Bui Thanh Ha. The team in Ho Chi Minh City had 14 members: Prof. Nguyen Quang Vinh (head), Van Thi Ngoc Lan, Luu Phuong Thao, Tran Dan Tam, Quach Thu Cuc, Ton Tu Anh, Nguyen Thi Nhung, Nguyen Huu Tuc, Dao Quang Binh, Tranh Anh Tien, Do Tuan Linh, Nguyen Ngoc Anh, Van Ngoc Dung, and Le Ngoc Phuong.

2 There are a couple of good reasons to include the Mass Organizations into the ensemble of Civic Organizations. For one, although most of the Mass Organizations have been established, financed and guided by the state and the ruling Vietnamese Communist Party, the point is that these organizations are not administrative subdivisions and agencies of the state. Therefore, they can be seen as societal organizations rather than organizations of the state.

The problem of including such organizations into the ensemble of Civic Organizations, which are to varying degrees non-state in character, touches on the issue "where does the state 'end' and society 'begin', and vice versa" (Kerkvliet 2001, p. 239). Since the boundaries between state and society are blurred not only in Vietnam, it seems always to be problematic to locate one entity either here or there (ibid., p. 240). Here we would like to express our support for Kerkvliet's proposal to take into account the roles such entities play and tasks they carry out in different "arenas" which are arranged around different policy issues and include a range of institutions and a variety of "players", instead of applying the notion of a dichotomy of state and society. However, we would agree with Koh's statement, citing Kjeld Brodsgard and Susan Young, that a "notional separation" between state and society is "theoretically useful" (Koh 2001, p. 300).

3 Since our survey intended to focus on organizations with a minimum of organizational structure (for example, such organizations should have by-laws; a chairperson and/or a board should be elected on a regularly basis, etc.) we excluded informal organizations at least for the purpose of our survey.

4 For Putnam the key is whether or not associational life is structured horizontally so as to generate trust. For him, only horizontally structured organizations are civic organizations (Putnam 1993, 167; 173). Since we could not know if all the Vietnamese Civic Organizations would fulfill this standard of a democratic organizational life, we could not presuppose this characteristic—at least not in the definition and from the very outset of our project. That means that we included organizations which might tend to feature internal structures of a hierachical nature.

5 The survey, titled "The Relationship between 'Civic Organizations' and 'Governmental Organizations' in the Vietnamese Transition Period", started in July 1999. The project is a German-Vietnamese cooperation, funded by the German Volkswagen Foundation and headed by Prof. J. Rueland (University of Freiburg, Germany) and Dr W. Pfennig (Freie Universitaet Berlin, Germany.

6 The questionnaire is available on request in either an English or Vietnamese version. Please send an email to joergwisch@yahoo.com.

7 Here we refer to Tarrow's definition of the concept of "Political Opportunity Structures Approach" (Tarrow, 1996, p. 54). We support McAdams suggestion to include the state's capacity and propensity for domination into the concept and definition (McAdams 1996, p. 27). The analysis of the impact of the whole set of political conditions, mentioned in this definition, is beyond the capacity of our project.

8 For an overview see Klandermans (1991); Kitschelt (1991); Mayer N. Zald (1991), McCarthy (1996) and McAdam et al. (1996).

9 That does not mean that these groups do not exist in Hanoi. But in the case of Hanoi the researchers have not detected and documented a group of businessmen/women similar to that of Ho Chi Minh City. The business related groups they identified in Hanoi had to be classified as Professionals' Associations.

10 The observation is related to the sample of organizations whose representatives were interviewed. The documentation of the total of Issue-Oriented Organizations reveals that at least two Issue-Oriented Organizations in Hanoi were founded before 1975.

11 This is due to the setting up of new districts in Hanoi, an exercise that also established concomitantly eight additional (branches of) Mass Organizations at district level.

12 42.9 per cent of the representatives of the Mass Organizations in Hanoi, 44.2 per cent of the representatives of the Professionals' Associations in Hanoi and 46.7 per cent of the representatives of the Professionals' Associations in Ho Chi Minh City indicate that the economic, political and cultural conditions have been favourable for what they intended to do.

13 In Hanoi 77.1 per cent of the answers of the representatives of the Mass Organizations refer to this wish, as do 55.8 per cent of the Professionals' Associations and 73.9 per cent of the representatives of the Issue-Oriented Organizations. In Ho Chi Minh City 69.2 per cent of the answers of the representatives of the Mass Organizations point to this reason, so do 56.7 per cent of the Professionals' Organizations and 72.9 per cent of the representatives of the Issue-Oriented Organizations.

14 Here we are talking about different sources the Vietnamese Civic Organizations make different use of. That means, for example, the Mass Organizations in Hanoi indicate that all of them (100 per cent) receive money from government agencies. But besides such contributions 74.3 per cent of them receive money from membership fees, 22.9 per cent of them receive donations from private domestic sources, 17.1 per cent of the Mass Organizations enjoy funding from foreign partners and 8.6 per cent of them receive money from services they provide.

15 This conclusion is drawn from summing up the absolute numbers of organizations, in both the North and the South, which indicate that "Sponsorship by governmental agencies" and/or "Fees for services provided" are their most important source of funding.

16 As mentioned in the introduction, the micro-level of our analysis, i.e. the analysis of the importance of the individual motivations, reasons, orientations and attitudes of the various actors for the development of a specific nature of relationship between Civic Organizations and Governmental Organizations, is still in its initial stages.

17 Due to understandable reasons, here as in other cases of citations from the in-depth interviews, we keep the name of the interviewee anonymous.

18 Excluded from this subgroup were associations that provide services.

19 Decision 35-HDBT of January 1992 of the Council of Ministers on the management of science and technology; Joint Circular 195-LB of November 1992 of the Ministry of Science, Technology and Environment and the Government Commission for Organization and Personnel promulgating implementing regulations for registration and activities of scientific research and technological development organizations.

20 One of the most important scholars, who has greatly contributed to the development of the "Political Opportunity Structures Approach", is S. Tarrow. See for instance, Tarrow 1996.

[21] This interpretation is inspired by Kriesi's remark concerning the possibility that different types of Civic Organizations are to a different degree dependent on such structures and that they might react in a different way to changes in the political conditions (Kriesi 1991, p. 31).

References

Diamond, Larry. *Developing Democracy: Toward Consolidation*. Baltimore and London: The Johns Hopkins University Press, 1999.

Ding, X.L. "Institutional Amphibiousness and the Transition from Communism: The Case of China". In *British Journal of Political Science* 24 (1994): pp. 293–318.

Hudock, Ann C. *NGOs and Civil Society: Democracy by Proxy?* Cambridge: Polity Press, 1999.

Kerkvliet, Benedict J. Tria. "An Approach for Analysing State-Society Relations in Vietnam". In *Sojourn. Journal of Social Issues in Southeast Asia* 16, no. 2 (October 2001): 238–78.

Klandermans, Bert. "New Social Movements and Resource Mobilization: The European and the American Approach Revisited". In *Research on Social Movements: The State of the Art in Western Europe and the USA*, edited by Dieter Rucht, pp. 17–44. Frankfurt/M. and Boulder: Campus Verlag and Westview Press, 1991.

Kitschelt, Helmut. "Resource Mobilization Theory: A Critique". In *Research on Social Movements: The State of the Art in Western Europe and the USA*, edited by Dieter Rucht, pp. 323–47. Frankfurt/M. and Boulder: Campus Verlag and Westview Press, 1991.

Kriesi, Hans-Peter. "The Political Opportunity Structure of New Social Movements: Its Impact on their Mobilization". Discussion Paper FS III Wissenschaftszentrum, Berlin, 1991 pp. 91–103.

Koh, David. "Negotiating the Socialist State in Vietnam through Local Administrators: The Case of Karaoke Shops". In *Sojourn. Journal of Social Issues in Southeast Asia* 16, no. 2 (October 2001): 279–305.

Mayer N. Zald. "The Continuing Vitality of Resource Mobilization Theory: Response to Herbert Kitschelt's Critique". In *Research on Social Movements: The Stule of the Art in Western Europe and the USA*, edited by Dieter Rucht, pp. 348–54. Frankfurt/M. and Boulder: Campus Verlag and Westview Press, 1991.

McAdams, Doug. "Conceptual Origins, Current Problems, Future Directions". In *Comparative Perspectives on Social Movements: Political Opportunities, Mobilizing Structures, and Cultural Framings*, edited by Doug McAdams, John McCarthy, and Mayer N. Zald, pp. 23–40. Cambridge and Melbourne: Cambridge University Press, 1996.

McAdams, Doug, John McCarthy, and Mayer N. Zald. "Introduction: Opportunities, Mobilizing Structures, and Framing Processes—Toward a Synthetic, Comparative Perspective on Social Movements". In *Comparative Perspectives on Social Movements: Political Opportunities, Mobilizing Structures, and Cultural Framings*, edited by Doug McAdams, John McCarthy, and Mayer N. Zald, pp. 1–20. Cambridge and Melbourne: Cambridge University Press, 1996.

McCarthy, John. "Constraints and Opportunities in Adopting, Adapting, and Inventing". In *Comparative Perspectives on Social Movements: Political Opportunities, Mobilizing Structures, and Cultural Framings*, edited by Doug McAdams, John McCarthy, and Mayer N. Zald, pp. 141–51. Cambridge and Melbourne: Cambridge University Press, 1996.

Nguyen Khac Mai. *Vi tri, vai tro cac hiep hoi quan chung o nuoc ta* [Position and Roles of People's Associations in our Country] Hanoi: Nha xuat ban Lao Dong, 1996.

Nguyen Van Thanh. *Nhin nhan lai vai tro cua cac to chuc phi chinh phi nuoc ngoai o Vietnam* [Reflections on the Role of Foreign Non-Governmental Organizations in Vietnam]. In *Tap Chi Cong San*, No. 17 (September 1998), pp. 27–8, 37–8.

Nguyen Viet Vuong. *Cac doan the nhan dan trong kinh te thi truong* [Mass Associations in the Market Economy]. Hanoi: Nha xuat ban Chinh tri quoc gia, 1994.

Putnam, Robert D. with Robert Leonardi and Raffaella Y. Nanetti. *Making Democracy Work*. Princeton: Princeton University Press, 1993.

Rodan, Gary. "Theoretical Issues and Oppositional Politics in East and Southeast Asia". Working Paper No. 60, Asia Research Centre on Social, Political and Economic Change. Murdoch University Western Australia, December 1995.

Sidel, Mark. "The Emergence of a Nonprofit Sector and Philantrophy in the Socialist Republic of Vietnam". In *Emerging Civil Society in the Asia Pacific Community*, edited by Takeshi Yamamoto, pp. 293–304. Singapore and Tokyo: ISEAS, and Japan Center for International Exchange, Tokyo, 1995.

Tarrow, Sidney. "Social Movements and the State: The Political Structuring of Social Movements". In *Comparative Perspectives on Social Movements: Political Opportunities, Mobilizing Structures, and Cultural Framings*, edited by Doug McAdams, John McCarthy, and Mayer N. Zald, pp. 41–61. Cambridge and Melbourne: Cambridge University Press, 1996.

Thayer, Carlyle. "Mono-Organizational Socialism and the State". In *Vietnam's Rural Transformation*, edited by Benedict J. Tria Kerkvliet and Doug Porter, pp. 39–64. Boulder and Singapore: Westview Press and ISEAS, 1995.

World Bank. *Vietnam 2010: Entering the 21st Century. Vietnam Development Report 2001*. Hanoi: World Bank with ADB and UNDP, 2000a, 133p.

———. *Vietnam 2010. Vietnam Development Report 2001. Part 1: Partnerships for Development*. Hanoi: World Bank with ADB and UNDP, 2000b, 129p.

Appendix

Box 1 The variety of Civic Organizations in Hanoi and Ho Chi Minh City: examples of the classification applied in the survey

We differentiate between 4 subgroups: Mass Organizations, Professional's Associations, Issue-Oriented Organizations and Associations of Businessmen/women.

For example, the following organizations are classified as Mass Organizations: the Women's Union, the Youth Union, and the Peasants' Association.

Professional's Associations are, for example: the Association of the Historians, the Union of the Science and Technology Associations or the Society for Ethnology.

As Issue-Oriented Organizations in Hanoi, we classified Centres such as the Rural Development Services Centre, the Centre for Research, Support and Empowerment of Ethnic Women or the Centre for Progress in Rural Areas, the Centre for Research on Energy and Environment, and the Centre for the Fight against AIDS.

In Ho Chi Minh City most of the Issue-Oriented Organizations are working in the field of social work. There we classified as Issue-Oriented Organizations organizations specializing in the theory and practice of social work such as the Social Development and Research Consultancy, the Centre for the Practice of Social Work or the Centre for Social Work with Kids; other organizations we classified as Issue-Oriented Organizations in Ho Chi Minh City are Buddhists Temple Associations such as the Bo De Free Kitchen of the Buddhists, the Nghia Nhuan Temple Association and centres that take care of street children such as The Club for the Sai Gon Train Station Kids or the Thao Dan Street Children Care Program.

As Organizations of Businessmen/women in Ho Chi Minh City we included, for example, the Association of Vietnamese Businessmen Living Abroad, the Leather and Shoes Society, the Weaving, Sewing, Stitching and Knitting Society, and the Foodstuff Society.

Box 2 Drawing of the Random Samples

Hanoi

Type of Organization	Total/Number	Percentage	Number of Organizations to be interviewed
Mass Organizations	98	19,7	30
Professionals' Associations	214	43,1	65
Issue-Oriented Organizations	185	37,2	56
Total	497	100	151

Ho Chi Minh City

Type of Organization	Total/Number	Number of Organizations to be interviewed
Mass Organizations	16	16
Professionals' Associations	46	46
Associations of Businessmen/ women	12	12
Issue-Oriented Organizations	137	137
Total	211	142

Total of the Organizations chosen to be interviewed: 293

Total of Organizations interviewed in the first stage of the survey: 257

Response Rate: 87.7%

FIGURE 2
Years of Foundation of Civic Organizations

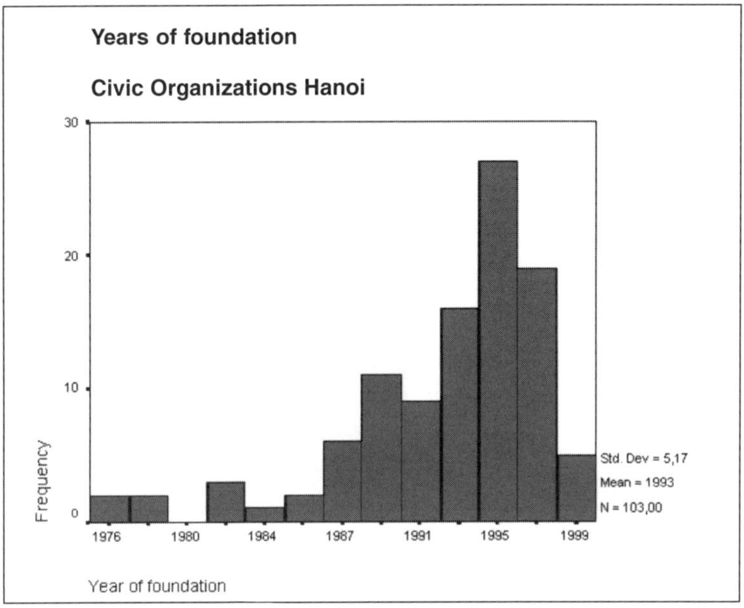

FIGURE 3
Years of Foundation of Professionals' Organizations in Ho Chi Minh City

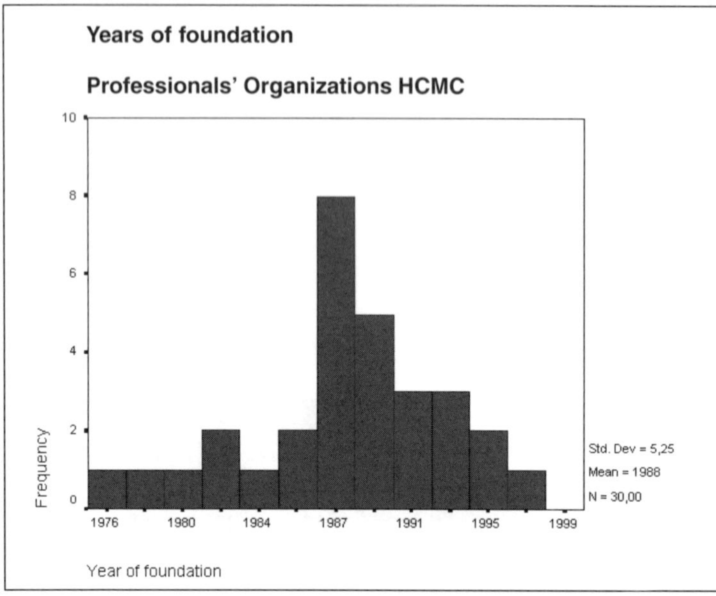

FIGURE 4
Years of Foundation of Issue-Oriented Organizations in Ho Chi Minh City

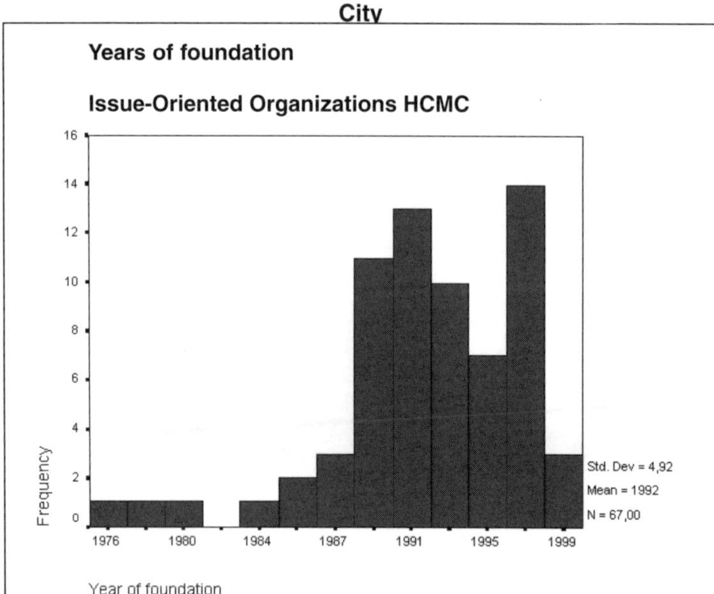

FIGURE 5
Years of Foundation of Issue-Oriented Organizations in Hanoi

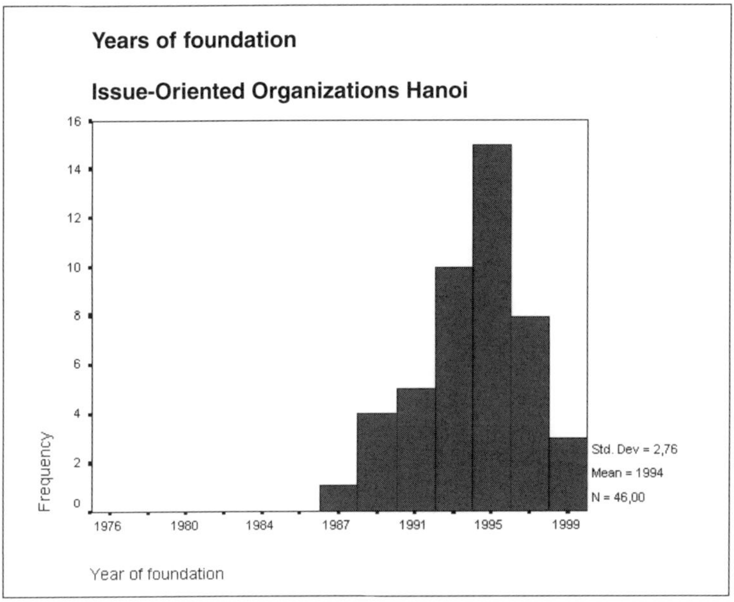

FIGURE 6
Years of Foundation of Professionals' Organizations in Hanoi

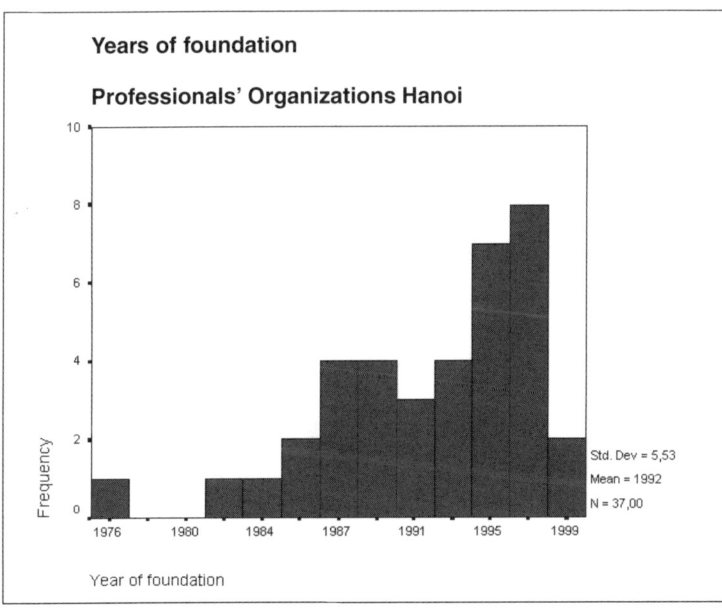

Note: In order to properly compare the development of Professionals' Associations in both cities, we choose the period 1975–2000. That does not mean that Professionals' Associations in Hanoi did not exist before 1975—on the contrary.

TABLE 1
The Distribution of Different Kinds of Civic Organizations

	Hanoi				Ho Chi Minh City				
	Mass Organizations	Professionals' Associations	Issue-Oriented Organizations	Total	Mass Organizations	Professionals' Associations	Issue-Oriented Organizations	Organizations of Businessmen/women	Total
Number	35	52	46	133	12	30	70	11	123
Percentage	26.3	39.1	34.5	100	10.5	24.2	56.5	8.9	100

TABLE 2
Size of the Staff of Civic Organizations

		Hanoi				Ho Chi Minh City				
		Mass Organizations	Professionals' Associations	Issue-Oriented Organizations	Total	Mass Organizations	Professionals' Associations	Issue-Oriented Organizations	Organizations of Businessmen/ women	Total
Full-time staff members	%	92.0	45.0	77.7	75.6	83.5	30.7	55.6	32.4	59.4
	Median	9	4	8	6	24	0	4	2	4
	Minimum	0	0	0	0	0	0	0	1	0
	Maximum	250	34	360	360	102	17	55	18	102
Part-time staff members	%	4.4	21.9	12.3	11.7	14.0	15.3	14.4	0.0	13.7
	Median	0	0	1.5	0	0	0	0		0
	Minimum	0	0	0	0	0	0	0	0	0
	Maximum	18	25	30	30	40	6	50	0	50
Voluntary staff members	%	3.6	33.1	10.0	12.7	2.5	54.0	30.0	67.6	26.9
	Median	0	0	0	0	0	2	0	5.5	0
	Minimum	0	0	0	0	0	0	0	0	0
	Maximum	20	35	25	35	15	50	35	26	50
Total staff members	%	100	100	100	100	100	100	100	100	100
	Median	11	8	14.5	12	40	7	9	8.5	9
	Minimum	2	1	3	1	5	1	2	3	1
	Maximum	250	42	360	360	102	50	880	28	102
	Mean	26.0	11.3	30.8	21.9	46.6	8.6	15.4	10.8	16.6

TABLE 3
Most Important Funding Resources of Civic Organizations

	Hanoi				Ho Chi Minh City				
	Mass Organizations	Professionals' Associations	Issue-Oriented Organizations	Total	Mass Organizations	Professionals' Associations	Issue-Oriented Organizations	Organizations of Businessmen/ women	Total
Membership fees	3 8.6	8 15.4	3 6.5	14 10.5	1 7.7	4 12.9	3 4.3	9 81.8	17 13.7
Donations from (private) domestic sources	1 2.9	9 17.3	1 2.2	11 8.3		4 12.9	15 21.7		19 15.3
Sponsorship by government agencies	30 85.7	17 32.7	4 8.7	51 38.3	7 53.8	7 22.6	10 14.5		24 19.4
Funding from foreign partners		1 1.9	12 26.1	13 9.8			17 24.6		17 13.7
Fees for services provided	1 2.9	11 21.2	25 54.3	37 27.8	4 30.8	14 45.2	12 17.4	2 18.2	32 25.8
Others		6 11.5	1 2.2	7 5.3	1 7.7	2 6.5	12 17.4		15 12.1

TABLE 4

General Assessment of the Relationships between Civic Organizations and Governmental Organizations

	Hanoi				Ho Chi Minh City				
	Mass Organizations	Professionals' Associations	Issue-Oriented Organizations	Total	Mass Organizations	Professionals' Associations	Issue-Oriented Organizations	Organizations of Businessmen/women	Total
Easy	24	35	17	76	11	21	42	8	82
	68.6	67.3	37.0	57.1	84.6	70.0	60.0	72.7	66.1
Sometimes there are problems	10	13	24	47	1	4	25	3	33
	28.6	28.6	52.2	35.3	7.7	13.3	35.7	27.3	26.6
No idea	1	2	4	7		4	2		6
	2.9	3.8	8.7	5.3		13.3	2.9		4.8
Other remarks		2	1	.3	1	1	1		3
		3.8	2.2	23	7.7	3.3	1.4		2.4

TABLE 5

Major Modes of the Relationships between Civic Organizations and Governmental Organizations

	Hanoi				Ho Chi Minh City				
	Mass Organizations	Professionals' Associations	Issue-Oriented Organizations	Total	Mass Organizations	Professionals' Associations	Issue-Oriented Organizations	Organizations of Businessmen/women	Total
We can work independently	17 48.6	33 63.5	24 52.2	74 55.6	8 61.5	19 63.3	44 62.9	9 90.0	80 65.0
The Governmental Organizations control and guides our work directly	13 37.1	12 23.1	8 17.4	33 24.8	3 23.1	2 6.7	13 18.6		18 14.6
They do not support certain plans			4 8.7	4 3.0			3 4.3		3 24
There is no pattern in the mode of this relationship	1 12.9	5 9.6	10 21.7	16 12.0	1 7.7	4 13.3	7 10.0	1 10.0	13 10.6
Others	4 11.4	2 3.8		6 4.5	1 7.7	5 16.6	3 4.3		9 7.3

TABLE 6
The Roles of Civic Organizations Arising out of the relationships with Governmental Organizations

	Hanoi				Ho Chi Minh City				
	Mass Organizations	Professionals' Associations	Issue-Oriented Organizations	Total	Mass Organizations	Professionals' Associations	Issue-Oriented Organizations	Organizations of Businessmen/ women	Total
Various forms of partnership	21 60.0	22 42.3	18 39.1	61 45.9	6 46.2	13 43.3	21 30.9	4 40.0	44 36.4
We play the role of an innovator		7 13.5	11 23.9	18 13.5	3 23.1	2 6.7	6 8.8	2 20.0	13 10.7
We act as a coordinator	29 82.9	35 67.3	34 73.9	98 73.7	8 61.5	19 63.3	23 33.8	5 50.0	55 45.5
We work as an implementor	26 74.3	30 57.7	22 47.8	78 58.6	6 46.2	11 36.7	26 38.2	3 30.0	46 38.0
We acts as a supervisor of governmental programs/policies	15 42.9	6 11.5	11 23.9	32 24.1	3 23.1	10 33.3	6 8.8		19 15.7
We work as a networker	17 48.6	28 53.8	20 43.5	65 48.9	1 7.7	4 13.3	20 29.4	1 10.0	26 21.5
We reflect societal concerns to political institutions	23 65.7	33 63.5	18 39.1	74 55.6	9 69.2	9 30.0	23 33.8	3 30.3	44 36.4
We initiate administrative or legislative reforms	9 25.7	6 11.5	10 21.7	25 18.8	4 30.8	4 13.3	1 1.5	1 10.0	10 8.3
Others	2 5.7	2 3.8	4 8.7	8 6.0	2 15.4	6 20.0	8 11.8	4 40.0	20 16.5

7

Donors, Local Development Groups and Institutional Reform over Vietnam's Development Decade

Scott Fritzen

International donors have attempted to contribute to, and indeed influence, the overall tenor of socioeconomic and governance-related reforms in Vietnam. They have done so in a number of ways: directly supporting policy research, establishing forums for debate of developmental issues with government counterparts, funding projects on administrative and legal reform and central level capacity building, and providing direct financial and sometimes indirect support for "indigenous" NGOs, primarily development service organizations working as contractors for particular development projects.

This chapter examines another modality through which donors sought to influence administrative reform over the heady "development decade" of the 1990s—donor support for rural development projects conceived as "policy experiments" (Rondinelli 1983). Though diverse in sectoral focus, these projects commonly attempted to introduce local institutional arrangements that promote greater responsiveness and accountability of local governments to rural communities as a whole, or to particular sub-groups such as smallholder farmers. To do so, local organizations or grassroots groups were typically established as new ways of organizing the rural populace to demand, plan for, access, or provide services underpinning rural development and poverty alleviation. "Local development groups" (LDGs) is the name I give to groups comprised of farmers and other end-users of project services (or representatives they choose) that were formed in the process of implementing particular development projects.

This chapter probes the experience of these development projects and LDGs over approximately the last ten years. It depicts how projects funded by a wide range of donors became an important part of the institutional landscape in many areas of Vietnam, leaving a significant mark on many sectors related to rural development. Five sections follow this introduction. The first examines how changing donor roles interacted with institutional developments to produce an opportunity for projects to influence policy. Section two presents a theoretical framework with which to assess LDGs and the policy experiments in which they were embedded. Section three applies the framework to a sample of 15 donor projects operational over the 1990s in Vietnam. Section four presents more qualitative detail on a few of the higher-impact projects. The final section concludes with implications for donors and the study of local institutional change in Vietnam.

Donors, Institutional Change and *Doi Moi*

Both centre–local relations and donor attempts to promote policy reform shifted significantly over the 1990s. The basic trends involved were: a) movement towards greater discretionary power for most provinces, coupled with an attempt to impose greater accountability for development outcomes; and b) a shift in the rhetoric of donors from an optimistic assessment of the government's capacity and commitment for institutional reform towards increasing pessimism and policy conditionality. Both profoundly affected the scope for donor-supported LDGs to contribute towards reformed state–society relations.

Centre–Local Relations in Transition

The Vietnamese system of centre–local relations has become significantly less hierarchical and centralized over the course of the *doi moi* policy reforms. Emerging from the pre-reform period of economic micromanagement and neo-Stalinist forms of political organization, one key component of *doi moi* reforms has been the attempt to redefine the role of the central state. The legal framework underlying centre–local relations was amended significantly over the past ten years, as exemplified by the 1996 Budget Law and national programmes. The Budget Law significantly expanded the role of Vietnam's 61 provinces, notably in the management and regulation of infrastructure, the development of provincial Socioeconomic Development Plans and coordination of line agencies. It also introduced a more stable framework for centre–local fiscal transfers, for which provincial shares would be relatively fixed for several years (Rao et al. 1999). "National programmes"—special-purpose central-level transfers to local governments in high-priority areas such as reforestation and employment creation—played a key role in the government's rural development strategy over this period, and these too have been increasingly decentralized (Fritzen 1999). Recent decrees attempt to institutionalize greater accountability of provinces to achieve targets set by the central level in exchange for increasing flexibility over line-item allocations (Nguyen 2000).

These changes still left the subnational scene rather centralized at the provincial level. This gave richer provinces much-desired room for experimentation in interpreting and implementing central decrees and programmes. The effect on fiscally weak provinces was less benign, as the system of intergovernmental transfers proved insufficient to shore up the gap between richer and poorer provinces. And, while accountability was the semantic focal point for decentralization, the centre has struggled with limitations on its ability to set meaningful performance goals for lower levels (to ensure *upward* accountability) and meaningful safeguards on the quality of local democratic procedures (*downward* accountability). The practical summation of what one might call overlapping fiscal, accountability, and capacity gaps was a yawning policy-implementation gap. In it could be found a sometimes astonishing variety of "interpretations" throughout the countryside for ostensibly unified national policies.

"Grassroots democratization" *(dan chu hoa tai co so)* became the idiom of choice for donors, the government and the state media for the importance of "downward accountability", a focal point for discussions on governance in the late 1990s. Expressed in several directives issued from 1997 onwards, the policy mandates that local governments take all necessary steps to ensure that procedural democracy is respected at the local government level. Particular attention is given to ensuring that all government investments (often through the vehicle of national programmes) at the grassroots level, and all taxes and labour contributions, are implemented equitably and transparently.

The roots of "democratization" lie in the government's response to unprecedented large-scale demonstrations, some of which turned violent, against local official corruption, particularly in the use of infrastructure funds in Thai Binh province over 1997–98. News regarding the incident was first suppressed, but the scale of the protests became too large to sweep under the rug. A Party response to this was a high-profile "rectification" campaign against corrupt officials, with emphasis on local government (EIU 1999; Kerkvliet 2001). The charge was led by conservative ex-General Secretary Le Kha Phieu, who emphasized the danger of corrupt local officials causing the people to "lose confidence" in the Party. Grassroots democracy was the ultimate legal expression of the campaign, and it dovetailed nicely with Hanoi's official post-mortem on Thai Binh—that the problem of corruption was one of a "few bad apples" in the Party (as opposed to being an institutional problem). Viewed this way, the problem of controlling corruption was one of asserting control and better internal vigilance over the Party and local government apparatus, and the democratization decree was viewed by the Party as one way of doing this.

While the grassroots democratization was greeted by donors as an "important move" (World Bank 1999, p. 90), some questioned whether it could survive the "policy–implementation gap", and indeed whether it was possible for the decree to work in the absence of carefully specified enforcement and quality control mechanisms. The government had formulated procedures for citizens to "raise complaints and make denunciations" *(khieu nai to cao)*, but use of such tools seemed to presuppose confidence in the ability of local administration to police itself. If preconditions for effective "procedural democracy control" included an active civil society capable of facilitating the collective expression of grievances against powerful local cadre, or a truly independent judiciary, then the decree's prospects appeared dim, as these goals remained largely off the policy agenda. In such a context, the best that might be expected is for the decree to reinforce progressive leadership in some localities that would serve as an ideal against which poorly performing localities could be held to some account.

Yet the issue of downward accountability or grassroots democracy is critical to donor policy experiments. In these, LDGs serve as a "surrogate" civil society (i.e. not self-organizing interest groups but also not formal parts of the bureaucracy) that probe the limits of downward accountability possible under existing local institutional arrangements.

Shifting Donor Roles

The donor community's profile increased significantly over the course of the decade, which began with only a minimal aid presence. Several factors accounted for this. The U.S. embargo, lifted only in 1994, prevented multilaterals from setting up shop; the legal and administrative environment for the processing of aid receipts was cumbersome; and *doi moi* or "renovation" reforms were tenuous (with hyperinflation still a real threat in the early years of the decade). By decade's end, the prominence of international development ideas and programme modalities on the developmental scene was arguably even more important than overall overseas development assistance (ODA) disbursements as a percentage of GDP, which was a modest 6 per cent in 2000.[1] The way in which developmental issues such as inequality, poverty, safety nets, participation and governance were talked about in 2000 was as much influenced by donors as by "indigenous" ideologies of development, in substantial disarray.

If the voice of the donor community became louder over the decade, what it was saying also shifted, at least in emphasis. The first half of the 1990s found donors such as the World Bank highly praising *doi moi* reforms and generally optimistic in outlook. Yet the heady pace of economic and social reform would not be sustained. Already by 1996, foreign direct investment (FDI) was beginning to decelerate, markedly so by 1998. Donors moved from offering policy advice with some confidence that it would be adopted in due course, to more or less comprehensive critiques of a perceived policy impasse in the wake of the Asian financial crisis. This impasse was viewed not just in economic policy, but also in "governance" terms: deficiencies in the administrative apparatus and the pattern of state–rural society interactions, it was claimed, were in danger of undermining prospects for sustainable poverty reduction.

Major policy reports reflect this more critical tone. The 1999 *Attacking Poverty* report by the World Bank in close cooperation with a number of NGOs was claimed to have "grabbed the attention of policymakers" (Turk 2001, p. 1). While applauding Vietnam's rapid poverty reduction, it also stressed increasing inequality, extremely limited government safety net coverage and, most significantly, continued marginalization of the poorest members of the citizenry in both rural and urban areas. The focus in this and other donor reports of the late 1990s (e.g. UNDP 1999) on "downward accountability" reflected three factors: the more general shift within the World Bank towards the idiom of governance; the seriousness with which it pursued collaboration with international NGOs in Vietnam; and a growing consensus in the donor community regarding the need to support government implementation of the grassroots democratization decree.

Donors over the period were increasingly more effective in interacting collectively with government to influence policy. Various donor–government working groups and policy forums on specific topics, from reforestation to the grassroots democratization decree, were formed. While donor coordination is notoriously difficult, these working groups helped donors contribute project-specific experiences and models to the debate over policy reform in various sectors.[2] In this context, experiences from LDG-related development projects that had proliferated over the decade served as important generators of the reform ideas for which donors wished to advocate (one example being the RIDEF case study presented later in the chapter).

By the end of the decade donors evaluated the policy environment to be ripe for contributing project-specific experiences to the policy debate. How they sought to do this—based on what kinds of projects and with what outcomes—is the subject of the rest of this chapter.

Towards a Conceptual Framework for Local Development Groups

One of the primary ways donors in Vietnam (and elsewhere) have attempted to support policy experimentation and learning has been through rural development projects designed as experiments in local institutional reform. Specifically, such projects have introduced various types of local development groups onto the local institutional scene.

The LDGs as defined in this paper constitute a category of organizations with two characteristics. First, they operate in the context of a donor-supported development project. As such, they may or may not have any viable organizational purpose or ability to exist once that project is concluded. They are neither a "self-organizing" part of civil society nor a formal part of the bureaucratic apparatus of local government.

Second, LDGs are supposed to have an impact on the interface between local governments and rural populace, typically to make the former more responsive to the needs of, and accountable to, the latter. LDGs manifest the long-standing debate in the development literature over how to improve the grassroots outcomes of rural development projects.

Two of the broadest answers suggested by the development literature have been *grassroots participation* and *local bureaucratic reform* (Feeney 1998; Charlick 2001). Strengthening local organizations and boosting local participation as a development strategy dates back to the 1970s, as discontent with the outcomes of state-led development became widely evident. The literature on bureaucratic reorientation, in turn, is concerned with reworking the apparatus of local government to achieve better performance. "Better" is defined variously as responsiveness to poor and vulnerable populations, greater local democracy or the achievement of substantive developmental outcomes. In recent years, analysts have begun shifting from a focus on an NGO-led, community participation strategy as a *substitute* for the local state towards ways in which the state can meaningfully *engage* with local organizations and civil society.

Donors have attempted to combine these approaches in order to push the boundaries of local institutional reform, using LDGs at the interface of local state–society relations. Working within the overall institutional parameters and constraints posed by a transitional context, donors have attempted to underpin the activities of sponsored LDGs with capacity building and a supportive administrative framework. Aiming to improve local governance, their intent has been to create local models of bureacratic reform and popular participation that local officials might wish to expand beyond the life of the project, and that donors might use to influence policy reform at central and local levels.

The case for a combination of local organization and bureaucratic reform strategies is arguably even more compelling for countries such as Vietnam. A facilitative policy environment for independent NGOs—say, Philippines-style—is not likely to be on the policy agenda anytime soon. Moreover, the policy–implementation gap stemming from dramatic capacity differentials among local governments makes optimism regarding decentralization naive. Vietnam is a *transitional* setting not just in the familiar sense of shifting to a market economy, but also in its ongoing decentralization of intergovernmental relations and in changing attitudes towards non-state-based social groupings (or incipient civil society).

Conceptual Framework for Assessing LDGs

This section begins to construct a basic framework for understanding how LDGs can have an impact on the broader pattern of state–society relations. An adequate framework would include two elements: a) a characterization of how LDGs develop over time and their success in influencing policy (outcomes of LDG experiments); and b) hypothesized factors underlying success or failure.

Outcomes

Outcomes here refer to the impact that donor engagement through LDGs has in terms of local institutional reform. Adapting from work on NGOs by Edwards and Hulme (1992), Carrol (1992), Uvin (1996), Lehman and Bebbington (1998) and Uvin and Jain (2000), I suggest four categories of outcomes indicative of the range of institutional outcomes experienced by LDGs over the course of their project life:

1. *Service coverage* relates to the extent to which services are valued by members and project sponsors.
2. *Scaling-up* describes the degree to which LDG institutional arrangements are replicated on a wider scale or become diversified in function.
3. The *institutionalization and sustainability* category examines how LDGs may become "normalized" in the normal institutional landscape in a way increasingly independent of project context; for instance, government agencies may increasingly direct resources for service delivery to LDGs outside of the project context.
4. *Policy impact* assesses the extent to which LDGs and the project context have a discernable influence on specific policy content at central and local levels.

Explanatory Factors

What factors might begin to explain LDG developmental trajectories and impacts? Categories of factors identified in the literature (Esman and Uphoff 1984; Uphoff 1986) and through personal observation as influential include project design, LDG-specific characteristics, environmental factors and institutional factors.

1. *Project design.* The most obvious potential impact on policy impact—particularly intuitive for those who have worked on a number of projects and observed their high failure rate (World Bank 1998)—is project design. Among the factors hypothesized to be positively correlated with high impact projects are the following:
   (a) Government counterparts that are institutionally powerful and in a coordinating capacity, since these would be in a prime position to institutionalize reforms emerging from a project context;
   (b) Donors that have either built up long-term relationships in a locality (particularly up to provincial level), or who enjoy significant national standing (such as multilaterals or U.N. agencies);

(c) Projects with geographical scope of sufficient scale to attract the attention of at least provincial level policy-makers;

(d) An explicit "policy experiment" orientation, typically expressed through project objectives underscoring such aims, a time-frame long enough to accommodate project experimentation objectives and strong orientation towards learning and adaptation, and well-developed documentation, monitoring and evaluation systems (Uphoff et al. 1999); and

(e) Intergovernmental linkages built into project design.

2. *LDG-specific characteristics.* The second category is in part a sub-category of programme design. It examines the organizational attributes of "higher impact" LDGs. For example, higher impact projects are likely to be those with more clearly defined organizational outputs that are highly valued by LDG members, particularly if economic services are involved.

3. *Environmental influences.* The socioeconomic and geographical contexts in which project efforts are pursued have a huge impact on the possibilities available for project action. Following earlier work (Fritzen 2000a) and the lead of Uphoff (1986), I hypothesize that project contexts with the following features offer more facilitative environments for policy impact, primarily through their impact on the facilitation of collective action: higher population densities; lesser inequality and social stratification; lesser ethnic diversity; and higher levels of social and economic development. They do this by facilitating both the demand for services and the ability to interact with the bureaucracy.

4. *Institutional factors.* A crucial category concerns institutional factors. A productive line of research (Grindle and Thomas 1991; Kingdon 1995; World Bank 1998) examines the great importance of the role of reform "champions" and the specific circumstances in which a reform proposal is transported into the agenda. Though apparently neglected in the study of development projects as policy experiments, I hypothesize these to be

> critical for the success of such projects. Such development projects typically are relatively localized and limited experiments, which to succeed in having a longer-term impact must attract the attention of senior officials at central and local levels—officials typically preoccupied with bureaucratic infighting and a multitude of other items on the national agenda, over which they rarely perceive themselves to be in significant control.

Three hypotheses are advanced regarding institutional variables. The first concerns the political sensitivity of reforms. Donors in Vietnam must walk a fine line in pursuing various administrative and policy reforms. Policy experiments that are allowed to proceed on issues that are potentially politically sensitive—such as grassroots democracy, or the status and welfare of ethnic minorities—are likely to draw higher levels of official attention and thus are more likely to have an opportunity to significantly influence policy.

The second hypothesis concerns the existence of what the literature terms "policy windows", which will also be highly influential for certain kinds of policy impact, particularly for national policy. Policy windows, according to Kingdon (1995), are typically short periods during which a confluence of external circumstances create the opportunity for specific, pre-formulated proposals to rise in salience and prominence onto the policy agenda, in a form that allows action to be taken (but does not guarantee it will be). In the Vietnamese context, issues relating to national programme implementation, centre–local relations (specific intergovernmental relationships), grassroots democracy and, to some extent, ethnic minorities and deforestation were "high profile" issues over the late 1990s.

Finally, "reform champions" (World Bank 1998) are well-placed officials at either the provincial or central levels who enthusiastically support or "champion" project efforts. Such individuals actively "own" project reform ideas by taking responsibility and seizing opportunities for adapting project-initiated local institutional arrangements and LDGs to become increasingly institutionalized, up-scaled or diffused to other localities. The success of subnational projects as policy experiments will be greatly enhanced by the existence of one or more well placed policy champions.

Local Development Groups in Vietnam: Findings from a 15-Project Study

This section applies the conceptual framework presented above to a number of rural development projects in Vietnam. It aims to get a basic overview of the phenomenon of LDGs in Vietnam and to make a preliminary test of the hypotheses expressed above. Implications are then further developed through a closer look at one case study in the following section.

Data. In the context of a research project I led in mid-2000 on "institutionalizing participatory approaches,"[3] some 15 rural development projects agreed to submit project documentation, fill out a self-evaluative questionnaire regarding project modalities and impact, and be interviewed for 1–2 hours.[4] Project selection included a mix of pre-identified and self-nominated projects. Field-level insights gained from consulting work I conducted in five of the fifteen projects from 1996–99 supplemented the analysis.

The projects are described in Table 1. Projects are not identified by name here (although some are discussed in the next section), because the analysis is not meant to suggest that projects with less observed institutionalization or policy impact were not successful; no meaningful information is thereby lost. As a sample, they form a reasonably diverse group, with NGOs, bilateral assistance, and U.N. agencies all represented. These are likely to be more successful projects than average, given that several were self-selected by the organizations involved and those which were invited were known to have generated interesting results.

Method. Based on accumulated documentation and interviews, coupled in five cases with my own work in the project sites, I first generated general findings (Fritzen 2000b). I then developed matrices that assessed each project in terms of each of the outcomes and explanatory categories posited above (with many sub-indicators for each category not shown here due to space constraints). Having assessed the existing variation found in the sample, I assigned scores for each indicator and variable, from 1–5, depending on the potential or observed outcomes and degree to which explanatory variables were facilitative of impact; these I aggregated to the summary scores for outcome and explanatory categories.

TABLE 1
A Basic Description of Projects Included in the Study

Project	Years	Scope	Primary activities	Type of LDG
Multilateral				
A.	5	One coastal province, saturation	Piloting community participation in planning and	Sectoral planning (i.e. health or forestry planning within
B.	5	One mountainous province (Tuyen Quang), saturation	Multisectoral rural development; natural resource management	Multisectoral planning (e.g. several types of social or productive services)
C.	6*	At present approximately 50 districts primarily in poor provinces.	Child services (primarily health, nutrition, education, water and sanitation).	Multisectoral planning
D.	8*	Farmer field schools present in most provinces; overlap with national programme.	Applied research, training and extension services for sustainable agriculture	Service-access
E.	5	50 communes in four of the poorest mountainous provinces	Credit and social services	Multisectoral planning and service-delivery
F.	5	6 communes in 3 districts of a coastal province	Multisectoral rural development with focus on agricultural extension and credit	Multisectoral planning and service-delivery (credit)

TABLE 1 (*continued*)
A Basic Description of Projects Included in the Study

Project	Years	Scope	Primary activities	Type of LDG
Multilateral				
G.	5*	Three communes in midland district of a coastal province, expanding over four years to most communes of district	Multisectoral rural development with focus on agricultural extension and credit	Service-delivery and service-access
Bilateral				
H.	6	Approximately 5 districts in 5 mountainous provinces	Piloting multisectoral planning; rural development and natural resource management	Multisectoral planning and service-delivery
I.	9	2 districts of 2 mountainous provinces	Extension services; forest land allocation	Multisectoral planning
International NGO				
J.	4	Three communes of one midland district of a coastal province	Agricultural extension, credit, reforestation and land allocation	Service-access and service-delivery
K.	4	One commune of upland district of a coastal province	Agricultural extension, credit, reforestation and land allocation	Service-access and service-delivery

TABLE 1 (*continued*)
A Basic Description of Projects Included in the Study

Project	Years	Scope	Primary activities	Type of LDG
International NGO				
L.	5*	Most communes in one coastal district	Savings and credit facilities	Service-delivery
M.	4*	Several communes in midland district of one province	Multisectoral rural development	Multisectoral planning
N.	5*	Small number of communes in four poor provinces of different regions	Primary health care support activities	Sectoral planning, service-delivery and service-access
O.	6*	One district of a coastal province	Multisectoral: social services and resource management	Multisectoral planning and service-delivery

*Denotes ongoing project

Findings

The overall assessment matrix for the 15 projects is given in Table 2. Both outcomes and explanatory factors were found to vary dramatically along the lines indicated in the conceptual framework.

From "whimper" to "bang": Outcome variation. In terms of *service* coverage, most projects and LDGs appeared relatively successful in producing valued outputs. Targeting of the poor was easier to achieve in areas that were overall much poorer. Few projects were able to create LDGs dominated by the relatively poor within a project area.

A large difference was found in the *scaling-up* capability between LDGs that appeared capable of diversifying activities and expanding geographical scope and those that could not. Projects that began at a sub-district scale (G, J, K and M) proved generally unable to scale up, suggesting that initial scope is an important limiting factor.

Greater capability differences were evident in the range of *institutionalization and sustainability.* Weakest were projects with LDGs focused on delivering multisectoral project-specific inputs not connected to the normal state planning process. Strongest were projects that targeted and eventually obtained a legal basis for local organizations to contribute to sectoral planning. No project was able to establish LDGs that show a high probability of continuing beyond the life of the project, except perhaps microcredit operations. In some cases, this was by design (i.e. projects did not have a long-term strategy for LDG sustainability).

In terms of *policy impact,* some projects were not in a position to have a policy impact due to their limited size or scope. Projects that did have discernable impact did so by serving as models for national projects at the central level, and/or influencing provincial policy towards particular sectors. Section five examines underlying factors for the seven projects in the sample identified as having significant policy impacts.

Variation in explanatory factors. *Project design* revealed four categories of projects: a) small-scale projects that while generally were designed as experiments in fact failed to cover sufficient intergovernmental scope to attract attention; b) large-scale, multisectoral projects covering up to provincial level or more, designed as policy experiments but often lacking in focus; c) provincial level projects that were sectoral in focus; and d) national or multiprovincial projects which were narrowly sectoral (focused on one particular high impact technology). The latter two had much stronger outcomes.

TABLE 2
Summary Scores for the 15 Projects*

Project	Key Explanatory Categories (average scores over variables)					Outcomes category (average scores over indicators)				
	Design factors	Institut.	Environ-mental	LDG-specific	Total explan.	Service coverage	Upscaling	Institut.	Policy impact	Total outcome
Multilateral										
A.	4	5	4	3	16	4	4	4	5	17
B.	4	4	4	3	15	3	3	4	4	14
C.	3	5	3	2	13	3	5	4	4	16
D.	5	4	4	5	18	4	4	4	4	16
E.	3	4	1	2	10	4	2	2	2	10
F.	3	4	3	3	13	3	3	2	2	10
G.	2	3	3	3	11	4	3	2	3	12
Bilateral										
H.	5	4	3	3	15	4	4	3	3	14
I.	5	4	1	3	13	3	3	4	4	14
International NGOs										
J.	2	3	2	2	9	2	2	3	3	10
K.	1	3	1	1	6	4	1	1	1	7
L.	3	3	3	5	14	4	4	4	3	15
M.	1	3	3	1	8	2	1	1	1	5
N.	3	3	1	3	10	3	3	3	2	11
O.	2	3	2	3	10	4	3	3	2	12

*Scored from 1–5, with 5 being most facilitative of impact (for explanatory categories), or highest potential or observed impact (for outcome categories).

Characteristics specific to LDGs included differential importance attached to the groups within the project and its design. More successful projects built up substantial capacity within the LDGs to deliver and demand services, and placed capacity development as a central aspect of the project aim. They also built tight linkages between LDGs and line services and authorities—a key first step towards their institutionalization. Training and other capacity building as a percentage of overall project expenditure tended to be higher than for comparative projects, though several had significant investment budgets as well. Sectoral rather than multipurpose LDGs tended to score higher, in line with the hypothesis regarding clarity of output.

Interestingly, there was little observed correlation between the *environmental characteristics* of projects described above (such as level of socioeconomic development) and their observed institutional impacts. As predicted, *institutional factors* were very influential. Facilitative institutional conditions included work in high profile areas such as rural infrastructure (due to its connection with the types of issues motivating the Thai Binh unrest), grassroots democracy, minority area development and reforestation issues. A tight overlap with national programmes was considered strongly facilitative, and some programmes indeed were technical support projects for national programmes. Policy champions could not be identified for all projects, but for a subsection proved to be correlated with higher policy impact.

Summary

The codings based on variations covered above suggest four primary points. First, the hypothesized explanatory factors are in general confirmed in their importance, except perhaps for the role of environmental factors. Scores on each explanatory variable category show high correlations with the various outcome categories.

Second, on average, environmental and LDG-specific factors were not as important in determining outcomes as the combined effect of design and institutional factors. Projects could have substantial policy impacts even when they were operating in difficult environments with only moderately successful LDGs, *provided* policy design created the right foundation for the possibility of taking advantage of policy windows.

Third, there is substantial variation within each of the three types of donor. Projects in which LDGs had a significant institutional impact are found in all three categories. However, projects very small in geographical scope—typically those with a "pilot commune" orientation within a single district—were found to have low institutional or policy impact. These projects were over-represented among NGOs.

Finally, projects observed to have a greater institutional impact showed diversity in the explanatory factors underlying that success. To explore this diversity, the next section examines one of the higher-impact projects in the sample (project A) in greater detail, followed by a brief comparison with four additional projects (B, D, H and I).

Case Study: the Rural Infrastructure Development Fund (RIDEF) and Comparable Projects

RIDEF Overview

RIDEF is one example of a provincial level policy experiment that has achieved relatively high impact to date.[5] It is funded by the United Nations Capital Development Fund (UNCDF) with technical backing by the United Nations Development Program (UNDP) and co-financing for one mountainous district by the Australian Agency for International Development (AusAid). Quang Nam province itself co-finances approximately 20 per cent of the total infrastructure budget for the project. Initiated in 1995, it was phasing out activities over 2002.

Quang Nam province is in the central coast region. It has a population of roughly 2 million, and its 12,000 sq km are split administratively into some 15 districts, divided almost evenly in number among lowland coastal, midland and upland districts. Although it ranks nearly average among Vietnamese provinces in terms of per capita income, the province's upland areas, overwhelmingly populated by ethnic minorities, are extremely poor by any standard; 22 communes there are classified by the central government as among the poorest 10 per cent of communes in the country.

RIDEF began against the background of a UNCDF/UNDP reorientation over the 1990s. Whereas previously UNCDF had focused directly on the funding of capital development projects—indeed, a precursor project in Quang Nam had built large-scale roads, bridges and power supply networks—under new leadership, the small agency had recast its mission as one of funding policy experiments. Quang Nam's RIDEF shared the primary characteristics of these experiments:

(a) Provision of small-scale infrastructure (small roads, health clinics, primary schools, local markets, small-scale irrigation canals, etc.);
(b) financed through stable, decentralized funding (in the form of poverty-targeted block grants); with
(c) community participation linked to the government's normal planning processes (UNCDF 1999).

Thus, while one of the project's objectives, as stated in the RIDEF project document, was "to alleviate rural poverty...through investment in small scale social and economic infrastructure", the policy-oriented objective was to "develop methods which local government and the community groups can use in the provision of social and economic infrastructure" and to share these methods "with those in the central government and other provinces who may be interested in applying them in other projects."[6]

Institutional Arrangements

There are three key institutional components in the RIDEF-sponsored local planning process. Together they constitute the local institutional innovation of this project. The first is the project management unit set up within the influential provincial Planning and Investment Service. The Rural Infrastructure Development Unit (RIDU) develops and supervises the allotment to each commune of an "indicative planning figure" (IPF) for budgetary allocations from the project. The IPF allocation is based on an index combining per capita income, population and a measure of the infrastructure need of the communes. It represents a move towards transparent, formula-based block grant allocations to the community level, even though the complexity of the formula itself is quite difficult for many immediately outside project circles to understand.

Based on the IPF, Planning and Technical Support Groups (PSG/TSG) from the district initiate a planning process at the commune level. They comprise a small number of personnel from technical line agencies based at the district level who have been trained in the project methodology. They report directly to the RIDU.

Commune Development Boards (CDBs)—the LDGs in this case study—are tasked with selecting local infrastructure projects for funding and supervising their implementation. These boards are composed of village representatives, commune People's Committee officials (certainly including the chairperson and/or vice chairperson), and various other commune notables (who typically have some abiding relationship to local officialdom). The CDBs convene "village problem and project identification" meetings in each of the commune's villages, develop a short list of potential projects, then ultimately decide on the prioritization of these projects based (in theory) on criteria established by the CDBs themselves, such as various shades of equity (sharing funds equally for small projects among villages vs. privileging the poorest villages) and efficiency (selecting the most urgent projects vs. those projects that would benefit the most people). To facilitate monitoring the construction and upkeep of works, Commune Development Boards also organize user groups of villagers affected by a particular construction project.

The CDBs in the RIDEF case demonstrate the ambiguous position of LDGs. They cannot be characterized as "pure" civil society, in that they involve substantial participation of local officials, but neither are they formal parts of the local bureacratic apparatus (in that their existence is contingent, at least initially, on the project implementation context). How do the CDBs, in combination with the other institutional arrangements noted above, seek to mediate between the preferences and demands of local villagers for small-scale infrastructure and the capacity of the local state (with donor assistance) to deliver? The key lies in the way CDBs function to heighten accountability to the end-users of project services.

Accountable Development, RIDEF-style

In many countries, infrastructure is notoriously a sector characterized by non-transparent, even corrupt, practices. Small-scale infrastructure provision in Vietnam is no exception, with articles in even the tightly controlled press repeatedly pointing to cases of cost overruns, bidding collusion or outright theft of funds in the implementation of national infrastructure programmes. The problem of corruption if anything is thought to be worse in mountainous and poor regions (Do and Le 2001).

The project aims to heighten accountability in this context by vesting the Commune Development Boards (the project's LDGs) with "project holder" authority, meaning that it is this board and not upper levels of government that enters into direct contracts with builders. The project also mandates that the CDBs hire an independent supervising engineer (i.e. one not employed by the builder of the works) to certify completion of constructed projects according to correct technical specifications. In addition, modifications to the process of bidding on contracts are introduced to reduce the scope for collusion, with cost savings in projects as opposed to "regular" infrastructure works said to average 20 per cent (Gardner et al. 1998). Costs in infrastructure projects are typically driven up by corruption, the built-in incentive for contractors to overcharge and the non-incentives for government officials to keep costs down (since they either enjoy kickbacks from the contractors and/or are uninterested in quibbling over how efficiently infrastructure funds allocated by upper levels of government are spent). Under RIDEF, communities have a strong incentive to actively monitor implementation and cost-effectiveness, as project funds are directly "owned" by the CDBs themselves. Communities that fail to enforce cost-savings and quality (as they are contractually enabled to do) find the value of their (fixed) allocation reduced.

Thus, RIDEF responds to the problem of low, unpredictable and non-transparently allocated funds for commune-level infrastructure through a formula-based block grant to communities. In contrast to the "normal" allocation process, which sees projects selected by upper levels and keeps project-selection and contract-negotiating authority within the central government, RIDEF decentralizes this authority to mixed government–villager Commune Development Boards. Projects selected should as a result correspond more closely to community priorities, and the quality of constructed works should be higher. Local ownership of the works has the further effect of positively influencing operation and maintenance of the works. These are high leverage points for change in a conceptually elegant package.

Summary: Explanatory Factors

Based on the above, the RIDEF has an *impact-facilitative design*. The RIDU is based in an institutionally powerful coordinating ministry; the project operates with an explicit policy experiment (or pilot) orientation at a significant provincial-level scale; and intergovernmental linkages (particularly through the role of the Planning and Technical Support Groups) are dense. The RIDEF's *LDG-specific characteristics* are also facilitative, with the CDBs functioning primarily as planning and service-access LDGs with a relatively clear "organizational technology"—emphasized through community ownership of the fund allocation. Quang Nam province is itself an interesting *environment* as it includes lowland districts with generally high socioeconomic development as well as some of the poorest communes in its upland region. This diversity can be thought to facilitate drawing out lessons for wider possible application.

FIGURE 1
RIDEF Project Institutional Relationships

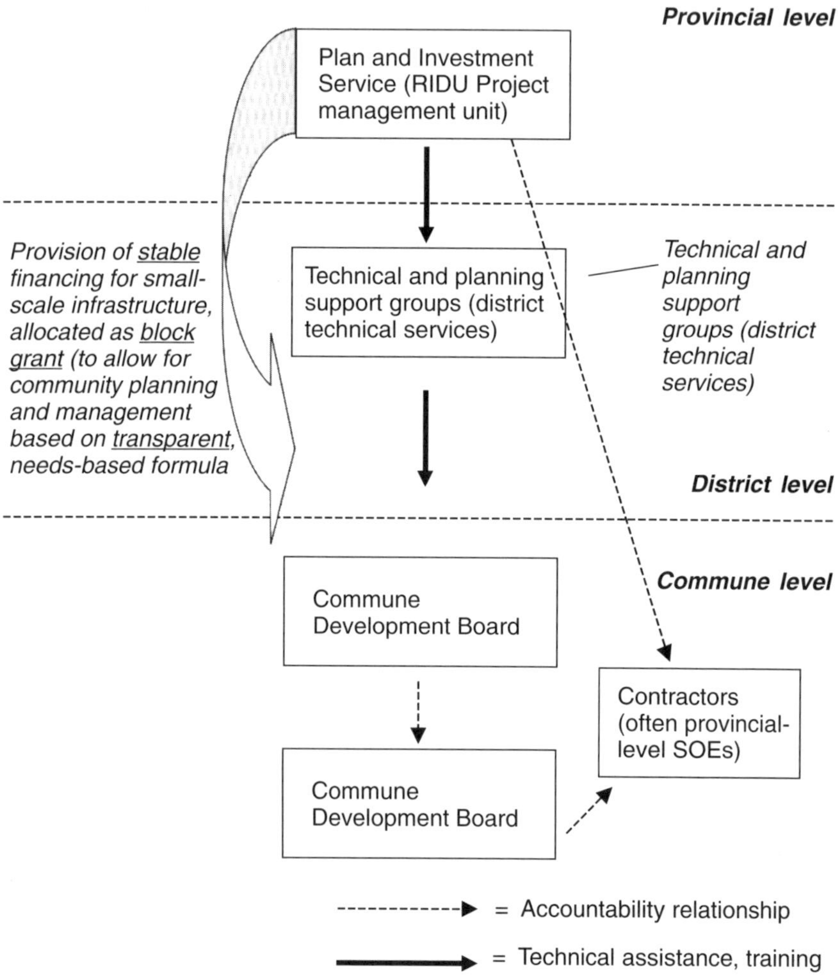

Most significantly, unusually positive *institutional factors* are evident in the RIDEF context. The political sensitivity and visibility of small-scale infrastructure programs in post-Thai Binh policy debates is very high (Kerkvliet 2001; Do and Le 2001). Moreover, project timing fortuitously corresponded to several "policy windows" opening, including the formulation of a major national programme for small-scale infrastructure provision in the poorest communes of the country and the formulation of guidelines for grassroots democracy. The more general issue of how intergovernmental administrative and fiscal relations should be structured for responsive and accountable local planning was, technically, very much part of the development debate over the late 1990s, as mechanisms for planning national programmes were increasingly decentralized. The project's focus on transparent block grants for small-scale infrastructure and a clearly articulated methodology for grassroots participation thus fit extremely well into this reform environment. Policy windows were opening at the right time for the RIDEF, both at central and local levels.

Finally, a "policy champion" is clearly identifiable. The chairman of the Quang Nam Provincial People's Committee, Dr Vu Ngoc Hoang, has been personally interested in RIDEF and has used it to further his own ambitious decentralization policy agenda, as the next section shows.

Outcomes

The RIDEF project was in the process of winding down in late 2001, but some evidence of significant impacts of the local institutional arrangements are evident. The project originally was implemented in three lowland districts, and subsequently was expanded to all 12 rural districts in the province (excluding only two towns).

In terms of *service coverage*, project evaluation reports suggest the local planning process, which has gone through several iterations, has been implemented with considerable success in lowland coastal, and some midland, districts. However, the RIDEF model for local planning and the relationships of accountability have not been easily transplanted into mountainous districts. The lower population densities, larger areas, difficult terrain, weaker administrative capacity and more complicated ethnic mix of these districts have contributed towards lower levels of grassroots participation on the Commune Development Boards. Problems relating to contractor reluctance to bid on individual, small contracts in high-cost mountainous areas, despite their higher unit cost pricing, have also been reported. Thus *upscaling* over the short project time-frame has been both unimpressive and problematic.

The *institutionalization* of RIDEF operates through virtually all of the mechanisms identified in the conceptual framework. Internal stakeholder support has been reinforced by the experience of many villagers who, through the CDBs, have been put for virtually the first time in a position of some authority over state resources being spent in their name. External stakeholder support has come mainly in the form of provincial leaders, who have unified behind a long-term decentralization agenda. "Opposition" (primarily resistance to implementing the local arrangements in earnest) to date has been evident in a few districts, including in mountainous areas, where long-term observers note tight linkages between local officials and contractors. An incipient foundation for institutionalization includes the gradual incorporation of the community development boards into the "normal" planning process of the province. This happened when finances were redirected from special project accounts to the state treasury. There was also the possibility of incorporating specific institutional innovations of the project into the province's ongoing decentralization policy, covered below.

Policy Impact

The provincial People's Committee administration is engaged in a potentially far-reaching and ambitious decentralization policy of increasing the responsibilities of districts and communes. This policy has many roots, but there is strong evidence—both in the structural form decentralization is taking (see Table 3) and in the statements of the leaders driving the new policy[7]—that the RIDEF experiment has been through its operational success to date, a strong influence on this policy. Changes in the central level policy and legal environment provided an opening for provincial leadership to pursue a decentralization agenda, but the decision to do so was very much a provincial-level one.

The province's "decentralization policy" has the following basic elements. The first is a set of long-term plans, articulated by the People's Committee chairman and the heads of planning and finance (both previous directors of the RIDEF project), to decentralize funds and authority to lower levels of government. The second is the establishment of several decentralized funding arrangements, strongly influenced by the RIDEF model, including the decentralization to district level of most of the province's capital budget for small and moderate-sized projects. Decentralization of *sectoral* capital budgets is however being phased in incrementally, due to the considerable resistance of sectors to this policy. The third element is an incipient implementation framework in the form of implementation guidelines for specific programmes to be decentralized, notably for small-scale infrastructure. These guidelines[8] specify the means of ensuring community participation in the decision-making process underlying this infrastructure, thus reflecting the influence of the RIDEF project. Taken together, these elements represent a convincing provincial intention to decentralize. Considerable provincial creativity and clarity of purpose is evident, as well as the ability to make noticeable progress within a short period of time (since 1999) in developing a legal and implementation framework. These are all positive signs that the decentralization process has some staying power.

Table 3 helps place the RIDEF in context by comparing four types of local institutional arrangements underlying planning and budgeting. The first is the "normal" state planning process, which is in effect for all non-RIDEF funds in recent years (up to changes introduced through the decentralization agenda). The second is a major national programme in this sector (the design of which RIDEF in fact partly influenced, although due to space constraints that story is not covered here), currently being implemented in Quang Nam in the aforementioned 22 communes on the "poorest commune" list. The third column summarizes RIDEF, and the fourth the province's evolving decentralization agenda, which post-dates RIDEF and was influenced by it. The first three columns represent a continuum of reforms to decentralize planning and budgeting, specifically in the direction of strengthening local institutional arrangements for accountability and grassroots participation. The shape that the decentralization agenda ultimately takes is still contested, but it represents a clear attempt to institutionalize many of the design elements introduced by RIDEF.

Nevertheless, the impact of RIDEF is probably best described as *potential*, at least if sustainability is the measure of it.[9] Several constraints on the realization of the decentralization policy—which represents the primary avenue through which RIDEF activities could become institutionalized—are evident. One is the fact that its potential beneficiaries—lower levels of government and communities—are not

TABLE 3
Comparison of Key Aspects of State Planning System, Programme 135 and RIDEF to the Current Decentralization Agenda

Aspects/ Models	"Normal" state planning and budgeting for infrastructure	National Programme 135: small-scale infrastructure for the poorest communes	RIDEF	Evolving decentralization agenda*
Local Planning System	Top Down: Province or District as Project Holder	Top Down: District Project Holder	Participatory: Commune Project Holder	Formative: District project holder: commune possible
Funding Sources and Allocations	Unstable, irregular and small. Political/ bureaucratic; not transparent; in theory based on "wish-list" forwarded by lower levels	Relatively stable/fixed (commune allocations can be changed by district)	Stable and regulated through IPF which is formula based on population, economic development/ infrastructure	More stable but depending on high levels of community contribution with no guiding formula
Community Participation	None	Some in project selection	Comprehensive in all areas of planning and decision-making	Some sub-programmes moving towards norms of community participation, but still in progress
Tendering	No tendering for small works	Little if any tendering	All works go out to tender	Unclear; policy direction not set
Human Resource Capacity Building and Training	Provincial Level	Provincial and District Level	District, Commune and Village Level	Proposed from Provincial through to the commune level
Management and Technical Assistance	"Command and control" along sectoral lines	District as primary coordinator in response to National Guidelines	Commune as Managers: Province and Districts provide technical assistance; monitoring	Provincial: provision of guidelines; District sphere of coordination being increased; substantial discussion of commune level management

* see n. 8 for legal basis
Source: adapted from Stanley and Fritzen (2001), p. 25.

mobilized to support the change; the decentralization "vision" has ironically been driven by the provincial leadership to date. Potential opponents are, in contrast, prepared to defend their turf; provincial line agencies and contractors perceive direct threats to their administrative control and profits, respectively, and are as yet unwilling to accept the shift in their roles that comes from a decentralized system.[10]

Another major difficulty is how to prevent decentralization from widening disparities between localities highly diverse in administrative and fiscal capacity, environmental conditions and the degree of "enlightened" local leadership. The ability of the province to set clear minimum standards for both service delivery and the quality of the local planning process itself in mountainous areas will depend on long-term financial transfers, capacity building assistance and information systems. For this, RIDEF does not yet have a mature model.

Ultimately, RIDEF must be assessed against the broader context of reform in Vietnam. Another look at the grassroots democratization decree can facilitate conclusions. This decree is a general statement of the Party's view of "ideal governance" at the local level that has not yet been systematically applied to specific programmes. But the high profile it is given by the government in the press means it might be used to motivate local change by providing an idealized measuring stick against which to compare the performance of local governments along this important procedural dimension.

As a policy experiment, RIDEF sought first to demonstrate its viability as a mechanism to efficiently deliver a rather large injection of infrastructure spending at the grassroots level of one province. Only then did it begin to attract the attention of provincial policy-makers as a means of imbuing the province's decentralization policy with local institutional arrangements that are supportive of grassroots democracy. Both RIDEF and the decentralization policy of the province are attempts to make the ideals underlying the grassroots democratization decree more meaningful and specific to the workings of local government.

Comparable High-Impact Projects

As noted above, in the summary analysis of the fifteen projects, seven projects ranked "significant" in impact (a score of four or above) in two or more of the outcome categories. One of these seven was the RIDEF project. This section briefly examines five others among those seven to explore the hypothesis that different *combinations* of explanatory variables may lead to overall significant institutional and policy impacts of the local institutional arrangements sponsored under the projects.

Impact through Design

Three of the seven (projects B, H and I) are multisectoral smallholder development projects. The fact that they were able to have a significant impact despite the apparent lack of a clearly identified "champion" and high-profile sectoral issues underlines the overall importance of project design of a sufficient scale. Two of these three worked in more than one province (with scattered coverage) with multiple levels of government, while one (B) was designed to saturate a particular province.

The key aspect linking these three cases was a project design facilitative of their role as policy experiments. Project activities were themselves too diffused to attract great policy attention or produce a "model" (as did RIDEF); institutional factors were only moderately supportive. These projects operated on a sufficient scale to be highly visible to provincial observers (project B), or combined moderate coverage with a long-term orientation towards learning and experimentation, lasting for nearly ten years with strong national-level participation (projects H and I). In so doing, they were able to moderately impact on policy at the provincial and, to a more limited extent, national levels. They were also able to build up sufficient human resources committed to the project concept—the "internal buy-in" aspect—to ensure some sustainability of local institutional arrangements. For projects H and I, provinces legalized the planning and service delivery roles of the LDGs through the issuance of decrees, though the relevance of this post-project is questionable.

The case of project B suggested even more clearly than RIDEF did the potential effect of a large-scale (by provincial standards) project on a province's decentralization strategy. At the beginning of the project, there was little provincial support for the idea of decentralization to district and commune levels, and this greatly hampered project implementation and conceptual development. Only with several iterations of failed local planning within a rigidly centralized system did it become clear to provincial authorities that resources should be devolved in tandem with planning responsibilities (UNOPS 1998).

Constituency-Building Service-Access Orientation

Another route towards high impact is shown by project D, the United Nations Food and Agriculture Organization's Community-Based Integrated Pest Management (IPM) support project (FAO 2000). This project supports the government's own IPM national programme, in which farmer interest groups access both training and technical services from district-level technical agencies. This training extends beyond pesticide management to a broader family of technologies for "sustainable agriculture". The IPM has served as a high-impact strategy for a number of reasons. First, it has effectively been able to link to a national programme to which the government is already committed. Second, it has identified a discrete and highly effective set of technologies and approaches which can be adapted to the diverse conditions of rural Vietnam and are directly related to production, leading to higher LDG effectiveness and sustainability.

Third, and most importantly, it has focused on the creation of farmer groups—the LDGs here—that are highly motivated and well positioned to effectively interface with district-level technical agencies that carry out the training (FAO 2000). There is considerable long-term potential for these groups to demand greater responsiveness from these agencies and/or to branch out into other production-related activities.[11]

Conclusion

While space constraints do not permit consideration of further case studies, the previous section presented more detail on several higher-impact projects. While demonstrating distinct avenues for project-initiated LDGs to have an impact on local institutional arrangements, all of them revolved around the concept of improved accountability. Accountability is understood here not necessarily as shifting decision-making power and resources *away* from government, as some advocates of community empowerment suggest (Osborne 1996), but of enhancing the ability of local levels of government and villagers to participate meaningfully in the governance processes that effect them, and to interface more effectively with higher levels of government. The heart of accountable development, in this view, is a reworking of institutional arrangements to build in incentives for upper levels to respond to the concerns and needs of lower levels and to the rural populace. The

LDGs initiated by donors, where meaningful (i.e. where they appear to have a chance of being sustainable and have influence on local state–society relations), represent diverse attempts to introduce such incentives and local institutional arrangements.

The idea of accountable development needs to be placed in a specifically Vietnamese frame of reference. This was provided by section one, which argued that several ongoing aspects of center–local and state–society relations in Vietnam are in flux. The overall framework for fiscal and administrative decentralization is changing; provinces are being offered greater control and discretion over funds, in return for improved accountability to the centre both to meet priority development goals and ensure a semblance of democratic process at the grassroots. The latter is related to heightened sensitivity at the national level to the potential for corrupt local governance to spark localized rural protests.

This increasing focus of the centre on process—in the form of the grassroots democratization policy—has served as an important "policy window" for donors eager to advance procedures, methodologies and local institutions that stand a chance of reducing the "grassroots democracy-credibility" gap. A truly facilitative framework for something approaching what the global development debate means by "civil society" cannot be said to exist in Vietnam (Marr 1994). There is, however, space for development-oriented local groups that operate increasingly vigorously in the defense of localized interests and with complex connections to the local state, as with the "new" cooperatives and microcredit groups mushrooming throughout the countryside.[12] Local development groups initiated in the context of donor projects are one part, to date unexplored, of this complex institutional scene in the Vietnamese countryside.

What implications does the analysis hold for donor-initiated projects and Vietnamese state–society relations in transition?

First, provinces are where the "reform action" is. The diversity of the country and historical factors have led to a highly decentralized system within a unitary or centralized framework (Shanks 2001), a tendency underscored by recent transfers of authority for national programmes to provinces. There are essentially 61 provincial experiments in public administration reform being carried out throughout the country. More remote and fiscally weak provinces are experiments in the sense that the centre finds it difficult to effect socioeconomic transformation there, while richer provinces are in a stronger position to negotiate greater autonomy from central controls. In both cases, provincial autonomy is substantial and, perhaps, increasing.

Second, there is clearly a space for donor efforts to impact on policy through provincial level development projects, and specifically, through projects which attempt to "tweak" local institutions to introduce greater accountability and responsiveness to locals. The conceptual framework was generally successful in identifying aspects of programme design and types of institutional arrangements likely to facilitate policy impact. Some of the lessons drawn from the above analysis are that donors will maximize their chances to influence policy through subnational policy experiments if they:

(a) Work in sectors corresponding to areas defined by central or local officials to be of high national priority *and* which are seeing significant institutional reform movement, and develop specific, workable methodologies that can address the policy–implementation gap in such sectors;
(b) Design projects as policy experiments, with strong learning orientation and information systems, a sufficient time-frame to allow support to grow, and a scale that commands the interest of officials at the provincial level, where most experiments are being carried out;
(c) Ensure LDGs have clearly defined functions that lower transaction costs for providing or accessing important productive services;
(d) Structure institutional arrangements in the project context such that local government agencies have an incentive to engage seriously with grassroots needs; and
(e) Cultivate "reform champions" and find ways to strengthen their hand.

Third, the institutional space occupied by project-initiated LDGs is likely to be contested. Elements of the local state and emerging élites linked to it (such as the contractors with close links to provincial line agencies, in the RIDEF example) will resist accountability-enhancing reforms. Strategic capacity building (the subject of the next point) may help reduce this resistance, while the creation of supportive constituencies at the grassroots—i.e. LDG members themselves—and well placed officials is vital to ensuring the local organizations sponsored by the project do not succumb to it.

Finally, the experience of donor policy experiments reveals the need for a long-term programme of capacity strengthening for local governance, particularly for the poorest regions that are experiencing the greatest gap between policy and implementation. Elements of a convincing demand-driven strategy would include:

(a) Reform of planning, budgeting and monitoring systems to make them more results-oriented and accountability-enhancing, both towards upper levels of government and the grassroots;
(b) Provision of real discretion in the use of centrally transferred resources (which will continue to be necessary in fiscally poor provinces) linked to the planning and accountability framework noted above;
(e) Attention to fiscal differentials through a beefed-up programme of interprovincial fiscal redistribution designed to help poor provinces meet minimum standards in high priority goals of national significance; and
(d) Administrative reform and training programmes that take a structural view of the capacities involved. Capacities should be understood in terms not just of the skills sets of lower officials, but also the incentives these officials work under, along with factors such as how local civil servants are recruited and promoted (Hilderbrand and Grindle 1997).

Local development groups are an important part of the story of local state–society relations in transition as well as institutional or policy reform. This is true both for the Vietnamese context and arguably for other transitional and/or authoritarian countries pursuing a state-led development strategy. Neither "pure" NGOs nor local organizations in a conventional sense, LDGs are usually neglected as focal points for analysis. LDG-sponsoring projects attempt to introduce new relationships of accountability of local government agencies to communities and to boost participation of the villagers in resource allocation and other decisions that affect them. In so doing, they become sites for contestation and negotiation between communities and local state actors with varying interests in the outcomes of such experiments, as efforts to meaningfully decentralize small-scale infrastructure decisions to communities in the

RIDEF project demonstrated. In a context in which a vibrant, genuinely independent civil society does not yet exist, these LDGs can be important sources of institutional change in the Vietnamese rural landscape. The influence of local policy experiments may grow in the coming years, as donors step up support for "accountable development" in a context in which the political leadership is supportive yet ambivalent, and watchful.

Notes

1 ODA pledges were stagnant over the latter half of the 1990s, and in fact were lower as a percentage of GDP in 2000 than in 1993. Figures from <www.vneconomy.com.vn>.

2 Personal communication by Nguyen Thanh Tung, UNDP Program Officer. See also World Bank and others (2001) for a detailed review.

3 The project was commissioned by the United Nations Development Program, the United Nations Capital Development Fund, and the Canadian International Development Agency.

4 See Fritzen (2000b), Nguyen (2000) and Tran (2000) for three outputs of this study.

5 Sources for this review include Gardener et al. (1998), Kammeier (1999), and fieldwork conducted during a Technical Review Mission in mid-2001 (Stanley and Fritzen 2001).

6 Project inception document, as quoted in Stanley and Fritzen (2001), p. 3.

7 This statement is based on several interviews conducted with Vu Ngoc Hoang, Chairman of the Provincial People's Committee and Nguyen Ngoc Quang, National Project Director of the RIDEF project as well as former head of the Provincial Planning Service and current head of the Provincial Finance Service.

8 Includes a 5–6 billion VND discretionary fund being decentralized to district level under provincial People's Committee Decision 13/2000; implementation guidelines and legal documents include Decision 35/1999/QD-UB and 19/2001/QD-UB of the Provincial People's Committee.

9 This overall assessment is based on fieldwork and interviews over two weeks in Quang Nam, as detailed in Stanley and Fritzen (2001).

10 Classic roles for the centre in a decentralized system include overall coordination, setting and monitoring minimum standards and capacity-building.

11 The IPM programme has been considering how it should address the issue of diversification. See FAO (2000) and <http://www.communityipm.org>.

[12] See contributors to Kerkvliet and Porter (1995) for more on Vietnam's agrarian transformation.

References

Carrol, T. *Intermediary NGOs: The Supporting Link in Grassroots Development.* West Hartford: Kumarin Press, 1992.

Charlick R. "Popular Participation and Local Government Reform". *Public Administration and Development* 21 (2001): 149–57.

Do Hoai Nam and Le Cao Doan. *Xay Dung Ha Tang Co So Nong Thon: Trong Qua Trinh Cong Nghiep Hoa, Hien Dai Hoa o Viet Nam* [Building Rural Infrastructure in Vietnam's Industrialization and Modernization]. Hanoi: Nha Xuat Ban Khoa Hoc Xa Hoi, 2001.

Economist Intelligence Unit (EIU). *Country Report: Vietnam (First quarter 1999).* London: EIU, 1998.

Edwards, M. and D. Hulme (eds). *Making a Difference: NGOs and Development in a Changing World.* London: Earthscan Publications, 1992.

Esman, M. and N. Uphoff. *Local Organizations: Intermediaries in Rural Development.* Ithaca: Cornell University Press, 1984.

Feeney, P. *Accountable Aid: Local Participation in Major Projects.* Oxford: Oxfam GB, 1998.

Food and Agriculture Organization (FAO). Community Based IPM Case Studies. "Intercountry Programme for the Development of Integrated Pest Management in Rice in Southeast Asia", mimeographed, 2000.

Fritzen, S. "Decentralization, Disparities, and Innovation in Vietnam's Health Sector". In *Market Reform in Vietnam: Building Institutions for Development,* edited by J. Litvack and D. Rondinelli. Westport: Quorum Books, 1999.

———. "Decentralization and Local Government Performance: A Comparative Approach with Application to Social Policy Reform in Vietnam". Ph.D. dissertation, Princeton: Princeton University, 2000a.

———. "Institutionalizing Participation: Lessons Learnt and Implications for Strengthening Vietnam's National Programs". Final report for UNDP/UNCDF/CIDA Institutionalization of Participatory Planning study. Hanoi, mimeographed, 2000b.

Gardener, J., R. Guild and A. Fforde. "Mid-term Evaluation of the Rural Infrastructure Development Fund". United Nations Capital Development Fund, mimeographed, 1998.

Grindle, M. and J. Thomas. *Public Choices and Policy Change: The Political Economy of Reform in Developing Countries.* Baltimore: Johns Hopkins University Press, 1991.

Hilderbrand, M. and M. Grindle. "Building Sustainable Capacity in the Public Sector: What Can Be Done?" In *Getting Good Government: Capacity Building in the Public Sectors of Developing Countries*. Cambridge: Harvard University Press, 1997.

Kammeier, H. "Towards Guidelines for Decentralized Management and Finance of Rural Development in Vietnam: A Profile of the Experience of the RIDEF Programme in the Provinces of Da Nang and Quang Nam (1996–2001)". United Nations Capital Development Fund, mimeographed, 1999.

Kerkvliet, B. "An Approach for Analysing State–Society Relations in Vietnam". *Sojourn* 16 no. 2 (2001): 238–78.

Kerkvliet, B. and D. Porter (eds). *Vietnam's Rural Transformation*. Boulder and Singapore: Westview and ISEAS 1995.

Kingdon, J. *Agendas, Alternatives and Public Policies*. 2nd edition. New York: Longman, 1995.

Lehmann, D. and A. Bebbington. "NGOs, the State and the Development Process: The Dilemmas of Institutionalization". In *The Changing Role of the State in Latin America*, edited by M. Vellinga. Boulder: Westview, 1998.

Marr, D. "The Vietnam Communist Party and Civil Society". Paper presented at the Vietnam Update 1994 Conference: Doi Moi, the State and Civil Society, 10–11 November. Canberra: Australian National University, 1994.

Nguyen Dinh Khoi. "Kinh Nghiem Cua Cac Chuong Trinh Quoc Gia". Submission for UNDP/UNCDF/CIDA Institutionalization of Participatory Planning study. Hanoi, mimeographed, 2000.

Rao, M., R. Bird and J. Litvack. "The Changing Requirements of Fiscal Relations: Fiscal Decentralization in a Unified State". In *Market Reform in Vietnam: Building Institutions for Development*, edited by J. Litvack and D. Rondinelli. Westport: Quorum Books, 1999.

Rondinelli, D. *Development Projects as Policy Experiments: An Adaptive Approach to Development Administration*. London: Methuen, 1983.

Shanks, E. Vietnam: Local Government in the Northern Mountains. DFID: manuscript, 2001.

Stanley, J. and S. Fritzen. "Viet Nam Technical Review Mission Report: Rural Infrastructure Development Fund". UNCDF, mimeographed.

Tran Huu Cuong. "Experiences from Donor-Assisted Projects on Institutionalization of Participatory Planning Approaches". Submission for UNDP/UNCDF/CIDA Institutionalization of Participatory Planning study. Hanoi, mimeographed, 2000.

Turk, C. "Linking Participatory Poverty Assessments to Policy and Policymaking: Experience from Vietnam". World Bank Working Paper Series. <www.worldbank.org/partipation/thematic1cs.htm> (accessed 19 October 2001).

United Nations Capital Development Fund (UNCDF). *Taking Risks: Background Papers*. New York: UNCDF, 1999.

United Nations Development Program. *Looking Ahead: A United Nations Common Country Assessment of Vietnam*. Hanoi: UNDP, 1999.

United Nations Office for Project Services (UNOPS). "Participatory Resource Management Project, Tuyen Quang Province: Case Study on Decentralization and Participation". Kuala Lumpur: UNOPS Asia Office, mimeographed, 1998.

Uphoff, N. *Local Institutional Development: An Analytical Sourcebook with Cases*. West Hartford: Kumarian Press, 1986.

Uphoff, N., M. Esman and A. Krishna. *Reasons for Success: Learning from Instructive Experiences in Rural Development*. West Hartford: Kumarian Press, 1998.

Uvin, P. "Scaling up the Grassroots and Scaling Down the Summit: The Relations Between Third World NGOs and the UN". In *NGOs, the United Nations, and Global Governance*, edited by T. Weiss and L. Gordenker. Boulder: Lynne Rienner.

Uvin, P. and P. Jain. "Think Large and Act Small: Toward a New Paradigm for NGO Scaling Up". *World Development* 28 no. 8 (2000): 1409–19.

World Bank. *Assessing Aid: What Works, What Doesn't, and Why*. Oxford: Oxford University Press, 1998.

World Bank and others. "Vietnam: Attacking Poverty". Joint report of the Government of Vietnam—Donor—NGO Poverty Working Group. Consultative Group Meeting for Vietnam, 14–15 December, 1999.

———. "Putting Partnerships to Work: An Informal Report for the Consultative Group Meeting for Vietnam". Hanoi, 7–8 December, 2001. <http://www.worldbank.org.vn/data_pub/reports/Bank1/rep35/partners2001.pdf>, (accessed 17 May, 2002).

Index

About the Contributors

Scott Fritzen has a Ph.D. in Public Affairs from Princeton University and is Assistant Professor of Public Policy at the National University of Singapore. His applied research and consulting practice focus on decentralization, public-sector capacity building and social policy reform in several Southeast Asian countries.

Michael Gray is a freelance writer and editor with an M.A. in Southeast Asian Studies from the School of Oriental and African Studies. He worked in Hanoi for four years, including two years with the local media and two years as a volunteer for the NGO Towards Ethnic Women.

Eva Hansson is a Ph.D. Candidate in the Department of Political Science, Stockholm University, currently teaching in comparative politics and in international relations. Her Ph.D. project "Civil Society and Democratization: Trade Unions in Liberalizing Southeast Asia" focuses on the role of trade unions in the process of political liberalization in Vietnam, Thailand and Indonesia. She is co-editor (with Beckman and Román) of *Vietnam: Reform and Transformation* (1997) and (with Beckman and Sjögren) of *Civil Society and Authoritarianism in the Third World* (2001).

Russell H.K. Heng is a Senior Fellow at the Institute of Southeast Asia (ISEAS) in Singapore. He has a Ph.D. from the Australian National University where he wrote a dissertation on the politics of the mass media in Vietnam. He looks at the development of civil society in Vietnam and other authoritarian polities.

Benedict J. Tria Kerkvliet, head of the Department of Political and Social Change at the Australian National University, does research on agrarian politics and state–society relations, particularly in the Philippines and Vietnam. He is currently co-editing a book on local government and authority in Vietnam.

David Koh is a Fellow at the Institute of Southeast Asian Studies in Singapore. A graduate of the National University of Singapore, he completed his Ph.D. studies at the Australian National University where he wrote a dissertation entitled "The Ward and State-Society Relations in the Socialist Republic of Vietnam." He continues to keenly watch Vietnamese politics, culture, and society, while developing a new interest in Political Islam.

Jonathan R. Stromseth is currently the Representative of The Asia Foundation in Vietnam. Prior to joining The Asia Foundation in 1998, he taught courses on Indochina and Southeast Asia at the School of International and Public Affairs at Columbia University in New York City. He holds a Ph.D. in political science from Columbia, where his research focused on political and economic reforms in Vietnam since the mid-1980s.

Thaveeporn Vasavakul has a Ph.D. in Government from Cornell University and is an independent researcher affiliated with the Centre for Vietnamese and Intercultural Studies, Hanoi, Vietnam, and the Institute of Security and International Studies, Bangkok, Thailand. She served as the Resident Director for the Council on International Educational Exchange's programme in Hanoi between 1998 and 2002 and its Southeast Asian Regional Director from 2000 to 2002. Her current research projects focus on the political reform in Vietnam and comparative political transition in Southeast Asia.

Ivo Vasiljev has a Ph.D. in Vietnamese language from the Oriental Institute, Czechoslovak Academy of Sciences, and is author of *In Search of the Heritage of the Ancient Viet* (Prague 1999, in Czech). Currently he is a freelance scholar and an overseas associate member of the Institute for Southeast Asian Studies, Hanoi.

Nguyen Quang Vinh is a sociologist affiliated with the Institute of Social Sciences in Ho Chi Minh City, where he was once Deputy Director. He also headed the Centre for Sociology at the National Centre for Social Sciences and Humanities, Institute of Social Sciences in Ho Chi Minh City. His research focuses on the sociology of urban housing, development and management, living standard and poverty assessment, and the development of urban societal organizations.

Joerg Wischermann has a Ph.D. in Political Science from Freie Universitaet Berlin, where he now works as Research Fellow and Lecturer. His research interests are: democratic transition in Southeast Asia (Vietnam, Cambodia and Laos in particular), new political movements and advocacy organizations in developing countries, the usefulness of the Internet for Southeast Asian studies and new social movements in Western Europe.